MIRROR THINKING

Also available in the Bloomsbury Sigma series:

MIRROR
THINKING

HOW ROLE MODELS MAKE
US HUMAN

Fiona Murden

BLOOMSBURY SIGMA

LONDON · OXFORD · NEW YORK · NEW DELHI · SYDNEY

BLOOMSBURY SIGMA
Bloomsbury Publishing Plc
50 Bedford Square, London, WC1B 3DP, UK

BLOOMSBURY, BLOOMSBURY SIGMA and the Bloomsbury Sigma logo
are trademarks of Bloomsbury Publishing Plc

First published in the United Kingdom in 2020

Copyright © Fiona Murden, 2020

A catalogue record for this book is available from the British Library

Library of Congress Cataloguing-in-Publication data has been applied for

ISBN: HB: 978-1-4729-7580-5; TPB: 978-1-4729-7581-2;
eBook: 978-1-4729-7579-9

2 4 6 8 10 9 7 5 3 1

Typeset by Deanta Global Publishing Services, Chennai, India

Printed and bound in Great Britain by CPI Group (UK) Ltd,
Croydon CR0 4YY

Bloomsbury Sigma, Book Fifty-Six

To find out more about our authors and books visit www.bloomsbury.com
and sign up for our newsletters

Contents

Why the Mirror System Matters

There is a picture of me that I treasure. It's a bright early summer's day, and I'm sat on a picnic blanket with my grandfather's fedora drooped over my tiny two-year-old head and his thick-rimmed glasses sat crooked on my nose. He is looking back at me, my little yellow cherry-embroidered hat perched on the top of his head. I'm told I put it there to make him smile, that it was the first time he'd laughed since my nanna had died. It's comforting to think this is true, to picture myself as caring enough and sufficiently wise at that young age to know how to give him a momentary respite from his grief. In reality, I was probably just doing what every child does, copying what I saw and mirroring his behaviour unthinkingly. That's what made him laugh.

This imitation is not just a human capability. To observe and copy what others in the 'clan' are doing is essential to all learning. Have you ever noticed a kitten watching her mother clean herself only to try doing the same? Or you may have seen footage of a sea otter opening a shellfish with a rock. A young pup cannot do this until they've witnessed the act and then tried it a few times themselves. This is the nature by which mammals know how to behave in different situations. We observe, imitate, assimilate and repeat, sometimes knowingly, but often without even noticing.

While on the surface this form of behaviour may appear basic and something we only do when we're little, without

it we would struggle to survive either as individuals or as a species. In fact, it is the power of mirroring that has enabled humanity to evolve to where it is today and conscious mirror thinking could be the key to unlocking the future of the human race; we just have to learn how to harness the incredible functioning of the mirror neuron system, embedded deep within our brains.

The brain and evolution

Increasingly, evidence points towards the human brain having evolved to the size it has in order to enable more effective social interaction, which in the time of our ancient ancestors aided our chances of survival. Being included within a larger group of people allowed humans to hunt bigger prey, choose from a wider range of sexual partners and watch out for lions or enemies with more pairs of eyes, as well as share the responsibilities of raising children and keeping them safe. The larger brain made it possible to store more information about different members of the tribe, to mentally hold a web of inter-relationships, to work out who was doing what with whom, who to avoid and who to befriend. All of these things are critical to getting along and cooperating with others[1] and, as we'll explore, totally dependent on the mirror neuron system.

Along with making us more socially adept, this evolution of the human brain has also enabled us to share our learning to a greater extent than any other species. It makes sense that this knowledge transfer originally happened via social mechanisms, passing understanding on from generation to generation through watching, doing, storytelling and imagining within our own mind. Without this we simply would not be where we are today. We wouldn't have an iPhone or running water, antibiotics for an infection or

aeroplanes to travel the world. This has all been built up from collective learning over thousands of years, which began at the most basic level. If we were to compare it to building a house, we had to put the foundations down before we could get anywhere near to putting a roof on. If we tried to construct the rafters with no frame it just wouldn't work.

Initially, we used our big brains to share knowledge about the most basic things – for example, learning how to spark a flame. Being able to harness the power of fire took humans leaps and bounds ahead of other animals. As a species food sources were opened up because we could cook things that were previously inedible, we were able to take over previously uninhabitable territories by clearing dense undergrowth, and we could ward away predators and generate light and warmth. If a single person in one place had learnt to light a fire and no one else ever imitated that, the accidental finding may not have repeated itself for centuries. Without it being shared and built upon, it would literally have been no more than a glimmer. We carry out the same iterative knowledge transfer today. While we don't need to know how to survive in the wilderness, we are constantly learning about social norms and group dynamics, and passing them on to those around us.

Given that it's our brain that permits this tutelage, it's useful to understand how it is structured. The model I have always found most helpful to explain the brain remains one that was proposed back in the late 1960s. The late physician Paul MacLean established the 'triune brain theory' to describe how the brain's structure developed from our evolutionary beginnings up until the point at which these changes stopped about 50,000 years ago. MacLean proposed that our brain evolved to its current size and capability while preserving features of two much more basic

formations, literally one layer on top of the next. The three parts have dramatically idiosyncratic structures and chemistry, reacting quite differently to stimuli even though they are interconnected.[2]

The first layer, known as the brain stem, resembles that of a reptile and evolved about 320 million years ago. This part of our brain monitors basic functions such as heart rate, breathing, and body temperature.

The second layer, known broadly as the limbic system, developed as reptiles evolved into early mammals about 160 million years ago. This takes care of our basic drivers: eating, sleeping, staying safe and procreating, and can be crudely described as the emotional part of our brain.

The third layer, known as the neocortex, was the final piece of the brain to evolve 50,000 years ago. It is this outer layer, that makes us most distinctively human and comes ready to be filled with experiences from the world around us when we are born. We rapidly feed our neural networks with insights specific to our society and culture in the early years of our life, allowing us to navigate our social world and 'fit in' with the customs, values and beliefs of the people around us.

The main aims of the first two layers are the same for humans as they are for other animals: they drive reproduction and self-survival. For the purposes of this book, we'll refer to this as the 'reacting brain'. The functions of this part of the brain are largely unconscious, responding quickly to environmental cues. For example, if someone throws something at us we duck before we actually think about what is happening. As a result, we avoid being hit by the object. The reacting brain is also surprisingly dominant in other aspects of our everyday lives, influencing things as varied as eating and sleeping, but most significantly it is also where our need to belong, to be part of a group in

order to survive, is rooted. As a result, we have strong drivers that motivate us to pay attention and conform to our social and emotional environment perhaps more than we care to admit. Although Western culture strives toward individualism, we are in fact highly interdependent and connected. Our instinct is to constantly watch and observe what is going on in our social environment in order to understand the nuances that in turn shape who we are and how we behave.

The more complex areas of life are the responsibility of the slower but more deliberate neocortex. For the purposes of this book, we will call this the 'observing brain'. The domains it looks after include more evolved behaviours such as finding purpose in our own personal existence and contributing to a society where we can all live agreeably. The neocortex also interprets messages coming from the reacting brain and allows us to search for the reason behind different emotions, to answer questions and to formulate language.

Arguably it's far more useful to think with our observing brain, which takes carefully considered action. But because our overall brain structure has remained largely unchanged, since the time of our ancient ancestors, our survival drivers are still powerful and override a whole range of situations where we may expect to respond more 'logically' with our observing brain. A simple example is eating more than we need to when we are trying to lose weight. Our core driver to feed overpowers our rationale that in the long run we want to get in shape. All of this applies today in spite of all of our mind-boggling advancements.

This means it is critically important to understand not only the interaction between the observing and the reacting brain, but also how our reacting brain is unconsciously directing us all of the time. For example, imagine walking

into an environment where everyone is whispering. Do you speak in your normal voice or do you find yourself speaking more quietly? How often have you looked across the table at the person you're talking to and found that their arms, head and hands are positioned in exactly the same place as yours? Have you winced when you've seen someone stub their toe or cried when you've heard someone tell a devastating story even though you haven't been impacted by the events yourself? Have you found yourself worrying about the look two friends gave each other when you were talking? These are the subtle, ongoing observations and imitations that we are constantly making in response to others. You may think you're aware of this, but the chances are you're not. And these little behaviours add up to habits and lasting behaviours that become part of who you are, altering your characteristics, beliefs and nudging your values without you realising. In fact, the complexity and distractions of our modern world make us even less aware, which can render outcomes even more unpredictable. Small everyday influences impact what we wear, where we shop, the cars we choose, who we follow on Instagram, the TV programmes we watch, how much exercise we do, what we eat. And it all comes down to our observations and interactions with others. This is what I call mirror thinking.

Role-modelling

The definition of a role model is 'a person looked to by others as an example to be imitated'.[3] It was the influential American sociologist Robert K. Merton who coined the term in the 1950s. The expression has become so proflific that it has filtered into everyday language across the globe. We are going to explore how interrelated role-modelling

and mirror thinking are. We're also going to explore a common misconception about role models; that they are heroes or heroines, people who are out of reach and infallible. In reality we are surrounded by role models both good and bad. We are also role models influencing others day in and day out ourselves.

What in Merton's time we saw on the outside – the act of observing and imitating – we can now see inside the brain, enabling amazing insights into the mechanisms that lie behind behaviours. Looking under the hood, we're able to see that role-modelling is not just about observation and imitation, but also dependent on our internal worlds in the form of imagination, empathy, storytelling and reflection. These are all part of mirror thinking and underly the creation of neural processes that refine and enhance our social and emotional experience of the world.

Monkey see, monkey do

Our understanding of the mirror system is still very much in its infancy, but has developed considerably since the intial findings, which were stumbled upon by chance. It was 1992 and the Italian neurophysiologist Giacomo Rizzolatti and his team at Parma University were trying to understand more about how the brain coordinates the muscles in the hand, *i.e.* what enables a hand to grab and hold things. Using electrodes inserted into the brains of macaque monkeys they were able to monitor the very smallest unit of the brain – the neuron. They were specifically interested in when these neurons 'fired' to pass on information to other parts of the brain and body. One day the team were eating lunch in the same room as the monkeys and noticed that the neurons fired when the monkey wasn't even performing an action. The monkey

was watching one of the scientists bring food to his mouth and the same neuron that was involved in the monkey bringing food to its own mouth was activated. The scientists quickly realised that this was a case of 'monkey see, monkey do'. Rizzolatti and his colleagues published their findings, naming the cells the 'mirror neurons'. It wasn't until 2000 when a neuroscientist and author called Vilayanur Subramanian Ramachandran began to publicise the findings that the mirror neuron became something of great interest. He was so taken with this functioning that he claimed 'mirror neurons would do for psychology what DNA did for biology' providing a unifying framework to 'help explain a host of mental abilities that have hitherto remained mysterious and inaccessible to experiments'.[4] Among those abilities and behaviours he listed: why people imitate the actions of others, how cultural norms spreads through populations, how people understand the intention of other people's actions and how children learn music. Even the anticipation of what is going to happen next – the prediction of someone else's actions or their next move – is dependent on the mirror neuron.[5]

As is often the case with anything that reaches notoriety, the criticism soon came. Other neuroscientists claimed that these specific neurons couldn't explain all of the intricacy involved in human learning, that in humans the system of neurons was far more dispersed and complex than in the macaque monkey. Perhaps this is true: we don't yet know and that is for the neuroscientists to investigate. Neuroscience is still in its infancy compared with other sciences, but what we do know and what we can use to help us understand daily life offers an amazing opportunity. This book isn't about proving or disproving neuroscientific theory, but rather about using the information we have so far as a

concept on which we can understand the broader nature of behaviour. And that concept is mirror thinking.

How mirror thinking is key to our social survival

When I was 13 my family moved to a different part of the country, which meant I had to change schools. I left behind a relatively sheltered environment where my fellow pupils were academically minded. In my old school being good at school was something to be proud of and diligence was respected. It may have had something to do with the transition that takes place in any teenager's life over the summer away from academia, but the world I entered when I joined my new school in the autumn that year was significantly different. A biology lesson in what must have been the second week of term is seared on my memory. The teacher was admonishing the class for not having made an effort with the homework with the exception of 'Fiona, who did a brilliant piece of work'. All eyes turned to where I was sitting, creating the feeling that the world was suddenly spiralling out of control and the ride was making me feel sick. It was so humiliating and not something I could easily shake – after all, first impressions last. This most certainly wasn't what a new girl trying to fit into what is basically a tribal environment (due to the hormones associated with adolescence) wanted to be labelled – the 'goody goody', the swot, the 'not one of us'. I realised something had to change – and quickly – if I wanted to belong.

In order to survive, I redefined who I was. My focus moved from getting good grades to seeing how little work I do to get by. Having previously been sporty I did anything I could to avoid being picked for teams and mastered the art of getting into bars and clubs underage. Before long I

felt like less of an outsider. It wasn't a 'tough' environment, but arguably it was a tough environment to fit into. It was thanks to mirror thinking that I was able to adapt in order to belong and became accepted.

Observing and imitating via mirror thinking of often the only way to learn the nuances of human behaviour and emotion. Think about it – can you remember how you learnt to tie your shoelaces, to swim or to ride a bike? Do you know where your value system came from? Can you recall who taught you how to do the job you do today? You may be able to pinpoint some situations in which you've learnt specific skills or people who've taught things to you. However, you, me, all of us are often completely unaware of the strongest influence in our life – the behaviour of those around us. In the same way we need to watch someone serve the ball in tennis – it's nearly impossible to do it correctly without having seen it rather than just following instructions – people have to see social and emotional aspects of learning role-modelled in order to assimilate them. We just aren't aware of this because it's so natural to us.

When we understand the mechanisms and make a conscious effort to 'observe' what's going on around us we can choose which behaviours to take on board and how we respond. For me, it took a significant jolt to make me aware, a conscious decision to do something about it and a concerted effort to change. It wasn't necessarily the right decision either, which is often the case with teenagers whose brains are not developed enough to make optimal judgements. The point is, becoming aware of the issue gave me a level of control; bringing us back to the idea that consciousness is central.

The scary thing is that when we are not consciously aware of something, we cannot judge it with reason and

therefore do not make a decision on whether to accept or reject that learning. We simply absorb that behaviour into who we are. For example, in 2007 a study published in the *New England Journal of Medicine* observing more than 12,000 participants for 30 years found that people are more likely to gain weight if those they interact with gain weight. The chances of gaining weight increased by an astounding 171 per cent if a close friend had done so. We almost absorb the behaviour of those around us – particularly those we're close to – by osmosis. And this isn't just true of gaining weight; it covers almost everything we do. If we can be more conscious of this, then we're able to judge it rationally and make a decision on whether we take on that behaviour or not. That can make a massive difference to how we live our life.

Where our attention is directed and what we absorb can dramatically impact our life outcomes, making the difference between; achieving at school or ending up in jail,

being fit and healthy or constantly at the doctor's, getting a promotion or remaining stuck on the bottom rung of the ladder at work, being socially adept or overlooked and ignored.

It can impact our financial income, social status, life expectancy, quality of life, how many children we have and how happy we are in a marriage. At a societal level it can make the difference between voting in good or poor leadership, maintaining or breaking the chain of abuse across generations, elevating or deterring terrorism, aiding positive or negative mental and physical health, and so the list goes on. And it's all the result of role-modelling.

As an adult I've spent my career carrying out in-depth psychological profiles and heard about the twists and turns of many different lives. I've seen the pain and joy experienced

across life stories. I've witnessed what has and hasn't worked, the highs, the lows, the tipping points. I have seen how what people do impacts those around them and how they themselves have been shaped by the people in their lives, through childhood and adolescence through to the present day. And this personal anecdotal evidence combined with what science has demonstrated paints the same picture – everyone has been shaped by the behaviour of multiple people in their lives. Whether or not we are aware of them, we all have role models in our lives, both good and bad. We have to see to be able to do. Observing allows us to make sense of a behaviour and translate it into our own actions. These role models are all around us, constantly imprinting on the neural networks of our brain. You are thought to, on average, meet 80,000 people in your lifetime. Each will impact you and you them. You play a role in passing on cultural norms and nuances, of teaching those around you how to and how not to behave. You are a part of shaping the human race.

We will see how those that have the greatest influence on us are people who we connect with, who we trust and who we are exposed to. These are the three fundamental factors that underpin who we learn from or imitate.[6] These connections can be forged in many ways – through family, friendship, school or work, or even through the stories we tell, the music we hear and the words we use. We'll explore each one of these connections and the incredible impacts they have on our brain, shaping us at each and every moment of our lives. We are far from being able to take full advantage of the mirror system – either individually as a way in which we can learn or at a societal level. To an extent the mirror system will have at times unwittingly taken advantage of us. The idea is simple and we have a choice. If we want to leverage and make conscious use of

mirror thinking in order to dramatically improve our own and others' lives, we have to understand and make a conscious decision to use it. If we are more aware of how our daily interactions influence and affect the workings of our brain, then we can deepen our understanding of what we can take from mirror thinking and how we can use it. This deeper understanding will allow us to exceed our personal expectations of what we as individuals can achieve and power us forward to the future we dream of.

THE MIRRORS OF OUR LIVES

Mirroring From Birth

Your birthday – it's indelibly etched on your mind whether you celebrate it or not. Officials want to know when you came into existence for passports, driving licences, mortgages, doctors' appointments. We know and expect those close to us to remember it each and every year. The date marks a monumental event in all of our lives, not just because it is when our family welcome us to the world or when various government bodies record our age, but for a far more profound reason. The moment you were born your brain began to feed off and be shaped by the people around you. Your basic brain structure started to mirror every person, every single action and every interaction. Neural pathways shaped by those around you began firing the moment the midwife lifted you into your mother's arms and your father first looked into your eyes. In fact, an astounding 180 million new neural connections[1] formed within the first three minutes of your life, and a large proportion of those were dependent on being able to mirror the actions of others, specifically your parents.

Neural connections in our brain are fundamental to who we are. They are responsible for how our brain communicates, sending electrical and chemical signals to one another to enable us to understand and react to the world around us. This structure provides the basis for learning and the memories that the learning is built on. Our neural networks start being built before we are born but continue to be shaped throughout adulthood. In fact, we now know that via plasticity our brain is able to change

and adapt throughout life – although this becomes harder
once we've passed our early years of development.

Our brain is built from the bottom up,[2] with the more
simple structures forming the foundations on which
increasingly complex networks are formed over time. The
reacting brain – the part of our brain structure that we
share with our mammalian relatives – has neural networks
that act as scaffolding to the formation of other more
complex characteristics, including those within the mirror
system, such as the aspects of behaviour that we learn
through observation and interaction with our environment.
The more basic emotional drivers include our drive to eat,
to feel pain, to form social bonds, to feel fear in the face of
danger. Our individual differences, the things that make
you uniquely you and me uniquely me, are influenced by
nature, your genetics, for example, and your environment.
These are housed in the parts of the brain that are more
uniquely human, our neocortex or observing brain, and
they are filled in as we observe the people and world around
us and take on board learning. The response to a core
driver – one that we all have, for example fear – may be
shaped uniquely by your specific experience. As a result it
becomes slightly nuanced depending on the person –
making them 'individual differences'. For example, one
person may be afraid of spiders (reacting brain – basic
driver), something which was reinforced by their mother's
fear (observing brain – shaped by experience); another
person may fear wasps (reacting brain – basic driver),
reinforced by being stung as a child and then being
encouraged by a scared parent to stay away from wasps
(observing brain – shaped by experience).

This, perhaps unsurprisingly, is also thought to reflect
how mirror thinking occurs, beginning with the simplest
aspects of mirroring, which are then built upon[3]. We first

observe then mirror a movement, behaviour or emotion, by synchronising that movement within our own brain and producing it ourselves. This enables it to be practised, refined and developed, and allows us to hone our mirror thinking along with it. A baby observing their mother or father's face may see them smile, which triggers mirror neurons in their brain associated with facial movement specifically in the area of the mouth: they may then try smiling themselves. That has a positive effect as their parent smiles back, which is mirrored in their brain. They then try again, and so on and so forth. Each time these interactions provide microlearning, helping the baby to understand the meaning of that smile within their social world and every instance builds a stronger neural pathway.

When an action or interaction is rewarded or repeated the neural connections are reinforced and become stronger. This is a bit like water repeatedly trickling down the same muddy path: if the water continues down one particular route it gradually carves a groove creating a path of 'least resistance', which encourages repeated use. The interaction between a child and their parents plays a huge role in the developing brain and the formation of these neural networks. It's estimated that a massive 65 per cent of Western infants' waking hours are not just spent in the company of their parents but in face-to-face contact with them.[4] Fascinatingly, the type of proximate contact has been found to differ between cultures. For example, in American culture mothers tend to respond to their baby's expressions with a pause, followed by their own facial expressions and vocalisations. Japanese mothers will also respond to their baby's expressions with a pause, followed by a reaction and then leaning in close to touch their baby. These interactions are thought to contribute to cultural differences, with American mothers encouraging more

independence and Japanese mothers the opposite –
encouraging more interdependence.[5]

Learning how to be a human

As humans we come into the world with less 'fixed' neural
networking. We are, if you like, less pre-programmed
than other animals, which means that we are helpless and
totally dependent on our main caregivers. As a result, we
need to rapidly learn about the world and how to survive
in it in order to stay alive. In the first few years of life,
more than 1 million new neural connections are formed
every second.[6] Much of this learning is about how to
become less helpless but not less dependent. We depend on
strong social ties to enable us to both survive and thrive.
That was the case in the time of our ancient ancestors and
it still is today. A majority of what we learn is focused on
how to be co-dependent and socially capable, which all
begins with our mirror system being shaped by interactions
with our parents. How can we tell that our parents so
strongly influence us? It's incredibly difficult to test, we
can't after all take children away from their mother and
father to see how they develop. However, an intriguing
insight into what we may be like growing up without our
parents can be seen in feral children.

The term 'feral' was coined by a man called Carl
Linnaeus, a Swedish botanist, physician and zoologist, who
in 1758 differentiated between humans living in society,
namely *Homo sapiens*, and those who grew up in isolation,
calling them *Homo ferus*. Feral children have been of
particular fascination to philosophers, psychologists and
scientists throughout history as they hold the key to many
secrets of socialisation. Are humans cultured because of the
society that they live in or in spite of that society? How

much do people learn through social interaction? What do people learn through cooperation with others? To what extent do we mirror the behaviour of those around us?[7] While it may be viewed as abhorrent that any child could be left to fend for themselves, it has happened and the cases have been studied to try to pinpoint the answers to some of these questions. One such example is the case of Oxana Malaya, who was born in a small, rundown village in Ukraine in 1983. Both of her parents were alcoholics and one night, 'too drunk to care', they left 3-year-old Oxana outside. Presumably looking for warmth and safety she crawled up to the stray dogs that roamed the area where she lived. The story goes that no one noticed she was gone or came to look for her and she spent the next five years living as a member of the pack until a neighbour reported a sighting and she was discovered by the authorities. By the age of 8, Oxana had become what is known as a feral child – she couldn't speak, walked on all fours, ate raw meat, scavenged through rubbish for food and barked like a dog. She had grown up through those years mimicking the behaviour of the dogs. Without parents to mirror she had not developed the ability to socialise, interact, communicate, talk, walk or even eat in the way we'd expect. This provides a strong representation of how the systems in our brain operate, particularly social systems. There needs to be a model in the environment to stimulate development. In a 'normal' setting this follows the iterative process of mirroring that begins when a parent or caregiver responds to a baby in face-to-face contact.

Shortly after you were born, a sibling, cousin or overzealous relative will most likely have stuck out their tongue at you. It's something that we tend to do to babies – a sign of playfulness and a way to interact with this little being who cannot talk or understand what we're saying. The likelihood is that you, as a

newborn, would have obligingly stuck out your tongue in
return. Research shows that babies as young as 41 minutes old
carry out this form of imitation.[8] This tiny, playful endeavour
is one of the very first demonstrations of the mirror neurons
in action. The baby observes the person sticking out their
tongue, their mirror neurons fire, rehearsing that action in
their own brain and they then reproduce it. Scientists are not
yet sure whether these mirror neurons are innately programmed
to imitate or if given the right conditions they begin to 'mirror'
behaviour soon after birth.[9] The most critical point, however,
is that the mirror neurons are almost certainly involved[10] and
the act of using them iteratively refines their capability.[11]

In our early years, when we are with our caregivers,
mirroring takes place roughly once every minute.[12] That's
a vast amount of time spent learning through observation
and imitation, and a huge opportunity for the mirror
neurons themselves to be shaped and refined. By 10 weeks
old our mirroring has escalated from simple gestures like
sticking out our tongue to spontaneously imitating happy
and angry expressions when they are displayed by our
parents.[13] During the first year of life, before language is
acquired, a parent and child can only communicate by
observation, making this capability essential to
development. Marco Iacoboni, professor of psychiatry and
biobehavioral sciences at the David Geffen School of
Medicine at UCLA, has carried out research to show how
this interaction triggers mirror neurons in both the baby
and the mother, providing a two-way imitation for
continued growth. Iacoboni and his team found that a
mother will synchronise her behaviour with the facial
expressions she sees in her baby and the baby will respond.
Scanning mothers' brains during this interaction, the
researchers were able to isolate the area involved, showing
mirror neurons triggering followed by activation of the

limbic system – the emotional centres of the (reacting) brain. The mirror neurons are associated with responses in the same area of the brain relating to the action (in this case the facial expression), which allows the mother to reproduce it and the limbic system to provide the emotional meaning behind it, enabling the mother to interpret and respond to their baby's intentions[14]. This creates a positive attachment and a virtuous cycle of mirroring, which leads to the development of the baby's mirror system and ultimately forms the basis from which they are able to understand and form social relationships. What's really interesting is that the capability of a mother to mirror and understand a baby's emotional state is greater with their own child than with someone else's. This shows that our parents, whether biological or adoptive, play a more significant role in providing mirroring than anyone else. This capability of a parent to 'share' their baby's emotional feelings is considered absolutely critical to healthy social and emotional development.[15]

Over time, each action mirrored and each step taken is seen, rehearsed and repeated thousands of times before something as seemingly simple as walking becomes a programmed neural pathway in the brain. It all starts with gestures that are as simple as sticking out our tongue, rewarded by a delighted smile, clap of the hands, excited 'look at this'. The majority of parents do not set out to spend their time deliberately teaching. While learning comes through intentional play – for example, throwing and catching a ball – most of the time the teaching is via incidental circumstances. Our caregivers inadvertently demonstrate how to talk, dress, clean our teeth, feed ourselves, say please and thank you, be kind to those around us and even how to use the toilet without a specific set of instructions. In spite of every keen new parent's effort to

accelerate their child's learning, the chances are that it won't work. However much you cajole your child to be the first among their peers – or at least not the last – to roll over, say their first word or take their first steps, it simply cannot be forced. These routine aspects of development, the factors around social and emotional intelligence, are learnt by watching, listening and mirroring what parents do when a child is good and ready, or at least when their brain is. It is mirroring and the mirror neurons specifically that form the critical link to enabling the vast majority of all early development.

From the mouths of babes

For the brain to become 'ready' to move from one stage to another, it's believed that the basic mirror neurons have to become established and adjust before the next level of neurons develop. It begins with the basic mirror neurons for vision, seeing what our parents are doing in order to mirror them, followed by the more complex aspects of behaviour – most notably the mirror neurons that assist language skills. Learning to babble and ultimately talk, learning a repertoire of language, a cadence of speech, an accent that relates to where you and your parents live, seems natural, effortless. Yet these are also aspects of our existence that take considerable time and ongoing practice. As an infant, from about the age of two, we acquire speech by mirroring the sounds we hear from our parents, learning up to 10 new words per day.[16] With no caregivers, as seen in the extreme case of Oxana, language simply doesn't develop. Studies have also shown that the rate at which children raised in a bilingual environment learn each language varies as a function of their exposure. The greater the exposure, the quicker the rate of development. So, if a

child has a mother who speaks Spanish and a father who speaks English, but spends more time with their father, the rate at which they acquire English would be quicker than the rate at which they learn Spanish.[17] The mirroring will be that direct.

Language in turn becomes the precursor for most of what we learn both socially and cognitively, forming the foundation from which to accelerate so many aspects of being human. At a neurological level, language is an incredibly complex phenomena involving multiple areas and mechanisms in the brain. For example, there is the 'what' and the 'where' of the sound itself that enables language recognition. Broken down further, within the 'what' of sound there is the ability to distinguish between the more melodic sounds: syllables, pitch, spoken words and different languages, between voices and other background noises. We are able to recognise voices as belonging distinctly to one person. If your friend calls you from a different number, when you pick up and they speak, you know who it is after just two words.[18] Even a toddler is able to recognise the voice of their mother on the phone.[19] This is critical to living in a social world if, for example, you are in a group of people and you need to be able to tell who is saying what. As with so many other factors it begins with a baby recognising their mother's voice as soon as they are born: a foundation that is then built on throughout life, and learning that needs to be nurtured even as adults if we want to remain socially and emotionally able.

The only way to learn how to speak and understand language is through imitating speech sounds, a capability that is enabled by mirror neurons in what is known as Broca's area in the frontal lobe[20] – a uniquely human part of the (observing) brain responsible for language generation.[21]

When parents are 'chatterboxes' it not only improves a child's language capabilities but has also been linked to better cognitive skills. Professor Sophie von Stumm at the University of York led research in 2019 that saw tiny audio recorders fitted to the clothing of 107 two- to four-year-old children for 16 hours a day. The research found that 'the quantity of adult spoken words that children hear is positively associated with their cognitive ability' as well as that 'positive parenting – where parents are responsive and encouraging of exploration and self-expression – was associated with children showing fewer signs of restless, aggressive and disobedient behaviours'. This powerfully illustrates how learning via the mirror neuron, even if it doesn't appear to directly relate to imitation, can quickly build into other more complex behavioural responses. In contrast, when these basics are missing, for example when a child has no or very limited language, as is the case for neglected children, these foundations of both social and cognitive skills do not form as expected. This then leads to issues with functioning effectively in life, school and as an adult within society and the workplace.[22] Mirroring our parents and early caregivers creates the foundations that set us up for life.

Shaping who we are

We don't get to choose our parents or caregivers, nor do we select the values, beliefs and behaviours we learn and mirror from them. We don't decide which language will be our mother tongue, which cultural norms we will grow up with, which faith we will adhere to. Yes, we can learn other languages later in life or convert from one religion to another, but those fundamentals that we learn as young children will always remain the foundation of our neural

network. What were those things for you? What beliefs and values have you grown up with and perhaps never questioned?

As we get slightly older it's not just our parents who we spend our time with. We're exposed to teachers, friends, relatives and other members of our community – and these are all factors that we'll come to later. As a child we may begin to wonder why we're different from our friends. A Muslim girl who wears a hijab in a mostly Christian school will at some level know she is not the same as everyone else. She may question why she has to wear it, feel proud of it, resent it or query whether it's the course she wants to take in life, but ultimately if that's what her parents want it's what she will do, because as children we generally do what our parents expect of us. In spite of interactions with friends who may be different, eat dissimilar foods or follow alternate customs, the most critical source of influence remains our parents. Dr Mary Thornton from the University of Hertfordshire and Dr Patricia Bricheno from the University of Cambridge carried out a study in 2007 involving children aged from 10 to 16 years old from four English schools in different socio-economic environments, and found that the majority of pupils chose one or both parents as their most significant role model. Thornton and Bricheno also cite research from the US and UK that 'broadly agree that the most frequently chosen role models are parents'. A survey carried out in 2007 by Weekly Reader Research on behalf of the American Bible Society involving 1,100 12- to 18-year-olds in the US found that 67.7 per cent of teenagers questioned said parents are the most influential role models in their lives.[23] A study carried out in 2014 involving black youths in rural South Africa also found that parents, specifically mothers, came out as strong role models for children. Mothers were

described as a 'steadfast source of support and mentorship', keeping families together.[24] The same is true across most if not all cultures across the globe – our parents are our main mirror through our early years and beyond.

An illustration of how much we absorb from our parents can be seen in children who are adopted. Take, for example, the case of an American girl called Kati, who in 2017 at the age of 22 met her Chinese birth parents for the first time. This story resonated with me – when I was not much older than Kati and travelling through rural southwestern China, I stayed with a couple who had given up their second child, the mother having hidden her pregnancy because of China's one-child policy for fear of fines or jail. This was what had happened to Kati's birth parents; she was the second and therefore illegal child and was given up, but left with a note that ultimately enabled her to find them. She was brought up in Michigan in the United States by her adoptive parents the Pohlers, a devout Christian couple. Kati is described by a newspaper report as a fiercely independent, outdoorsy, Christian all-American girl who has travelled widely. In contrast, her biological sister was brought up to be far more dependent on the family; she has never travelled and the government of China officially advocates state atheism meaning that they practise no religion. Simply the act of going and meeting her birth parents highlighted the contrast in behaviour, as her father told the reporter: 'Foreign girls and Chinese girls think differently. A Chinese girl who was given away would never have forgiven her birth parents. It's cultural.'[25] Beyond these variations there are the language disparities. Kati's birth parents do not speak English and she does not speak Mandarin, and then there are the traditions practised, foods eaten and everyday way of life. Although we are socialised by society and community, it is primarily our parents who teach us these

things. Once again this illustrates that being human and being social first comes down to being raised by and mirroring our parents, whether biological or adoptive.

A given between parent and child is that there is trust, connection and exposure. These unfortunately can lead to massively negative impacts on children, as well as providing the foundation for positive development. With children whose caregivers have histories of childhood abuse and neglect there is an increased chance of sexual abuse and neglect in the next generation,[26] as offspring may model the approach they grew up with. And living with a parent who smokes dramatically increases the chance of an adolescent taking up smoking.[27]

The same repetitive generational cycle is true of crime, drug abuse, alcoholism and divorce. While we may infer that these come from the broader social environment in which people grow up, these studies have stripped out and controlled as many other factors as possible in order to examine the direct influence of parents on children. Mirroring is powerful and nowhere more so than in the concentrated environment that is our childhood home, with those we love and need to love us most – our parents. All of these examples, both positive and negative, have massive implications for how we operate as a society – from how we break cycles of obesity, through to building social economic strength.

The influence of our parents is still so important even to adults in their mid to later life. If you think about your own parents, you probably still look for their affirmation on major life decisions. The influence of caregivers in shaping who we are and who we become is so critical that it's something people such as myself – psychologists who work with leaders – must explore in order to understand how and why as adults we do the things we do.

Once genetics have been accounted for, between 35 per cent and an incredible 77 per cent[28] of who we are is open to the influence of the world around us, to mirroring behaviour in order to learn how to behave. Given that the time our brain is most malleable is when we are growing up, it is our caregivers who shape who we become through mirroring. Even when we are counter-mirroring – seeing something and doing something different – it is typically our parents who we are using as a point of reference.

In exploring the childhood and specifically the influences of the hundreds of people I've worked with over the years, it's always interesting to see how they react to being asked about their parents. Some have reflected on their impact, particularly how similar or different their parents are from them, others have not given it much thought. Regardless, looking back as an adult with a more objective viewpoint almost always results in surprising insights. We tend to carry the same narrative with us throughout life unless it's examined and while we question many things on a daily basis, for example, why doesn't that person like me or how could I have done that better, there are many other things we ignore. Unless someone encounters an issue or is for some reason encouraged to look at the influence certain aspects of childhood have had on them, they do not make space to explore it. Why would they? There's so much to think about in just living life today and worrying about tomorrow. But it can be an incredibly powerful exercise, something I have seen time and again when working through people's personality profiles. The purpose of this is not to dig up dirt or to place blame, but to understand what makes you, you; how you have or have not mirrored your parents.

Other factors influenced by our parents include our level of self-control, which as a child is a strong predictor of how things turn out for us as an adult. The ability to manage our emotions and overcome short-term wants and needs is a critical life skill that we begin to develop when we are young. While some of this is inevitably genetic – you only have to look at siblings to see stark differences, for example – it's also heavily influenced by mirroring or counter-mirroring our parents. Studies have shown that being given responsibilities as a child or a young adolescent – for example, being expected to assist with household chores or having a part-time job – helps to build self-discipline. This is partly due to the expectations or intentions of parents, but seeing a mother or father who works hard often instils the same work ethic in their child, simply through the child watching and being immersed in their world. Well-known instances of this include the former first lady Michelle Obama, who credits her parents for her strong work ethic. Michelle graduated from Princeton with a law degree despite her working-class background. Or Taylor Swift, one of the best-selling music artists of all time, who said: 'My parents raised me to never feel like I was entitled to success, that you have to work for it. You have to work so hard for it. And sometimes you don't even get to where you need to go.'[29]

Our parents' expectations, and the intentions they have for us, have a huge influence on the career path we take and what we achieve, regardless of the child's own upbringing or income. Studies show that teenagers often set out to mirror their parents' footsteps, whether as an entrepreneur, shop assistant, council worker, small business owner or doctor, and those whose parents are in 'top' jobs are more likely to find themselves in a similar position.[30] Considerable research has been carried out on this when it comes to

entrepreneurism in particular. One study led by Professor
Johan Lindquist at Stockholm University, published in 2012
by the IZA Institute of Labor Economics, took an approach
that strongly indicates the impact of mirror thinking.
Looking at Swedish adoptees and examining the
occupational status of both their adoptive parents and their
biological parents, they show that the effect of post-birth
factors (traits from their adoptive parents) is approximately
twice as large as the effect of pre-birth factors (traits from
their biological parents).[31] In other words, the adoptive
parents and their role-modelling plays a more important
part in predicting behaviour than genetics.

Well-known examples of children following in their
parents' footsteps can be found across professions. Take
acting, for example. Actress Dakota Johnson, daughter of
actors Don Johnson and Melanie Griffith, is quoted as
saying: 'I grew up under the impression that I wasn't capable
of doing anything else.'[32] Other examples include Kate
Hudson, daughter of Goldie Hawn, and Kiefer Sutherland,
son of Donald Sutherland. George Bush, President of the
United States from 1989 to 1993, was followed into office
by his son George W. Bush in 2001; and Ivanka Trump,
daughter of Donald Trump, is senior advisor to her father
the President. In many cases the children who follow in
their parents' footsteps are exposed to comparable situations,
meaning what they mirror is similar. In some they may be
given opportunities as a result of nepotism, being given the
chances they had in these careers simply because their
parents were already embedded in the industry.

Other children deliberately 'counter-mirror' a decision
to not be like their parents. But even that comes from
observing what they do and making a decision not to take
that path, which is in some ways an even more powerful
use of mirror thinking because it's conscious.

The influence of parents is particularly important when looking at the science, technology, engineering and mathematical (STEM) fields where women are typically underrepresented.[33] Theories focusing on their development of gender roles suggest that across their lifespan people perceive certain roles to be more or less appropriate for their gender[34]. As a study specifically published in *Frontiers in Psychology* in 2018 states: 'Parents are the role models young children are exposed to most.'[35] This means that parents' occupations have a significant impact on not only career aspirations but also the gender stereotypes of roles. This review highlights numerous studies that have found evidence of 'the role model effect' of parents, specifically mothers' occupational roles on their daughter's aspirations. With exposure to mothers in counter-stereotypical roles such as leadership, politics or STEM, daughters are encouraged to aspire to counter-stereotypical roles themselves. Although not following in her mother's footsteps per se, former Microsoft general manager Melinda Gates is a good example of parental influence. Melinda's father was an aerospace engineer and in an interview she gave in 2019 she said:

Some of my most treasured memories of Dad are of the nights he let us stay up to watch the Apollo *launches on TV in the late 1960s. Those were exciting nights for a lot of families – but they were especially exciting when your father was an engineer who contracted with NASA.*[36]

Even though I didn't know a lot of women who worked outside the home, I always knew that I wanted to have an exciting career like my dad's …

Dad was … the first person I ever heard talk about the importance of diversity in STEM. He made a point of hiring women when he

could because he believed the best teams he'd worked on were the
ones with women mathematicians on them. That stuck with me.[37]

It's not hard to see how Melinda ended up doing what she was doing. While she may have had a genetic propensity toward scientific thinking, it was mirroring her father, hearing of his attitude towards women in STEM and having encouragement from both parents that enabled her to flourish. Interestingly, a study carried out in 2000 by professor of psychology Glenn Geher at the State University of New York suggests that we gravitate toward romantic partners who are similar to our opposite-sex parent.[38] Could this explain Melinda's attraction to Bill Gates as a spouse?

Even if we see less of our parents, for example if both work long hours in full-time jobs, we still tend to place higher value in the meaning of what our parents do than we do in anyone else. They are our main caregivers; we look to them for guidance and protection, and as young children we trust that they know what they are doing and we have a blind faith that they are wise and always correct. You may of course change your outlook, but during this incredibly powerful phase of learning and development your brain is being programmed along the lines of what your parents believe, how they behave and what they choose to do. The leaders I work with find they are often frustrated or even surprised by the fact that they still feel a strong pull towards the expectations of their parents and a need to seek their approval. Just because we're adults doesn't mean we stop caring what they think. Those foundational neural networks will always be there.

Mirroring our parents when we were growing up also influenced the development of our social skills. A broad set of characteristics such as how empathic we are, how kind

and how co-operative, have been shown to come from parental influence. These facets of who we are impact our interpersonal skills throughout life, which in turn have a massive influence on our success more broadly as well as our emotional well-being.

Being a parental role model

One of my core reasons for studying psychology was trying to understand the intentions of others: why do people do certain things and what motivates them to choose that course of action? This is critical to what I do in my day-to-day job, helping people to understand how to interact more effectively, communicate, lead and become more self-aware. It may seem like a big jump to get to that from the basic foundations of social and emotional life that we've explored so far, but beyond these core foundations of mirror thinking that allow us to thrive in early life, the mirror neurons also serve another incredibly important function. Mirror thinking also gives us the ability to understand why we or someone else is carrying out that action. For example, the same action can have different intentions and we begin to learn how to interpret what someone is going to do next in childhood. Your mother may have looked out of the window to check the weather to decide if she should hang washing on the line. Her intention was to understand what to do with the laundry. My mother may have looked out of the window to see who was coming to the front door. Her intentions was to understand whether or not to let someone in. These are the same actions for different reasons. It's this inference of meaning that makes the mirror neuron so incredible. This allows us to understand not only the intentions, but also the expectations and motivations of others based on watching and unconsciously modelling that behaviour, and

incorporating it into our own. As we are growing up we constantly watch our parents for guidance on not only how but why to do something.

It's hard, however, parenting in a world where we have no role models to demonstrate how to behave when it comes to screens. Today parents have to navigate totally uncharted territory. When I was a child I would have to wait until after 6pm (free local calls) to speak to friends on the phone, or ride my bike around to their house. There was no texting and no social media. My daughter hardly even uses her phone to speak and the roads are too busy for her to cycle to a friend's house. Instead, like many other teenagers around the world, she spends hours sending messages to not just one friend but to groups of friends. Our parents taught us not to speak to strangers, to avoid anyone who looked like they were behaving oddly and never to get into the car of someone we didn't know. Yet now children have open Instagram accounts where thousands of people can see what they're doing, they have followers with no face, they are in constant danger of being groomed and as parents we may not even know. When I was growing up there were only four TV channels and we only had one TV in the house. My mum knew when a programme with 'inappropriate content' was coming on and the television could be switched off. Today, on iPads, iPhones and a multitude of other devices, children can watch anything, broadcast by anyone at any time they wish. It may be violent or have sexual content; it may be on YouTube and never have been screened by any governing body of any sort. We haven't seen how to parent this because it never existed before. As parents we look to our peers for guidance, but they are as uncertain as we are. Should devices be put down at 6pm or 9pm? Should they be allowed an iPhone or not? Should they be allowed on

Instagram? Should an account be locked or open? Should they be allowed their phones in their bedroom? Because we have never observed how to parent in this technological world we are left with no behaviours, beliefs or values to follow. It makes us aware of what's missing and how much our parents provided a role model not only of how to behave but how to parent. And while we clumsily navigate the digital world for ourselves, we often inadvertently model the 'wrong' behaviours to our children. Too much time staring at our screens, phones by the bed, endless texting and emailing, never switching off. Which perhaps makes it even more important that we do take responsibility to model the behaviours that we know positively impact our kids.

This understanding of mirror thinking adds depth to the saying 'do as I say, not as I do'. When we say one thing and do another it confuses the message. You may think that's common sense, yet people, including parents, so often don't practise what they preach, which in terms of mirror thinking makes understanding – and therefore learning – disjointed. For example, in an article for *The European Journal of Public Health*, Dr Stephanie Schoeppe showed that the more time parents spent watching screens meant more screen time for children. This study and others have shown that 'telling' children not to watch screens is not enough. The behaviour has to be modelled. In other words, the intention and action have to match. In contrast to the sedentary behaviour of viewing a screen, when parents role-modelled more physically active behaviours, children were far more likely to be physically active themselves. The researchers explained this by saying children were inspired by their parents' lifestyle, and 'incidental' physical activities such as walking and cycling as a means of transport became integrated into family life.

They also said that active parents were more likely to provide support whether in the form of equipment, fees or encouragement. These forms of role-modelling from parents, following through with intentions, encouragement and integration into family life, all represent aspects that are initiated via mirror thinking and then reinforced as neural networks through repetition and reward.

What we role-model to our children can even go as far as impacting their physical health. For example, a 2018 study led by Amber Vaughn, associate director of the Children's Healthy Weight Research Group at the University of North Carolina, showed that parents' purposeful or conscious modelling of healthy food choices was positively associated with a child's diet quality.[40] Other studies have shown that parents are the single most important influence over their children's diet.[41] Although anecdotal, this is reflected directly in mine and my husband's diets, which are both quite different. He, having been brought up by a Chinese mum, eats a heavily meat- and rice-based diet. I on the other hand had a mum who preferred vegetables and salads over meat and I eat a largely vegetarian diet. Our children eat a mixture of both.

Beyond the research there will be so many quirks and daily habits that are unique to you, influenced by your parents and that you pass to your children. Take my situation for example. My husband and I share a lot of values, with a similar take on how to treat others and what matters most, which comes from our parents. Strangely, after we met we found out that our fathers had both worked together years before, so maybe it's not surprising to learn that we have similar views on life. But on a micro level there are quite big differences. For example, when it comes to doing the dishes, he cleans them under a running tap. I clean them in the way I was taught by my mother: using

the same bowl of water, starting with the glasses, then cutlery, followed by crockery and finally the pots and pans. An added twist from my stepmother is that I then rinse each item to get the bubbles and dirty water off. If you look at how you carry out daily tasks and how your partner or close friends carry out the same tasks, you'll notice that you've picked up so many of these little quirks from mirroring your parents. Unlike your values these daily habits are probably something you've never questioned and have no need to change. They are also the things that your children will carry with them into their adulthood.

Being conscious of all of the things we say and do, the way we behave, and the values and beliefs we impart is so important. It may feel like too big a responsibility but it's one that we take on the moment our first child is born. In the same way you could not and did not choose your parents, your children did not choose you, yet you are the ones shaping their brains more than anyone else in this world.

It is hard to constantly role-model the 'right thing'. We have bad days where we fly off the handle. We say things that on reflection we shouldn't have. We navigate difficulties in a way that we're not always proud of. But we can make a conscious choice to immerse our kids in the positive: to eat healthily and exercise because that will set them up well for life; reading lots of books because we want them to do the same; being caring and considerate to others; working hard; and displaying self-control. Even when we don't behave in the best way, it helps to then explain why and what we should have done differently so that our kids understand how to behave. Doing this also provides insight into how to show humility and understanding.

It's worth exploring your own values and purpose, the influences on your own life that have shaped you and the

negative tendencies that you may never iron out but could be more aware of. These things will help you as well as helping your children, if you're a parent, and enable you to live a more fulfilled life even if you are not. Ultimately, it's your choice.

Our parents have a huge influence on the development of our mirror neurons and mirror system from the moment we are born, impacting many adult outcomes from how empathic we are to what language we speak, shaping our beliefs, values, behaviours and the lens through which we see life. As parents, we ourselves have the same massive impact on our own children, and understanding that can be the most important parenting lesson we'll ever learn.

It's All in the Family

Sibling thinking

In the early autumn of 2016, the Triathlon World Series was held in Cozumel, Mexico. Despite the time difference, UK TV viewers keenly watched two Brits competing, hopeful to see them finish in the top rankings. At the time the Brownlee brothers were world leaders, having won myriad titles from Olympic gold medals to Triathlon World Championships, and if 26-year-old Jonny won this race he would secure the world title. He was in the lead, but as he rounded the corner, heading toward the finish line, he began to wobble. At first it wasn't clear whether he'd just lost concentration, but quickly his legs started to look as if they were going to fail him. Exhausted, he stumbled from side to side, on the brink of collapse. Rather than powering over the line, he started to look seriously ill and fell to the side of the track with only 700m to go. Cycling, swimming and running in the scorching 34°C heat had taken their toll on his body. Then suddenly, his older brother Alistair appeared from around the corner. He later said: 'I was thinking: This is perfect – Jonny's ahead of me, he's going to win the world title, I'm going to come second or third. This is a great end to the year.'[1]

But instead he saw his little brother in desperate need of help. Without a second thought, Alistair took hold of Jonny, pulling his brother's arm around his own shoulders enabling

him hobble to the finish. Despite being overtaken by Henri Schoeman they still took second and third place. Alistair, having helped Jonny to finish, let go of him and gently nudged him over the line, meaning that Jonny secured second place, while Alistair took third for himself. The strength of their bond meant that despite competing against his brother, Alistair put Jonny's welfare first. Not only did he stop to help, giving up his chance of first place, but he maintained Jonny's position ahead of him.

How does such a strong bond form? I once profiled someone who had trained with the Brownlee brothers and he described the hours and hours that they put into training – running at the track and cycling across the Yorkshire countryside. Over the many hours, days and years, the two men had been not only been exposed to the elements, but also to each other in a way that influenced their attitudes, values, behaviours and beliefs. There often tends to be a natural trust and deep connection between siblings. When you are with someone for so long it is inevitable that you are close due to the level of shared experience that influences your life, your memories and who you are. Even if you don't particularly like one another, you and your siblings share common ground that no one else can. Growing up you go on the same holidays, live in the same house and have the same relatives. But some siblings go to different schools, live in different houses and go on different holidays. Does that impact the strength of their mirroring?

My big brother and I have an incredibly close bond. I was teased when I began senior school for starting almost every sentence with 'my brother'. Some friends to this day say that they never knew his name. He did, without a doubt, have a huge influence on me. Family folklore says he was the first person I ever smiled at, that we were the siblings

who never argued, he was the brother who would show his little sister off proudly to all his friends. I adored him and still do, although now I see him more as a great friend. When I was growing up not only did I idolise him, but I also overtly mirrored his behaviour: he climbed trees so I climbed trees, he played the piano so I played the piano, he played the clarinet so I played the clarinet, he did athletics so I did athletics. Everything he did, I did. As far as the mirror neuron was concerned, I'm guessing it was pretty much triggered with that first smile and ultimately his behaviour, attitudes and values all played a huge role in shaping my brain and who I am today. Our parents separated when I was seven; my dad had custody of him and my mother of me, yet my brother still shaped me. Was the connection and trust so strong that the level of exposure mattered less? Or was it that I was deliberately and consciously mirroring his behaviour, making it more powerful?

The factors that play into the behaviours we mirror are multifaceted and complex. The Brownlee brothers' lives very much reflect one another's. There are aspects that are obviously the same for both of them; having grown up together with the same parents they will have developed a shared approach to life both morally and pragmatically. Inevitably this shared parenting will have formed the foundation for mirroring each other as well as their parents. Added to this, the Brownlee brothers went to the same schools and the same university. Hence, they had more in common with each other than anyone else. Whereas parents would naturally be the strongest source of mirroring with these siblings, this provided a multiplier effect, reinforcing those preferences, habits and approach to life that they may initially have got from their parents but then sourced primarily from each other. We can assume that

they differ in genetic make-up; Alistair has slightly lighter curly hair and is an inch taller than Jonny, for example, and they have different personalities. In an interview with the *Independent* Alistair joked about Jonny, saying: 'I call him Gnome because he's so boring. He's more intense and uptight – a bit more of a worrier.' Jonny agreed, saying: 'Yeah, Alistair's a bit more ... relaxed.'[2]

These differences make the similarities in what they've striven for and achieved even more interesting. Surely this commonality cannot just be due to family and environmental influences, but largely to their own mirroring of each other? According to Jonny: 'Without a doubt he [Alistair] has been a massive influence on me. From coming home with some international kit for the first time and me thinking "I want some of that", to prepping for the biggest races of our lives ... he has guided and shown me the way. I've not always agreed with him, but we are brothers after all.'[3] Such influences are inevitable as a result of social proximity[4] – bonding as a consequence of the density of their interactions and the interdependencies created.[5] This phenomenon leads to a strong level of influence and semblance even in decision-making, simply through exposure.

A study carried out by Professor Susan McHale in 1996 at Pennsylvania State University showed that by the time a child reaches the age of 11 they spend approximately 33 per cent of their free time with their siblings; more time than anyone else, including friends, teachers and even parents.[6] This continues into adolescence despite the many activities that by that age are filling our lives, with an average of at least 10 hours and up to 17 hours per day spent in the company of a sibling. That's an awful lot of time. Yet we often don't consider how that has influenced the way we behave or who we are today. When profiling it's critical that we hear about a

person's siblings. The relationships we have with our brothers and sisters have been found to predict a whole host of adult outcomes, from academic success to how we respond to people in our social environment and even our health.

If you think about it, the impact of sibling influence can be seen across all walks of life. Looking to your own upbringing, that of your parents or grandparents, or even that of your nieces and nephews or children of friends, the patterns are there to be found. I've met a number of CEOs who have a sibling who is also a CEO; entrepreneurs who have a sibling in a similar field; and many psychologists who share their profession with a brother or sister. There are also numerous public examples of the influence that siblings have on one another. In the sporting world, tennis alone provides three current examples with Serena and Venus Williams, Andy and Jamie Murray, and brother and sister Marat Safin and Dinara Safina. In other sports, it's easy to name myriad examples: Kurt and Kyle Busch (Nascar), Jonny and Alistair Brownlee (triathlon), Vitali and Wladimir Klitschko (boxing), Justine and Jordan Mowen (beach volleyball), Irfan and Yusuf Pathan (cricket), Melvin Upton Jr and Justin Upton (baseball), Kareem and Brandon Rush (basketball) and Ardie and Julien Savea (rugby union). Beyond sport there are businessmen, such as Adolf and Rudolf Dassler, founders of Adidas and Puma; in politics the Kennedy brothers; in film Ben and Casey Affleck; John, Ann and Joan Cusack; and so the lists go on.

On the surface of it, despite the connection and trust and the massive amounts of time spent together – the exposure – it may be difficult to understand the mechanisms of how a sibling can have such a big influence on mirroring. One area that's of particular interest in the work I do is studying how siblings have approached academic life. An individual's decision to go to university, for example, is

often based on what an older sibling does, and even where they go. My husband went to the same university as both of his older brothers and the same was true of the Brownlee brothers. It may be that your sibling was the first in the family to go on to higher education, making it feel like a natural step for you, or that you chose your subjects based on what your sibling did or didn't like. Part of the reason for this is demonstrated by a 2019 study led by Professor Cheti Nicoletti at the University of York.[7] Nicoletti and her team looked at a staggeringly large data set of 230,000 sibling pairs from across the UK. Tracking the data over the course of four years, they examined what is known by psychologists as 'the spillover effect' of academic achievement – where one sibling's performance has a knock-on impact on another's. However, Nicoletti herself is not a psychologist but an economist, revealing another interesting component of this impact – the influence is so great that there is a) reason to study it from an economic perspective and b) a tangible measure of the outcome. Nicoletti found that not only did an older sibling's academic achievement have a significant positive influence on a younger sibling's subsequent attainments, but she also demonstrated that these impacts were equivalent to the effect of spending an additional £1,000 a year on education for each younger sibling. The influence was biggest when the older siblings had 'top grades', which the authors attribute to role-modelling effects of positive educational aspirations, values and academic behaviours. This may on the surface appear to be quite noble – a big brother or sister helping out their younger siblings – but it can also arise from a competitive relationship with a younger sibling spurred on to do as well or better. This mirroring often happens without any explicit awareness. These effects may even be felt with very little interaction at all

due to mirror thinking creating a norm or benchmark for how to do things in the way that a big sister or a big brother behaves.

It's not just academics that have this kind of 'spillover effect'. The vast amount of time spent mirroring, trying out different behaviours, feeling the outcome and adjusting behaviour impacts a far deeper level of your psyche. Think about your life as an adult and the people you spend most time with – a work colleague who, like a sibling, you have no choice in being with for several hours a day, a best friend or a partner. All of these relationships have highs and lows, good days and bad. Then imagine how those relationships might have developed when you were a child, before you had developed an understanding of how the world works, how social interactions operate, how to manage your own emotions or how to take conscious control of what you're mirroring. At this early point in life, your brain was not developed enough to control many of the more nuanced aspects of your emotions, let alone consciously decide the more subtle aspects of your behaviour. You had far less control over how much something annoyed, upset or frustrated you or what you could do about it because the connection between the pre-frontal lobe in your observing brain and the emotional reacting brain is not fully developed. You experienced your siblings as companions, opponents and confidantes, you also compared yourself to them both at home and within your social environment. All of these interactions, combined with your developmental vulnerability as a child, created emotionally intense interactions both externally and in our inner world. From this standpoint it's not hard to see how each interaction, whether good or bad, teaches a sibling about cooperation. The consequences of an action or behaviour, how to work things through and negotiate, and how to practise and

refine their navigation of the social world. You may also look to a sibling to see what has worked with a parent, friend, relative or teacher and then role-model that behaviour, trying it on for size in your own social environment. Over time this develops the mirror system itself. Working through these interactions time and again improves social skills. Thus sparring with a sibling or watching how they did things could have led to you becoming a more socially adept adult – more able to get on with others at work and at home and consequently achieve many successful outcomes in life.

This continued social and emotional interaction also helps build empathy, which is a crucial life skill developed and shaped all through childhood. Empathy begins with a level of self-awareness of our own feelings and the gradual development of the recognition of those emotions in others. For many years research[8] has demonstrated that people who have grown up with an older sibling tend to develop higher levels of empathy themselves. However, a 2018 study has shown that this does not just benefit the younger sibling. Canadian psychologist Marc Jambon at the University of Toronto, together with Dr Sheri Madigan, led an ambitious effort looking at 452 sibling pairs to figure out whether there was a two-way impact on the development of empathy. The sibling pairs were part of the Kids, Families and Places project, from a range of socio-economic backgrounds, and comprised 18-month-olds with a four-year-old sibling. Jambon was interested in knowing whether empathy levels in the siblings at the beginning of the study would predict changes in empathy 18 months later. At the start[9] all of the participants' mothers completed questionnaires and the siblings were filmed interacting with an adult researcher in their family homes. The researcher pretended to either be distressed due to breaking

a 'cherished object' or hurt after hitting their knee and catching their finger in the zip opening of a bag. The psychologists then measured empathy levels using the questionnaire and painstakingly reviewing the footage for behavioural and facial responses in the children. This was repeated after 18 months. The results revealed a surprising difference with what had been reported previously – both the younger and older siblings' empathy increased over the 18-month period. In an interview with *Science Daily*, Jambon said: 'These findings stayed the same, even after taking into consideration each child's earlier levels of empathy and factors that siblings in a family share – such as parenting practices or the family's socio-economic status – that could explain similarities between them.' In other words, they were able to show that the increases in empathy were uniquely related to the influence that these siblings were having on one another.

The results have fascinating implications for our understanding of the influence that siblings have on one another. Not only are siblings far more significant in the development of each other than may have previously been thought, but it was also found that the impact is not just from older to younger sibling. As Jambon says: 'Although it's assumed that older siblings and parents are the primary socialising influences on younger siblings' development (but not vice versa), we found that both younger and older siblings positively contributed to each other's empathy over time.'

A younger sister may run to their older brother's aid at school if they've hurt themselves; an older sister may shout at a younger sister for 'not getting how it feels to be me'; even brothers, who tend to be more likely to be hide their feelings[10], will generally share hurts, pains and worries with a brother over a friend. These behaviours, observations and discussions all add up over time to have the iterative

impact that researchers report. What's more, scientists are pretty definite that the ability to empathise is deeply rooted in the mirror system.[11,12,13] The mechanisms of this will be explored in more detail later.

However, not all outcomes of sibling mirroring are positive. Take, for example, a 2005 study looking at smoking habits carried out by Richard Rende, professor of psychiatry at Brown University. Using the US National Longitudinal Study of Adolescent to Adult Health, Rende was able to examine over a thousand pairs of siblings, combining genetic information with measures of how close brothers and sisters were and frequency of smoking. The findings clearly indicated that the level of siblings' social connectedness – trust and connection – and how much time they spent with each other – exposure – significantly influenced the frequency of smoking in adolescence (even after the effects of genetic similarity were excluded and parent or peer smoking were taken into account).[14] Rende's study also found that increases in drinking and 'delinquent' behaviours were related to the triumvirate of connection, trust and exposure between brothers and sisters. These results have been replicated in a number of other studies.

Research shows that siblings even influence life events like getting pregnant. The likelihood of a younger sister becoming pregnant as a teen increases significantly if her older sister was also pregnant as a teen.[15] We tend to think of these impacts lessening once we've left home and begun to live separate lives. But in the same way that parents continue to influence, so do siblings. One remarkable and surprising study carried out in 2010 looked at 110,000 sibling pairs in Norway, finding that sisters trigger each other in having their first child – one gets pregnant and the other follows shortly after.[16] The increased impact of

same-gender mirroring has been found across a range of sibling studies. The effects are stronger between sister and sister or brother and brother than between brother and sister. We do, after all, have more naturally in common with someone of our own gender, especially when going through the developmental stages of life.

In most cases this sibling mirroring is unconscious, but sometimes a sibling may intentionally try to carve their own way – to be different from their sibling in every way possible. After the Brownlees won gold and silver in the Rio Olympics of 2016, media coverage of the brothers was immense. Twitter went crazy with notes of congratulations, but one user made a very important point, which had been completely overlooked. SimonNRicketts wrote: 'Alistair and Jonny Brownlee have a brother, Edward. I hope he's sitting at home on his couch, necking a beer and chucking stuff at the TV'. Another user wrote: 'If you ever feel overshadowed by your siblings, spare a thought for Edward Brownlee.' Ed, who is seven years younger than oldest brother Alistair is also athletic, but prefers rugby and is training to be a vet. He has said: 'I did some triathlon locally when I was little but I didn't want to be the same.' It's this not wanting to be the same that drives counter-mirroring – a deliberate recognition of what someone is doing and a decision to take a different course. A child may choose not to go to university or to go to an alternate one to a sibling as an act of defiance. If one sibling plays the violin then another will set out to be the fastest runner, intentionally carving out their own identity and perhaps craving their parents' attention to see them as distinct and recognise their achievements. You may have chosen different subjects at school to your brother or sister, to purposely take a different career path, to live somewhere at the other end of the country or even the world as an act of

rebellion, independence or simply to be your own person. We have each experienced a unique interplay with our brothers and sisters, which in turn shapes who we are even when we have deliberately counter-mirrored their behaviour.

But what about those at the extreme end of the spectrum, whose quarrels go beyond a learning tool for empathy or creating their own path through life? What of those siblings whose friction becomes too much to bear and turns into an almost bitter hatred for their siblings? This type of relationship is often dramatised in TV shows, but also exists in myriad real life examples. Take Joan Fontaine and her sister Olivia de Havilland. The story goes that their disputes lasted for more than 40 years, beginning when both were up for Best Actress at the 1942 Academy Awards and Joan won. Olivia was furious and it all went downhill from there. Then there's Liam and Noel Gallagher of Oasis who frequently got into physical fights on stage. The feud came to a head when Liam broke up the band and Noel sued him in response. With the connection and trust gone we may expect mirroring to disappear. However, these sibling relationships still serve to drive certain behaviours, whether mirroring or counter-mirroring, the motivation simply comes from a different place and is often just as powerful.

German brothers Adi and Rudolf Dassler are a prime example of this. Initially working together, they set up a successful shoe company in their mother's laundry room called the Dassler Brothers Sports Shoe Company, and their growth boomed when the shoes were worn by athletes in the 1936 Berlin Olympics. The rise of the Nazi Party, which prioritised athletic teamwork, also gave the company an economic advantage. However, it all turned sour when a growing rift between the two brothers escalated following

a misunderstanding. During a bomb attack in 1943 Adi and his wife climbed into a shelter that already contained Rudolf and his family and reportedly said, 'The dirty bastards are back again,' referring to the war planes. Rudolf mistakenly believed his brother meant him and his family.[17] Rather than being resolved, the mix-up led to growing mistrust between the brothers and when Rudolf was captured by US troops, he believed that it was his brother Adi who had denounced him. The family split even beyond the brothers' relationship with their mother siding with Rudolf and sister siding with Adi. Rudolf moved across the river in the same town, and the brothers divided all of their assets and never spoke again.[18] Adi renamed his part of the business Adidas, based on a combination of his first and last name, and Rudolf originally opted for a similar approach with Ruda, which he later changed to Puma.

In her book *Sneaker Wars*, Barbara Smit, a Dutch author and journalist, explains the competition and rivalry as the businesses unfolded. German sprinter Armin Hary, who typically donned Adidas, asked Adi for payment to wear them at the 1960 Olympics, something that he had previously done with no fee. Adi refused, so Hary then went to Rudi who agreed to pay him to wear Pumas. He went on to win gold in the 100m final wearing Rudi's shoes. But when Hary appeared on the podium he was wearing Adidas. Smit writes: 'With a keen business acumen, Hary hoped to cash in from both with the trick' but it backfired; 'Adi was so outraged he banned the Olympic champion' from ever representing the brand again.[19] This represents the sort of feud that was ongoing between the businesses of the two brothers, and was so powerful that it even divided the city of Herzogenaurach, with Puma on one side of the river and Adidas on the other. It reportedly became the norm for citizens to look

down to see which brand of shoe someone was wearing in order to decide whether or not to speak to them. It wasn't until 2009, long after both brothers had died, that the companies ended the 60-year feud.[20] With the case of Adi and Rudolf this rivalry and competition drove and influenced the behaviour of both brothers, resulting in two shoe companies from the same city becoming global giants. They were both mirroring and counter-mirroring. As much as mirroring one another, the rise of their companies came in many ways from imitating the same innovations, such as the screw-in stud for football boots. Both claimed this as their own idea, but it was Adi who saw it rise to global acclaim in the 1954 World Cup. Arguably the connection between them remained, even though it was one based on hatred and no longer empathic, but the history of growing up together remained the same; the shared memories, values and beliefs. Would they have been as successful without the initial positive influence and support of each other that turned to rivalry? Perhaps the conscious behaviour that the dispute drove in each of them made their behaviour more powerful, certainly more overtly within their control. This demonstrates how being aware of mirroring and role-modelling can be so incredibly powerful. Even in the case of loving brothers competition drives behaviour, in part because behaviours become more conscious and deliberate. Ed Brownlee, for example, said of his older brothers: 'They know they wouldn't necessarily be [where they are] … without each other.'[21] The brothers really enjoy each other's company when training but also clearly use it to spur each other on. We will never know for sure if it was powerful hatred that drove the success of Adidas and Puma, but ultimately relationships between brothers and sisters — whether positive or negative — are not only

incredibly influential, but also often our longest lasting. Beyond childhood we typically spend 40–50 years with our parents, but life with siblings can last between 60–80 years.[22]

If you're an only child you may well be reading this and thinking: 'Well, none of this applies to me.' What if you don't have a sibling? Does that make any difference to how you turn out or how situations shape your brain?

In 1979, concerned about a booming population, China introduced a mandatory one-child policy that remained in place until 2015. This unique situation gives researchers the opportunity to study huge numbers of people who have grown up without a sibling. In 2017 researchers at Southwest University in China recruited 303 college students to explore whether only children demonstrated neurological differences from their peers with siblings.

They underwent various tests and brain scanning using fMRI (functional magnetic resolution imaging). The results showed that only children had more flexible thinking, indicating higher levels of creativity, but lower levels of agreeableness on personality measures. At a neurological level, only children showed more volume in areas of the brain associated with language, but less in areas relating to emotional regulation. The reasons hypothesised for these elevated levels of creativity and language was a more intense focus from parents on learning. The researchers also suggested that lower emotional capabilities could be a result of 'excessive attention' from family members, less exposure to external social groups and more focus on solitary activities while growing up.[23] This study represents a snapshot in time of one particular cultural group, but nevertheless provides powerful neurological evidence of the impact that siblings – or a lack thereof – can have.

The outcome would of course be different for other generations and parts of the world, but not so different that there would be no bearing at all. For example, my mother was an only child born in London during the Second World War. While she carried out a lot of solitary activities, she was not given excessive attention and, with an expectation that she would be independent and self-sufficient, she spent a lot of time out and about on her own being exposed to a whole range of different social settings. As an adult she is definitely charming and very socially adept. The results of the Southwest University study point to how differences can and will appear in any culture as the result of what and whom children mirror, whether that's parents, siblings or their broader social groups. The huge amount of time typically shared or not shared by siblings during childhood and adolescence will most definitely shape behaviour as well as social and emotional development.[24] As Sheri Madigan says, referring to the study she co-authored on sibling empathy with Jambon: 'Our findings emphasise the importance of considering how all members of the family ... contribute to children's development.'[25]

Intergenerational wisdom

Moving on to other members of the family, it's interesting to consider the influence of grandparents. Several generations ago, before the Industrial Revolution, it was far more common for people to live in extended family networks. Grandparents, parents, children, uncles, aunts and cousins were all within close proximity, if not under the same roof. The same is still true in some Asian and African societies, but in the West industrialisation saw a move toward the nuclear family and looser ties, accelerated by ease of travel and relocation. As a result, many people

moved away from family and set up their own independent lives. However, with an ever-increasing life expectancy, grandparents in particular are starting to play a far more significant role again today, although in a slightly different capacity than in years gone by.

My husband's parents live quite some way from us, but they have been on holiday with us many times and also looked after our daughters while we've been away for weddings, anniversaries and on work trips. My mum plays a huge role in the girls' lives, picking them up from school, taking them to activities and having them at least one day a week in the holidays when I work. In many families grandparents play an even bigger role when it comes to childcare. I know of a number of couples who both work full time: the grandparents take over the household during the week while the parents spend time working.

Roughly one-fifth of children under 12 in Australia and a quarter of pre-school children in the US are regularly cared for by grandparents. In the UK it's estimated that almost £15.7bn is saved in childcare costs per year as a result of grandparents helping out.[26] While the role of grandparents will clearly differ across cultures and individual families, it's clear that on the whole they play a significant role in looking after children.

In a day-to-day environment, I see the influence that my own mother has on my children's beliefs and behaviours, particularly my youngest. I hear phrases, ideas and attitudes mirrored back in a way that's almost disconcerting. She walks around parroting what my mother says. For example, my mum has sparked in her a deep interest in nature and at six years old my daughter knows the names of flowers that I've never even heard of. Her mirrored attitude towards life, such as what's right and wrong, comes across quite strongly, too, even her knowledge of the weather. She has

an uncanny knack of being able to look at a cloud and tell whether it's going to rain or not, something that my oldest daughter and I find both amusing, impressive and coming from nowhere other than my mum. And both girls have a strong connection with her, a trust in her and are exposed to her frequently, more so than any of their other grandparents. The strength of the connection and trust I have in her as my own mother, plus the fact that I most probably mirror many ways in which she parented me, will have a multiplying effect, too. I didn't see a huge amount of my grandparents when I was very little, but many of the things my paternal grandfather said to me have stuck to this day. His thirst for life and way with people was eternally positive, and his phrases and comments frequently play through my mind. In effect I am mirroring him even though he is no longer here.

Research by Professor Ann Buchanan, director of the Centre for Research into Parenting and Children at the University of Oxford, showed that a higher level of involvement by grandparents increases the emotional and social well-being of children. A real life example of this is Obama who certainly seems to be more socially and emotionally rounded than his successor Trump. This may well be down to the influence of his grandparents who were responsible for bringing him up, although this is anecdotal so we cannot be certain. Buchanan studied more than 1,500 children and showed that those who had a higher level of grandparental involvement also had fewer behavioural and emotional issues.[27] Another study carried out by Wade Peterson and Lauren Wild at the University of Cape Town in 2017 with adolescents in South Africa looked specifically at mental health and substance abuse. The results showed that involvement with grandparents was associated with prosocial behaviour even when the involvement of the parents was

taken into account. It is believed that this is because they provide support and serve as positive role models. The role-modelling specifically appears to relate to being able to offer a range of social interaction styles to mirror, providing a 'model of empathic behaviour which adolescents then imitate in their own relationships'.[28] Research suggests that the social and emotional pathways are the most direct route of influence between grandparents and grandchildren, beyond the genetic, which is 'mediated' by the parents. In other words it is more about connection, trust and exposure providing opportunities for mirroring than hereditary influences. Sharing the more traditional values often brought by the older generation, such as respect, the importance of education and strong work ethics, clearly has a strong positive influence.[29]

But it's not all good. Grandparents can also be guilty of passing less positive aspects of behaviour on to grandchildren, which given the levels of trust, connection and exposure shouldn't come as a surprise. Researchers at the University of Glasgow led by Dr Stephanie Chambers were interested in the potential implications of the changes in childcare towards grandchildren. They made a very bold claim that grandparents could unwittingly be helping to encourage increases in non-communicable diseases like cancer. Taking 56 studies with data collected from across 18 countries, Chambers' review aimed to uncover any potential influence that grandparents' habits may have on their grandchildren's health. The results are quite surprising, showing that across all of these studies grandparents had an 'adverse impact' on their grandchildren's health when it came to weight, diet, physical activity and smoking. Grandparents were found to not listen to parents' requests to, for example, not smoke around their grandchildren, which consequently role-modelled the behaviour to them and increased the take up of smoking. The effects of grandparents were found to be

particularly strong when it came to weight and diet. Most studies conclude that this is due to overfeeding through 'treating' grandchildren and fostering a lack of physical activity, with grandparents probably in part conscious of what they're doing but unlikely to be aware of the impact. Dr Chambers concluded that these behaviours in turn lead to an increased risk of cancer as a result of exposure to these risk factors in childhood, which has been linked to cancer mortality in adulthood.[30] Another study led by Nelly Elias at Rutgers University in New Jersey, US in 2019 looked at 356 sets of grandparents who took care of their grandchildren aged two to seven years old at least once per week. They found that during an average four-hour visit, the children spent two hours either watching videos or playing games on electronic devices.[31] This is considered especially worrying given the negative effects media use can have on children's development and well-being.[32] The experts believe that this reflects a lack of knowledge and understanding. In the same way parents don't know about new technology or how to regulate it, nor do grandparents – they have never seen anyone role-modelling the expected behaviour to them.

However, overall, the effects that grandparents have on children seem to be more positive than negative. Our elders have wisdom and a knowledge of the world that cannot be replicated without those same experiences. That's one of the key reasons why their stories are so valuable. The role of grandparents is all the more precious in a world where elders are increasingly disregarded. By overlooking the older generations we're missing huge opportunities for knowledge transfer as well as the transmission of social and emotional learning.

The wisdom of elders was once passed on because of the way communities were set up, enabling everyday cross-generational interaction. While we do not have that today,

we could still be sharing their knowledge. Take the example of Nelson Mandela, who grew up in the company of tribal elders and once said: 'In my youth in the Transkei I listened to the elders of my tribe telling stories of the old days. Amongst the tales they related to me were those of wars fought by our ancestors in defence of the fatherland.'[33] While this may have taken him down the wrong path as a younger man, it later meant he upheld the values of learning from those who have gone before us. He spent his 27 years in prison listening to others, learning from people he wrote to and reading biographies. He allowed his mirror neurons to shape his mental world into an open and constructive attitude, which ultimately led to him being awarded a Nobel Peace Prize for his efforts to end apartheid. Yet in our modern civilisation, where technology and culture move incredibly quickly, we are less likely to listen to people whose formative experience occurred in a very different era and often think less of them. They have a grasp on the 'timeless' truths of human behaviour honed over a lifetime and so much to pass on. Grandparents, like siblings, are perhaps a big part of mirroring and influence that we often forget or overlook, yet when we are lucky enough to have them they have a hugely formative impact on who we are. The consciousness of their role-modelling makes it powerful, the stories add to connection, and the time and patience increase the impact of their exposure.

The aunt and uncle effect

Another major influence in our lives comes in the form of aunts and uncles. My husband is an example of someone who didn't really know his grandparents. He only met his paternal grandparents and his maternal grandmother once when he was very little. He has, however, spent a great deal

of time with his aunts and uncles – his mother is one of nine and his father one of five children. Although they are scattered across the globe, their presence, even now that he is an adult, is very strongly felt with frequent family get-togethers, emails and phone calls, letters and parcels. It's easy to see how growing up with this kind of interaction, in spite of the distance separating them, must have had an effect on who he is. The trust and connection are there, and exposure through the constant contact, but not to the same intensity as seeing someone face to face, of course, which provides an immediate limitation on how much exposure the brain of the role modelee has. When teenagers are asked who they see as their role models, parents inevitably come first; however, research then differs with some showing grandparents or siblings as the next most influential and others suggesting that aunts and uncles have the subsequent greatest impact.[34]

The effect of these familial relationships, particularly those that are supplementary to parents, are considered a critical facet of adolescent development.[35] My mother was an only child, but her mum's sister played a massive role in her life, particularly during her teenage years. My great aunt was single her whole life and ran a telephone exchange during the Second World War, enabling her to be socially and financially independent. Her strong character and belief in what was possible still shone through in later life. When my mum was growing up, simply as a result of their own upbringing, my grandparents didn't know how – or probably more accurately it didn't even occur to them – to role-model values around education or striving to get ahead. It had not been modelled for them by their parents so they did not think to model it themselves. To do so would have taken a conscious effort and possibly someone calling their attention to it in some way and stressing the importance of

it. They had both left school in their early teens and their work ethic was directed toward getting their heads down and being dutiful employees in order to make ends meet. My mother's aunt, however, had a different view on life. She frequently took care of Mum and spent time quizzing her on her knowledge of all things, testing her spelling and times tables, taking her on educational outings and igniting my mother's fiery and determined nature.

The influence of aunts and uncles is often positive – you may be able to think of your own experiences in that light – but not always. For example, studies looking at children from less privileged backgrounds find aunts, uncles and cousins are among those most likely to lead them astray. Dr Noelle Hurd from the University of Virginia is passionate about promoting healthy adolescent development, and led a study in 2011 looking at both the positive and negative impacts of role models on marginalised teenagers. Hurd's study 'Role Model Behavior and Youth Violence' showed that exposure to negative adult behaviour by aunts or uncles was associated with increased violence, levels of anxiety and depression, and substance abuse, as well as negative attitudes toward school. Witnessing their role models engage in antisocial behaviours primed teenagers' own aggression and strengthened their attitudes in support of violence. This was made worse still when they saw resulting rewards in the form of power and respect via street codes. Hurd believes there is a strong behavioural imitation component associated with adolescents' exposure to role-modelling these antisocial behaviours.[36] On the flip side, the study also showed that when a role model displays prosocial behaviour this indirectly relates to less violent behaviour in adolescents, having a protective effect on the other factors.

On the whole, in less marginalised communities aunts and uncles play a significant role in shaping our brain but

in a less direct way. In an interview with *The New York Times*, Urie Bronfenbrenner, a child development expert at Cornell University, said:

> *The most important thing is to have an adult to turn to when it's necessary for the child and not convenient for the adult. Youngsters can do that only with people on whom they have a special claim, and who have a special claim on them – namely family. Aunts and uncles are made for the part because they're related to the child but they generally don't live under the same roof, so they are at the same time connected and detached – part of the family but not part of the household power plays.*[37]

Siblings and grandparents undoubtably shape us, and are quoted as the biggest influence outside of parents in most studies. Following this, uncles, aunts and cousins influence who we are, but the extent to which that happens is clearly dependent on an individual's circumstances. Only you know yours. The level of their connection, trust and exposure will steer the degree that they have shaped you. Although the chances are this influence is greater than you might have expected and most certainly less conscious, sometimes by virtue of the exposure alone. It's also important to mention that stepfamilies can play as significant a role as direct family. I grew up with a stepmother, stepfather and all of the other 'steps' that come with that, which definitely influenced who I am. Each circumstance is unique, each impact and influence complex. What is definite is how much our relatives shape who we are and how we respond to the world. In the next chapter we'll explore another group of people who have a huge impact on us despite not being a big part of our family lives.

CHAPTER THREE

What Are Friends For?

One time, I told you I was gonna make you somebody. That's what you done for me. You made me somebody they're gonna remember.

Clyde to Bonnie

In January 1930, at a house party in a suburb of Dallas, Texas, two young people met and fell for one another. Bonnie Parker was 19 – a slight, blonde woman, well dressed despite her poor background, and Clyde Barrow, a good-looking 20-year-old with a swagger, wilfulness and determination about him. This couple went on to lead one of the most notorious gangs in modern history, travelling around the United States, robbing banks and stores, breaking criminals out of jail and killing numerous people along the way. From the moment they met they were inseparable.

We've all had a friend that our parents have worried wasn't the right influence on us, and Bonnie Parker and Clyde Barrow are certainly a case in point. Bonnie's mother was deeply unimpressed with her daughter's choice of partner and tried many times to persuade her that he wasn't good enough, but Bonnie was devoted to her boyfriend and saw her 'new real-life role as a convicted criminal's supportive lover'[1] as exciting.

How did Bonnie go from being the hardworking daughter of a respectable woman, a good Christian girl who went to church every Sunday, to becoming a hardened criminal? This dramatic transition into the role of lawbreaker could only have come from being around

someone else who was themselves one. She didn't suddenly hop across from dedicated churchgoer to gangster's moll because one day she woke up and it occurred to her that it would be a good idea. This was far from the Hollywood screen or Broadway stage that she reportedly dreamed of. She had to see and then assume that behaviour, which happened through her acceptance and commitment to Clyde. She also had to observe what to do and how to do it in order to undertake such a dramatic change in identity, and this is where mirror thinking came into play.

Bonnie and Clyde met as adolescents, a developmental stage that technically reaches from early teens to early 20s. This is a time of life when we move away from the safety of our parents and prepare to be independent young adults with a strong need to learn more about the world around us. Interestingly, recent neuroscientific research led by Locke Welborn at the University of California has shown that parents still remain a significant influence on adolescents, but it tends to be values and morals that are mirrored, as opposed to social and everyday behaviour where peers have a stronger impact. It's at this stage of life that the part of the brain known as the 'social brain' is undergoing huge structural development.

Researchers such as Adriana Galván, associate professor at UCLA, explains how teenagers 'begin to appreciate the influence they have in enacting change, either through political movements, activism for causes they believe in, or lending social support to a friend in need'. From an evolutionary perspective this came about because adolescents need to extend their social connections to reproduce and survive as an independent unit, influencing the group and being an active member of the community.

Eva Telzer, associate professor of psychology and neuroscience at the University of North Carolina, recently

showed how malleable the brain is at this age. She also showed that it's particularly oriented towards the social world, hence the heightened susceptibility to social influences giving the behavioural cues from peers the most weight in impacting behaviour. Once Bonnie had decided that Clyde was the man for her, she was with him and his fellow gang members constantly. Each time she saw a behaviour her brain mirrored it, imprinting it into her neural networks and reorganising her neurological connections in order to mirror what she saw and heard from her peer group. This led to her more extreme and criminal actions seeming and feeling more natural and 'normal' day by day and will even have improved her ability to carry out those behaviours. The way mirror thinking works meant that her brain had been practising long before she ever took any action herself.

The social brain

Neuroscience is increasingly being used to study social behaviour. The advantage of neural studies is that we're not just looking at the outcome or behaviour of an individual but also at how their brain is responding in real time. These studies support previous research suggesting that as humans we have a unique facet to our brain – the social brain, which is specialised for social interactions. This encompasses all of the brain processes that allow us to interact with one another, from perception of facial expressions, body posture and eye gaze, to the evaluation of other mental states such as intentions and desires. This allows us to predict what people will do next, to understand others' feelings and behaviour and to choose how we respond, which is critical for social understanding, to maintain healthy relationships with others and to facilitate prosocial behaviour. All of

these factors give us an evolutionary advantage – we are a social species and need to be with a group to survive, so our brain is wired to facilitate this. Within the modern world it enables us to function as part of our society, community, within work environments and in our family unit.

The social brain covers many different aspects of neuroanatomy, making it hard to localise. However, if we look at just one example, that of facial expressions, it's possible to see how the factors involved play out. From an evolutionary perspective fear was an incredibly important mechanism to keep people safe. It makes sense, for example, that if someone has seen an enemy they feel scared and other people in their tribe will also feel fearful without having even seen the enemy. This mechanism enables everyone to become more alert and quicker to respond if they are attacked. Elizabeth Phelps, a professor of psychology and neural science at New York University, has found that fear can indeed be felt through direct experience, but also through other social means such as verbal warnings or simply observing others. Phelps' research has shown that socially learned fears, such as those passed on by seeing someone else afraid, share the same neural mechanism with fears that have been acquired by direct experience (seeing or coming into contact with the enemy). Both trigger similar levels of activation in a part of the brain known as the amygdala, which processes these emotions. The experience of the same emotion is therefore mirrored by people who see only the fearful person and not the source of that fear.

The clearer picture we are gaining through neuroscience, and specifically where the social brain is concerned, helps us to see what's going on at a neural level: how the brain is affected by social influence and the contexts in which peers,

parents and other factors may have a significant impact on decision-making processes. For example, research shows that peer influence is associated with heightened activation in areas within the network that are involved in thinking about the self and others. The cortical structures it encompasses fall within the mirror system.

It's not hard to see how, given the malleability of the brain, that the impressions made at this time of life begin to shape our identity, defining the relationships we will have as adults, the roles we will play within society, and the core passions and interests we will build on as we move through life. When I profile people we always start at the beginning of adolescence and walk through their life to where they are today. I find it fascinating how much this stage of life, most significantly the peers we have, impacts who we become as adults. Take, for example, Jerome, a French national who grew up in Paris. He had always believed, in large part influenced by the way his parents had encouraged him, that he wanted to work in the car industry. While still at school Jerome described how, in his own words, he hung around with 'gays and fashionistas' – that was his life at that time. After school he began working at a well-known automotive company with a reputation for fantastic training and opportunities, but less than a year in he left and began working for a luxury fashion label. Today he is director of buying for a leading department store and, as he always says, he deals with those same 'gays and fashionistas' who he grew up with.

If you think back to your own adolescence, if you really look objectively (with your observing brain) you'll see patterns in how influenced you were by those around you. At the time of adolescence we don't like to think of ourselves as being drawn in or along by anyone. We see ourselves as becoming independent and self-sufficient,

but it's the age when we are more impacted by our peers than at any other time in life. Who influenced you during your teens and how? Does it remain an impact on your life today?

It will also come as no surprise that teenagers tend to be more susceptible to risk. As adolescents struggle to be accepted by their peers, they conform to some quite radical and risky patterns of behaviour in order to fit in. Bonnie and Clyde are a classic example of this. This is an evolutionary driver – for our ancestors it was critical to be part of a group at this age to aid our chances of survival – in order to remain safe and reproduce. This need to belong often comes hand in hand with a need to show off in order to be accepted. For example, Sarah-Jayne Blakemore, professor of cognitive neuroscience at University College London, carried out research in 2018 showing that adolescents take more risks when playing a simulated driving game when being watched by friends. Neuroimaging suggests that this is due to an increased activation in an area of the brain linked to reward (the ventral striatum), which in effect 'eggs on' the mirroring behaviour in spite of any risks involved. The way that the brain responds supports and rewards risk over playing it safe or following moral codes and beliefs that act as a stronger compass later in life. Brain structures respond more to the 'reacting brain', giving a preference for small immediate rewards versus the potentially larger or longer-term rewards we associate with meaning and purpose.

Clyde closely mirrored the behaviour of those around him. His older brother was a convicted criminal, and once Clyde had spent time in jail his peer group became entirely populated with lawbreakers. So, his behaviour, however extreme it may seem, was simply mirroring those peers.

This was heightened by being a young man and further still through being in the company of a female he was keen to impress. Research done by Australian psychologists Richard Ronay and William von Hippel at the University of Queensland in 2010 showed the impact this can have. They carried out an experiment looking at what happens on a biological level when men are in the presence of an attractive young female. After setting up their equipment in the unusual setting of a skateboard park in Brisbane, they observed 96 male skateboarders with an average age of 22. As part of the experiment, the psychologists asked the boarders to choose one easy skateboarding trick (one they could do well on most attempts) and one difficult trick (one they were still learning and could do well approximately 50 per cent of the time). They were told to do each of these tricks 10 times while being filmed by a male researcher. Following a short break, they were then asked to make 10 more attempts of both tricks. Some of the skateboarders performed their second attempts for the male researcher, while the others did them in front of an attractive 18-year-old female. Rosie had been rated as attractive by the researchers using widely recognised scientific criteria (symmetrical face, distance between the eyes just under half the width of the face, distance between eyes and mouth just over one third the height of her face). She was totally unaware of the conditions of the experiment and didn't know that she had been chosen to take part because she was deemed to be so pretty. However, her attractiveness was also confirmed by the skateboarders, many of whom made positive comments about her looks and a few even asked for her phone number. One of the most remarkable and relevant findings was that the skateboarders took far greater risks on the difficult trick when Rosie was watching. The researchers also found that testosterone levels were

significantly higher among the guys who skateboarded in front of Rosie than the ones who skateboarded in front of the male researcher. Having demonstrated a measurable reaction from the reacting brain (driven by the more primitive aspects of behaviour), the experiment demonstrates how young men will risk physical injury to impress an attractive young female.

Conversely, another study carried in 2010 out by Blakemore showed that lower testosterone levels in men are associated with higher levels of sympathy. This suggests that while young men mirror the more risky behaviour of their peers, the mirror system (also used to empathise) can become 'blocked' by high levels of testosterone. As a result, these young men become single-mindedly focused on one thing, without consideration of what is going on more broadly or the risks involved. They mirror behaviour and then miss the typical nuanced modifcations that happen when we typically 'read' those around us. They become in effect socially and emotionally blind.

Despite being one of the healthiest developmental periods, according to the National Center for Health Statistics, in the US morbidity and mortality rates increase 300 per cent from childhood to adolescence, with more than 70 per cent of adolescent deaths each year due to risk-taking behaviors such as reckless driving. Risk-taking is inevitable, but it's not all bad. It also promotes healthy neurological development enabling teenagers to become independent adults and establish their identity. The question is how to redirect teens away from negative and towards positive risk-taking – activities like rock climbing, mountain biking and martial arts, which involve 'safe' risks. Sports that are competitive or performance based are also preferable as they incorporate the possibility of failure – in itself a risk, yet one that provides the opportunity for

building self-esteem, confidence and the ability to grow. Research shows that an adolescent girl who is involved in sport is less than half as likely to get pregnant as a teenage girl not involved in sport. Alternative beneficial activities include getting involved with a social or political cause, or running for a leadership position in or outside of school. Even meeting new friends involves an element of risk through rejection and the fear of trying something new. However, most importantly, if you are around teens, watch how you're behaving as their mirror thinking is ripe for picking up anything you do. What do you do that you wouldn't want them to mirror?

Someone like me

A large body of research suggests that adolescents select and maintain friendships with people who are similar to them; we also do this as adults, but the effect is not as strong. Bonnie and Clyde shared many similarities both in terms of background, outlook and personality. They were fed up with life, feeling dejected about their social status, and longed for a more glamorous life that crime offered up in a perverse way. When it came to their personal characteristics they were both feisty, headstrong and most probably extroverted. In his book, *Go Down Together: The True, Untold Story of Bonnie and Clyde*, author Jeff Guinn describes Clyde as a 'social sort of boy who made friends easily', and both Bonnie and Clyde sought out excitement. This attracted them to one another, but also then made them more and more similar as they mirrored each other's behaviour and beliefs. Research within school settings in the US has shown that this can cause issues of homogeneity even where diversity is the intention. Black pupils become friends with black pupils

and white with white, rich with rich and underprivileged with underprivileged. This is called the homophily principle, which states that people are more likely to form friendships and social connections with people who are like them based on characteristics like age, race, gender, occupation and income, with ethnic origin and race being one of the strongest factors. David Brooks, columnist for *The New York Times*, has written about how neighbourhoods have a strong tendency to develop based on similarity and preferences. Brooks gives the example of new suburbs in Arizona and Nevada, which 'start out reasonably well integrated. These communities don't yet have reputations, so people choose their houses for other, mostly economic reasons. But as localities age, they develop personalities (that's where the Asians live and that's where the Hispanics live), and segmentation occurs.'[2] The same is true in suburbs and neighbourhoods across the world. You can probably see it around you and where you live. Are people like you? Overall homophily leads to stronger role-modelling, when people see someone who is like them they are more likely to emulate their behaviour.

In addition to the homophily principle, we know that individuals who are more susceptible to peer influence are more likely to have problems with drug and alcohol use, and are more likely to have friends who also engage in risky behaviour. Research carried out in 2002 shed more light on this. Antonio Terracciano, a professor at Florida State University College of Medicine, and psychologist Paul Costa examined data on over 1,600 people and found that smokers do, overall, have certain personality traits. They also found that smoking initially starts through mirroring the behaviour of someone, typically a peer. The characteristics they identified include an inability to resist cravings (shown as a high level of impulsiveness), a search

for stimulation (known as a high level of excitement seeking), a lack of perseverance (or low self-discipline) and a lack of careful consideration of the consequences of their actions (another sign of impulsiveness).

The cordial teen

Research into the influence of peers focuses largely on the negative aspects of mirroring – for example, dropping out of school, smoking, taking drugs, sexual promiscuity. But because the people that adolescents associate with largely shape what they are mirroring, they can also have an impact in a more positive way. For example, recent studies have shown that peers also promote prosocial behaviour during adolescence, which relates to helping other people as a result of seeing or learning about 'positive' behaviour in others. A study carried out in 2016 by Jorien van Hoorn, a senior postdoctoral researcher at the Brain and Development Research Centre at Leiden University in the Netherlands, showed that 12- to 16-year-olds were more prosocial when doing so was approved of by their peers. Another study carried out in 2015 out by assistant professor of psychology Sophia Choukas-Bradley and colleagues at the University of Pittsburgh found that 12- to 15-year-olds were more likely to volunteer or help people in their community if they believed that other pupils in their school were doing the same. This use of mirror thinking is known as 'imitative altruism' and represents the mirror system responding to positive behaviours in the same way as more risky behaviours. It is so powerful that it can even limit the impact of behaviours like dangerous driving. For example, Telzer, a psychologist and neuroscientist who examines how social and cultural processes shape adolescent brain development, found that when young people drove in the

presence of a 'cautious peer' they took fewer risks and drove more safely.[3] Even school engagement can be influenced in this more constructive way with exposure to positive role models as peers, improving school attendance and academic achievement.

Social 'norms'

As an adult these mirroring behaviours creep up on us, but with the exception of risk-taking (which is affected by age and hormones) all of what we've discussed in relation to Bonnie and Clyde is also true of you. In adulthood, we are all still influenced by our social brain and we gravitate towards people who are similar to us. Counterintuitively, the difference is that as adults our brain merrily mirrors others without us having a conscious awareness of it. While it may seem to make more sense that this is what happens to adolescents, given many of their often surprisingly extreme behaviours, in reality adolescents are more proactive and conscious in monitoring their own attitudes compared with those of their peers than we are as adults. As grown-ups it's still critical to fit into our social environment in order to thrive in life, whether that's at work, in our community or among friends. As teenagers we were often conscious of mirroring because what we were imitating was new and ever changing. As adults we don't notice, a bit like not noticing how time passes. Things change and we change with them. Do you, for example, wear the same style of jeans now as you did when you were a teenager or has that style changed over the years? If you don't wear the same now, have you consciously changed your choice? Our mirror system carries on adapting our attitudes and behaviour often without us noticing. The need for conformity or to align with our peers means our behavioural nuances and attitudes

are constantly being shaped by the people around us. The mechanisms that we've discussed as impacting adolescents are also impacting you, nudging you so gently that you don't even notice. It's a bit like a tap dripping into a sink with a plug: it may not look like much water is in each drip, but it will eventually fill and overflow. There is almost an arrogance in our belief that when we become an adult we don't get influenced by those around us, but the fact is that when it's unconscious it can be even more dangerous. Professional cyclist Tyler Hamilton has gained a particularly sharp insight into how these dynamics can affect someone over the years. In his book *The Secret Race: Inside the Hidden World of The Tour de France*, he attests to the extraordinary intensity of relationships within the team saying: 'There is no friendship in the world like the friendship of being on a bike racing team ... Other sports teams like to call themselves "families". In bike racing, it's close to true.'

Hamilton spent an ordinary and stable childhood in a small Massachusetts town. He describes his upbringing as one without too many demands from his parents, except to 'always tell the truth, no matter what'. His mother and father instilled honesty as the core value to live by and that straightforward morality was ingrained in every decision the family made.

Cycling is a notoriously difficult sport to break into. There is an unofficial code of secrecy known as the *omertà* – a term derived from mafia culture – which enforces a tacit rule of non-disclosure to anyone outside of the elite inner circle. Put simply, the top level of cycling is a closed club with an exclusive membership and unwritten rules, which can only be understood by those on the inside. Once Hamilton chose to be a professional cyclist, it took him a number of years to break into the inner circle – at which point he began to glimpse a much darker side to the sport.

Doping in sport is regularly in the news headlines now, but the true scale of the issue was far more hidden back in the 1990s. Given his scrupulous upbringing, Hamilton was shocked by the prevalence of doping among his team members. He was determined to defy the pressure that he must dope in order to win. The problem was turning a blind eye in effect excluded him from that inner sanctum of the cycling elite. He did defy the pressure for three years, until one day he finally accepted 'help' from the doctors in the form of illegal drugs. Hamilton described this as the moment that 'I did what many others had done before me. I joined the brotherhood'. Fast-forward a number of years and a couple of positive doping tests, and in 2010 he was ordered to appear before a Los Angeles court to provide testimony in the doping investigation against Lance Armstrong. Only then did he finally admit to a jury that he had taken banned performance-enhancing drugs. This once honest boy had fallen prey to conformity. He was so ashamed of what he had done that it wasn't until the following year that Hamilton admitted the truth to his own family. This is not a hot-headed teen like Bonnie and Clyde, desperate to escape a certain lifestyle. This was an adult who by letting the mirror system take its own, unguided course became blind to the moral implications of what he was doing. Research carried out by Dr Jessica Nolan and colleagues at the University of Scranton shows that social norms, which largely relate to the behaviour of our peers, can have a dramatic effect on influencing our attitudes and behaviours, yet we are usually unaware of how influential they are. Many other horrendous and surprising examples exist, such as the Holocaust, gang membership and terrorism. Psychologically speaking, almost all of us modify our behaviour in order to fit in, but not necessarily in a negative way or to such extremes. However, people, for the most

part, don't blatantly flout the rules of a group. A person who causes trouble or someone who makes people unhappy is typically excluded from a group fairly swiftly. This fundamental conformity even applies to those who feel themselves to be strongly individualistic or resistant to following the crowd. Psychologists have shown that supposed non-conformist behaviour is in itself a group behaviour: when we rail or rebel against the mainstream, we are almost always doing it to align ourselves with another group. We can see everyday examples all around us, from people who cover themselves in tattoos to be 'individual' to the clothes people wear and the hair styles they choose. We often accept social norms that we think we reject, mirroring behaviours and attitudes that we don't even believe are impacting us. The only way to stop that is to pause, look up and around, and be deliberately and consciously curious about the world around us and 'check' that we are making our own decisions.

Neuroscience enables us to understand what is happening at a biological level when it comes to social conformity – in effect, how we are mirroring those around us, and how in the case of Bonnie and Clyde they were influenced by the criminals they came into contact with. An intriguing study on this was carried out in 2009 by Vasily Klucharev, a researcher and lecturer in economic psychology at the University of Basel, who asked participants to rate the attractiveness of different faces. Once subjects had rated the faces, they were told the average score for each face given by the rest of the group. They were then asked to rate the same faces again. There was a significant change in results the second time around with the majority of people shifting their opinions to align with the average ratings of the group. Although the extent to which people did this differed, all the participants did it to some degree.

Fascinatingly, Klucharev's research showed that when participants recognised a difference between their rating and the rest of the group, an 'error signal' was activated in their brain.[4] This signal in our brain alerts us that the group has responded differently, that we are not mirroring the behaviour of those around us, that this is 'wrong', and we need to adjust our behaviour to overcome that 'error' and align with other people.

Conversely, research has also shown that the reward circuits in the brain are activated when we agree with others. Daniel Campbell-Meiklejohn, professor of neuroscience at Aarhus University in Denmark, worked with Chris Frith, professor of psychology at University College London, in 2010 using music taste to study the rewards of mirroring those around us. They found that people would unconsciously realign their music preferences, or the value placed on a particular song, to match with others in a group. When they moved their tastes away from their own preferences to align with and more closely mirror the people around them, dopamine pathways were activated in the brain.[5] So, our brain mechanisms ensure that agreeing with and mirroring other people feels good, even when it goes against our own values. This is illustrated in the story of Bonnie and Clyde. For example, following one stint in prison, Clyde had actually intended to 'go straight' and made every effort to earn a decent living, but when a friend from prison approached him about a job he quickly returned to his life as a career criminal and robbed a bank. It takes considerable conscious effort from the observing brain to override these processes. Science has shown that when it's peers and close friends who are concerned, as opposed to fellow subjects in an experiment, the impact is even greater.

Working in a broad range of organisations I see adults unwittingly mirror each other in many ways and I see the stark contrast between different settings. These individuals are

not so aware that they are in fact dressing a certain way, choosing a specific restaurant to go to for lunch, following others' suggestions on where to buy coffee, even speaking in a language that becomes exclusive to the company they work for. This is about people conforming to the expectations of their peers. It's the work of the mirror system helping them to fit in mostly without any conscious awareness. This allows us to feel accepted, to feel like we belong, which is a fundamental human need.

While that feeling of belonging at work is positive, the need to be like the people around us can also cause issues. For example, 'hiring in your own image' is a common problem across work environments, and seems to catch people out time and time again. Even senior leaders need reminding that they will always have leanings known as affinity bias, unintentionally favouring someone who has similar attitudes, beliefs, values and capabilities to them. This isn't deliberate; it happens at a subconscious level to all of us. Yet broader diversity is essential for optimal performance. Research by the global consultancy firm McKinsey shows that businesses which are diverse deliver 35 per cent better results than those that are non-diverse. Even business psychologists with a deep understanding of these phenomena believe there is a need to remind ourselves before stepping into any assessment of candidates. My personal pitfall is someone having a shared passion for skiing and snowboarding; if that comes up I have to deliberately and consciously check myself so as not to get swayed in my decision-making.

You are a mirror of your closest friends

The impact of close friends and peers on our behaviour is clearly demonstrated in research on obesity. This validates one of perhaps the most surprising everyday examples of how dramatically our peers influence us and how much

we unwittingly mirror those we care about. Obesity spreads in a way that's been described as being 'just like a virus'[6] and really reflects how the mirror system operates on a daily basis without our conscious awareness. The study led by Dr Nicholas Christakis, a sociologist and physician at Harvard Medical School, was conducted over the course of 32 years (from 1971 to 2003). The team carried out detailed analysis of a social network of 12,067 people, mapping who was friends with whom, who were siblings, who was married to whom and even who were neighbours. Staggeringly, they found that people were most likely to become obese when a friend (*i.e.* peer) became obese, with the chances increasing by 57 per cent. With mutual close friends, if one becomes obese then the chances of the other also becoming obese increased by 171 per cent. This was impacted more by social distance or closeness than by geographic distance.[7] In other words, if people are close friends, even if they do not live in the same area, they have a huge influence on each other's behaviour and attitudes. Christakis said: 'You change your idea of what is an acceptable body type by looking at the people around you.' It's not hard to see how this extends to a whole host of other behaviours from how you dress, where you shop and how you decorate your house, to what car you buy and where you go on holiday. It's all influenced by your peers. Other contagious behaviours, spread unconsciously via the mirror system, include having affairs, suicide, bulimia, depression, anxiety and financially risky decision-making.

The good news is that this contagion also applies to positive behaviours in the same way for adults as it does for adolescents. For example, learning about other people's prosocial actions is associated with an increase in donations to charity and an increase in fairness when playing games. If you think of the recent fire in Notre-Dame cathedral,

billionaire Francois-Henri Pinault, owner of Gucci and
Yves Saint Laurent, pledged to donate €100m (£86m). He
was swiftly followed by a €200m (£172m) donation from
the Arnault family of Louis Vuitton, and then €200m
(£175m) from the Bettencourt Meyers family, owners of
L'Oreal, and many more donations from millionaires across
the globe. These people were mirroring the behaviour of
their peers.

I have seen how this positive peer influence can have an
incredibly powerful effect within organisational settings.
As stated in a *Harvard Business Review* article written by Jon
R. Katzenbach and Zia Khan: 'Peers in large organisations
are invaluable in spreading behaviour change across an
enterprise ... Whenever significant numbers of peers
interact formally or informally, they constitute a force to
be reckoned with. When they share mutual respect, they
will listen to, learn from and secretly support one another
in ways that can shape opinions, create resistance or
generate energy.'[8] Organisations are constantly undergoing
change and searching for ways in which to create the buy-in
of employees, to 'bring them along on the journey'.
Engaging employees with change is a relentless concern for
the leaders I work with. What those who are savvy do,
beyond communication, is leverage this implicit mechanism,
which works via the mirror system. One of my clients has
used this very effectively through the simple mechanism of
values ambassadors. Choosing enthusiastic, positive
influencers from the population of employees, they carried
out workshops to help educate them about the company
values and to help them really understand why they matter
not only to the overall success of the organisation but also
to individuals. They carried out several one-day workshop
sessions where they came together to carry out exercises,
listen to talks and engage in discussion about how the
values mattered, why they mattered and what they could

do to help engage their particular areas of the business. This played not only on the positive influence of the group of ambassadors when they were together, influencing one another to engage with the values, but also planted strong influencers back within the broader population of employees to carry the messages of the behaviours within and across the organisation.

But what does this mean to you? Put quite simply it's about what you focus your attention on and both the conscious and unconscious decisions you make. A lot of peer influence, both positive and negative, will take place whether or not you are aware of it. You may see someone do something that you feel is wrong, for example, someone being rude and disrespectful to waiting staff, and your value set, buried deep within your subconscious, will tell you it's wrong. Even if your mirror system reflects that behaviour, you don't. However, if you keep seeing that behaviour over and over again there will come a point at which it is normalised, your brain no longer pipes up to tell you it's wrong and you risk mirroring the same behaviour yourself. As we have seen through the various examples, this can have devastating consequences.

However, there are also stories of people who, despite being exposed to certain ways of behaving, will speak out. There are numerous examples of whistleblowers who stand up against conformity. For example, Sibel Edmonds, who was hired by the FBI as a translator shortly after 9/11. Edmonds reported cover-ups of security issues, political espionage and incompetence and as a consequence was fired from the FBI. These are things that many other people will have seen, yet chosen to ignore. That resistance on her part to the beliefs and behaviour of those around her will have taken a continuous conscious effort. In everyday life the effort to be aware of and continually evaluate what and

who you are mirroring may feel like too much. It's a bit like going on a diet and trying to resist what our brain is pulling us towards. An easy way around this is to carefully choose who you surround yourself with by spending time with people who are going to influence your behaviour in the direction you want to go without you even having to think about it. It's as simple as that.

If you want to eat healthily, hang out with a friend who does; if you want to succeed as a business leader, spend time with a friend who is already one. Evidence shows that if you have peers who are successful entrepreneurs it makes it far more likely that you will be too. Take, for example, entrepreneurs Steve Jobs and Steve Wozniak, or innovators such as Henry Ford and Thomas Edison. In fact, the influence of friendships on one another litter the history books. Other examples include John Adams and Thomas Jefferson, who had differing political views but as US presidents could learn from one another; Wolfgang Amadeus Mozart and Joseph Haydn, who had a mutual admiration for one another; Ella Fitzgerald and Marilyn Monroe, with Fitzgerald attributing her big break to Monroe; Virginia Woolf and Katherine Mansfield, who would discuss projects at length and push each other on to be the best writers they could be. All of these people positively propelled each other in their fields, and proactively choosing who you spend time with and get close to can do the same for you.

However, you don't want to suddenly cut off all your friends who don't behave in a way that takes you in the direction you want to go. For example, if you don't want to put on weight, you also don't want to suddenly dissociate yourself from a friend who is gaining weight, or never see a friend who's had an affair again because it goes against your values. You can, however, be conscious of their

behaviours and choose whether or not you emulate them, what it is you take on board and what you consciously move away from.

The mirror system has a huge impact on the formation of identity and direction in life as an adolescent and then on into adulthood. For anyone who knows, is parent to, grandparent to, or uncle or aunt to a teenager, the extreme nature of this has worrying consequences. The implications reach beyond who they are, extending into factors such as involvement in crime and drug use, through to health-related behaviours such as the spread of STIs and obesity. Later in the book we will look at the worrying influence that social media platforms such as Instagram have on peer role-modelling, and how in effect this technology hijacks the mirror system, blocking optimal brain development.

However, it's not all bad. Equipped with knowledge of how the more positive aspects of peer influence operate and harnessing that understanding of the mirror system with adolescents and in adults, we have the ability to make huge differences within society. For example, enabling positive peer influence can encourage school engagement, influence academic results and facilitate anti-bullying campaigns.[9] With adults, other prosocial behaviours can be leveraged through an understanding of the mirror system, such as combating obesity, enhancing climate change initiatives and encouraging positive change within organisations.

At a personal level, understanding how the mirror system works when it comes to peers enables you to become more conscious of what you mirror and who you are mirroring. Simply by becoming more conscious of what you observe, what you want to take on and what you don't, can make a huge difference to your everyday life through to moving you towards the life you want.

PART TWO
WHAT THE MIRROR TEACHES US

In Your Shoes

On 2 September 2015 a story stirred something in thousands of people across Europe. For months the news had been inundated with stories of the Syrian refugee crisis, a mumble in the background as we all carried on with our busy lives. But on that morning the image of a small lifeless figure on a beach in Turkey, lying on his front, the palms of his hands and the soles of his tiny shoes facing towards the sky, drove through the shell of oblivion. The image appeared on 20 million screens in just 12 hours.

Another image shows an unsettled policeman carrying the toddler's body up the beach, cradling it as if he were still alive.

Three-year-old Alan Kurdi drowned with his five-year old brother Ghalib and mother Rehenna while attempting to cross the Aegean Sea[1]; only their father Abdullah survived. He describes the confusion as the flimsy boat was tossed around by the sea: 'I was holding my wife's hand. But my children slipped through my hands. It was dark and everyone was screaming. I tried to catch my wife and children but there was no hope. One by one, they died.'[2]

The story of one boy brought the crisis into sharp focus. The human connection was made so much more visceral by seeing one boy and one grieving husband and father. We could understand the pain of one where the 'many' had become a blur of data and reports. The crisis of people fleeing civil war in Syria suddenly made sense. The image quickly went viral on social media with the

hashtag #KiyiyaVuranInsanlik ('humanity washed ashore').[3]
Charities supporting refugees saw a dramatic upturn in
donations. The amount given to the Swedish Red Cross, for
example, was fifty-five times greater in the week following
Kurdi's death.[4]

Perhaps before this the Syrian refugee crisis was too
intangible to relate to. A dead child, however, was not.
Perhaps most Europeans living in peaceful countries
simply could not imagine the terrors faced by these
refugees; or maybe up to this point they were the
'out-group', people different from 'us', which limited our
empathic concern.

A study carried out in 2010 at the University of Würzburg
by Swiss psychologist and neuroscientist Grit Hein looked
at just such a scenario to explore the neurobiological
mechanisms involved during in-group and out-group
interactions. She studied football fans with the aim of
seeing how in-group and out-group membership affected
their willingness to help someone in pain. The in-group
members were other fans supporting their favourite team
and the out-group were fans supporting a rival team.

Participants, whose brains were being scanned, watched
fans from their team and rival fans in pain after receiving a
painful electric shock. They could select one of three
options:

1. To help the fan from their team or rival fan by
   receiving half of that person's pain themselves. This
   would reduce the intensity of the other person's
   pain by half.
2. Not to help and watch a football video instead
   while the fan from their team or rival fan
   experienced pain. Watching the video provided a
   distraction from seeing the pain being inflicted.

3. Not to help and to watch the other person suffering from the pain.

Grit and her colleagues assumed that empathic concern would motivate participants to help the people in pain, which is indeed what happened. They also predicted that people would be more likely to act upon this empathy when it was directed towards an in-group member rather than an out-group member, which also proved to be the case. Participants were less likely to help reduce the pain of a fan who supported a rival team. Remarkably, from studying the activation patterns within the brain, they found that people not only felt less empathy for rival fans, but seeing them in pain actually activated the reward centres of the brain. Worryingly, people derived pleasure from the misfortune of those not in their group.

We have evolved to favour the in-group over the out-group. The driving force for this is simple: not being part of a group causes psychological distress. In that sense, we closely resemble other animals. Individual sociability may vary, but we are innately social beings that yearn to be accepted by other people. Research indicates that people invariably favour other members of their in-group over people who are outside of the group. If someone exhibits unusual personality traits – such as a sardonic sense of humour or quirky dress sense – we subconsciously accept them if they are part of our group but tend to see the same tendencies as flaws if that person is not in our in-group.

Hein says that 'deficits in empathy enhance conflicts and human suffering. Thus, it is crucial to understand how empathy can be learned and how learning experiences shape empathy-related processes in the human brain.'[5] This has led her to carry out further studies to explore whether we can learn to empathise with out-group members.

To investigate the interaction between learning and empathy, Hein and her team used what they called 'an ecologically valid intergroup conflict in Switzerland' where the study was based. The Swiss participants were paired with individuals of Swiss descent (in-group members) and individuals of Balkan descent (out-group members) who frequently encounter prejudice from nationals. Using a similar pain-based experiment, Hein and her colleagues showed that positive experiences with someone from the out-group created a shift in neurological response, increasing the levels of empathy. Other research has also shown that empathic responses increase as we amass more knowledge about others.

Empathy as a phenomenon is deeply rooted in prosocial and social behaviour. It's what we unwittingly direct toward other 'in-group' members and, conversely, using it can help us overcome the tendency to view someone as 'not one of us'. The word 'empathy' was coined in 1858 by German philosopher Rudolf Lotze as a translation of the Greek word empatheia. The meaning behind the word is an ability to feel into, or project oneself into something else. It means understanding another person's experience by imagining oneself in that other person's situation.

Statistics across the globe are showing a decline in levels of empathy: for example, a YouGov survey published in 2018 showed that 51 per cent of Britons think empathy has declined since the onset of Brexit.[6] Sara Konrath, a Canadian social psychologist and director of the Interdisciplinary Program on Empathy and Altruism Research at the University of Indiana, carried out a study in 2010 showing that younger generations in particular are less empathic.[7] And another study led by Konrath showed that levels of empathy fell by 48 per cent between 1979 and 2009. Given how important empathy is, from maintaining

peaceful international relations through to our individual experience of life and human connection, it's something that should be of great interest to all of us. Being empathic enables understanding, and allows us to make a connection and build trust. We use empathy to quickly read levels of vulnerability, respond to different needs and therefore to understand how to give others hope. This is critical for anyone in a helping profession, especially the ability to read a situation quickly, as so often the other element – time to make that connection – is missing.

When it comes to the study of empathy in pragmatic settings, one area that has received a great deal of attention is healthcare. While nurses and doctors can give us immense hope by simply telling us everything will work out OK and motivate us to get better if we take care of ourselves, equally they can quickly pull us down with one thoughtless comment or ill-fitting piece of advice. They can make us question ourselves: 'Maybe I'm not in that much pain, perhaps there is nothing that is wrong with me?', even when we have been in agony for days. 'Maybe my son isn't that sick?', even though as a parent we know when something is not right with our child. Healthcare professionals can have a dramatic impact on patients without even realising it, through both verbal and non-verbal communication. These social interactions are a juncture at which they can have either an immensely positive or colossal negative influence on our lives for days, weeks or years after. For example, the average nurse interacts with 1,000 patients a year. That's 1,000 lives impacted and 1,000 brains shaped by the experiences for better or worse.

Imagine you are a tourist overseas. You have had severe abdominal pain for several days. You've tried taking normal analgesics, but it's gone on for so long that you are getting

quite worried. It's also debilitating, so you can't go anywhere or do anything on your holiday. You go to a local pharmacy. You don't speak the language so you charge your phone with your translation app and take your little language book. Once facing the pharmacist, as hard as you try to explain you cannot get yourself understood. The pain is making it nearly impossible to concentrate, let alone try to work out how to explain your situation in a different language. You leave feeling exasperated and helpless. When you get back to your holiday villa you pass out from the pain and one of your travel companions, back from their day at the beach, comes in to find you on the floor. You wake up in a hospital with people speaking over your head in a language you don't understand. You don't know what's wrong with you and you don't know how to ask. You just want to go home, but don't even know if and when that will be possible.

After what feels like an excruitating wait lying in the hospital bed, a nurse comes over to you and takes your hand, looks you straight in the eyes and smiles gently. It is a warm, caring and considerate smile. Her eyes don't shift from yours, she looks at you with a reassuring intensity. She doesn't speak English and you still don't know what's wrong with you, but you feel yourself let go of a breath you've been holding onto. Your body relaxes slightly. There is still a communication barrier, there are still cultural barriers, but you trust her and feel more hopeful although you don't know why. What is the difference between this and everyone else you've seen? Aside from the obvious – being understood or being acknowledged – what's the essence of this? How can we help everyone have it? And, what has any of this got to do with mirror thinking?

The difference is empathy. The nurse reads your emotions by looking you in the eye and seeing how you

respond, and the micro-movements give away what you are feeling. She then responds accordingly by reading your reaction as she touches your hand. We have all had both positive and negative experiences, you know as well as I do what each can feel like. However, the problem with empathy is that it is elusive and hard to define. It's even harder to work out how to be empathic if it's not something that comes naturally. And empathy, while positive, can go the wrong way and cause burnout and distress to those exhibiting it. This is the case for many who work in the 'caring' professions, such as social services, emergency services and healthcare. It can also spark negative reactions, even when well-intentioned, if whoever is displaying it is not using it in the 'right' way.

The link between the mirror neuron and empathy was first made when scientists were exploring the 'affiliative communication gesture' – the non-verbal behaviours that increase levels of intimacy between two animals or two people – in monkeys. In humans these bonding gestures may take the form of a hug or a kiss, which are made only in friendly or intimate situations and strengthen the bond between people. Researchers found that if monkeys were watching gestures that were purely social in nature, both in monkeys and in humans, their mirror neurons were activated. When an researcher standing in front of the monkey smacked their lips together or protruded them (both friendly social gestures to monkeys), the corresponding mirror neurons fired in the monkey's brain.[8] The monkey was seeing and feeling what the researcher was doing even when they were not carrying out the action themselves. Neuroscientists believe that this same mechanism in the human brain allows us to feel what other people are feeling, creating the basis for our truly unique feature as humans – the ability to deeply bond with others. If someone is crying,

we may feel discomfort or sadness even when we are not crying ourselves. If someone is laughing it may make us laugh or feel happier.

Replicating the same experiments in humans isn't possible. These poor monkeys had the tops of their heads removed to measure single neuron activity. This is what provided the minute level of detail and accuracy in the results that allows scholars to pinpoint what was going on and how. However, neuroscientists have been able to look at the mechanism in the human brain both at a broader level and in a couple of one-off cases to explore these mechanisms at the level of the single mirror neuron.

In 1999 a study led by Dr William Hutchison, professor of neurosurgery at the University of Toronto, gave a unique opportunity to insert micro-electrodes into a human brain. Hutchinson was performing surgery on people with severe OCD (obsessive-compulsive disorder). Nine of the patients agreed to undergo procedures for single neuron analysis while having surgery and the results showed fascinating and exciting outcomes. During this experiment Hutchinson was specifically interested in looking at the brain's response to others in pain.[9] Pain is a remarkable evolutionary tool, which when expressed overtly motivates helpful behaviour from other people. Thousands of years ago this meant that the rest of a tribe would stop and assist if someone was hurt, improving their chances of survival. The same is true today – if we see a person who is suffering we will typically see if there is any way in which we can help. During these experiments the researchers found that a part of the brain known as the anterior cingulate cortex (ACC) responded both when the person received a painful stimulus themselves and when they observed or even anticipated the same painful stimulus being delivered to someone else. In other words, even when we don't actually feel someone else's

pain, we mirror the response enabling us to understand their distress.[10]

Another study that took advantage of a rare set of circumstances was performed by Professor Itzhak Fried at UCLA in 2010. During this experiment 21 patients undergoing surgery for epilepsy were implanted with intracranial depth electrodes. This was to identify seizure foci for surgery, but it also offered the opportunity to study other brain systems, specifically those relating to the mirror neuron and empathy. To explore this the neuroscientists asked patients to perform two facial expressions – smiling and frowning – and then to observe the same expressions in others. The findings were similar to the previous study: the same mirror neurons fired when the patients made the expressions themselves as when they observed them in someone else. The only differences were a reduced firing rate in the brain of the observer, which is typical for all mirrored behaviours. This was a huge breakthrough for scientists, indicating that not only are mirror neurons responsible for imitating actions, but also for mirroring emotions. When someone else feels something, we feel it too.[11,12]

Empathy on prescription

It feels like common sense that empathy is a fundamental requirement in all healthcare professions. Indeed, empathy is considered to be a critical component of healthcare across many different cultures, and not just by psychologists like myself who understand the power of social and emotional skills. In fact, it's considered to be central by medical professionals themselves: the American Board of Internal Medicine recommends that 'humanistic values and empathy should be cultivated and assessed as an

essential educational activity in graduate medical education'.[13] The General Medical Council in the UK states that in order to promote excellence in standards for medical education and training, 'Organisations must demonstrate a learning environment and culture that supports ... sensitivity and empathy.'[14] Empathic communication skills have been linked to positive outcomes in patient satisfaction levels, increased diagnostic accuracy, a positive impact on the extent to which patients adhere to treatment plans[15] and more broadly support the patient's healing process. Empathy has also been found to provide positive outcomes such as improved quality of life, lower levels of emotional distress and reduced anxiety and depression. Even physiological outcomes can be related to a healthcare provider showing empathy, including lowering blood pressure and reducing blood glucose levels.[16] Scholars have shown that patients diagnosed with the 'common cold' via a communication style from their doctor that is empathic show reduced symptoms and even produce positive changes in their immune system.[17]

Sadly, despite empathy being seen as a critical component of healthcare, it doesn't follow that it's taught, encouraged, recognised or rewarded. As an end result, the varied experiences that we all encounter give direct evidence. Why is that? One longitudinal US study from 2009, led by Dr Mohammadreza Hojat, a researcher professor of psychiatry and human behaviour at Thomas Jefferson University in Pennsylvania, found that in the third year of medical school, the year in which patient care starts being taught and therefore when empathy becomes most essential, empathy levels start significantly declining.[18] This study was unfortunately not a one-off; plenty of others have shown the same for medical students across the globe, including in India,[19] Bangladesh[20] and Belgium.[21] This is

not just in doctors, but also paramedic students in Canada,[22] Nigerian dental students,[23] nursing students in the US[24] and a decline across nursing, dentistry and medical students in the West Indies.[25] However, the disappearing nature of empathy is consistently most severe in medical students. We know that it's needed, as both intuition and research show as much, and we know that healthcare professionals themselves want to display it, so what is preventing them? What is getting in the way?

While there are many possible causes, three interrelated themes stand out. The first is cultural, the second is the pressure that exists within the system of healthcare and the third relates to the individual.

Let's first explore the culture in medicine. Have you ever watched the TV series *House*? It's an American medical drama in which Hugh Laurie plays the role of Dr Gregory House, who is described as a medical genius. In each episode, House leads his diagnostic team to uncover the causes behind unusual and unexplained illnesses. It is in effect a caricature of medicine with an uncanny resemblance to the ideals that are instilled in young healthcare professionals, especially medical students. Young Gregory went into medicine with good intentions. He did exceptionally well at school, studied hard and was ambitious. His parents were proud – there is a certain status attached to becoming a doctor. This inadvertently encouraged a focus on continuing to get good grades and achieve. And while empathy may be extolled in medical councils, it is exam results that get a young medical student through and noticed by their seniors. Dr House's ability to solve problems inadvertently encouraged him to focus more and more on learning medical problem-solving above all else as he passed through medical school[26] – and as a consequence he focused less and less on the patient as a person. In real-life

settings the Dr House-type persona – the erudite medical sage – is instilled in the culture of old-school surgeons and specialists. Those in these prestigious positions role-model an ability to adeptly problem-solve with an air of cynicism and without an incredible bedside manner. The former is rewarded through social norms and expectations, whereas the latter becomes more and more of an afterthought. As a result, so does empathy.

A fascinating experiment relating to this using fMRI looked at patterns of brain responses in physicians and those without a medical background. Jean Decety and colleagues of the University of Chicago looked at physicians who also practised acupuncture. Both groups of people were shown videos of needles being inserted into someone's body (*i.e.* pain). They were then shown a video of the same areas of the body being touched by a cotton bud instead of a needle (*i.e.* no pain). You'll remember that the earlier study looking at empathy showed that people responded to seeing someone else experiencing a painful event as if they were feeling it themselves, albeit to a lesser degree. On the other hand, their mirror neurons[27] didn't respond when people were experiencing a non-pain event. This same result was replicated for the people who were not from a medical background and didn't practise acupunture. Their mirror neurons fired in response to seeing someone being pricked by a needle, but didn't when the person was simply touched by a cotton bud. In comparison, the physicians' brains showed a far lower level of activity in their mirror neurons when people were experiencing pain. The researchers concluded that these doctors had down-regulated their response to pain in order to protect themselves. Over time they had in effect learnt to numb the pain and avoid being empathic so that they didn't have to experience the emotion.[28]

Added to this conundrum of rewarding problem-solving over 'feeling', there is the added problem of stress in the system. This points towards the effects being seen in the caricature of *House*. Others' pain is typically deprioritised in response to problem-solving. In the UK it's no secret that the NHS is under huge pressure. I've worked with medics looking at how to enhance emotional resilience in order to protect both healthcare professionals from stress and other mental health outcomes and to enhance positive patient outcomes, but at times it can feel like we are fighting a losing battle. Even without the bureaucracy of the NHS, all healthcare professionals work in immensely pressurised situations due to the very nature of what they do. My stepsister, who has been an intensive care nurse in Australia for years, says she often seriously considers whether or not she can continue. Why? Not because she doesn't love her job, but because of the pressures and lack of support, which makes it feel unsustainable. Ask anyone you know in healthcare and you are quite likely to hear a similar story.

When you're under immense pressure it's hard to keep your own head above water, let alone show empathy and concern to someone else. Think about when you're late for an important meeting and rushing to catch a train. If you see someone upset, you're unlikely to stop and ask if they're OK. You may even be irritated if they get in your way. That doesn't mean that you're not an empathic person, just that you are stressed and in a rush. Indeed, scientists have found that empathic ability can be dramatically harmed as a result of extreme pressure, noting that: 'Once pressure, fear and stress are present, everything that depends on the system of mirror neurons stops functioning: the ability to empathise, to understand others and to perceive subtleties.'[29] It makes logical sense

that this is one reason why some healthcare professionals seemingly lack empathy.

At an individual level every medical professional, on top of these pressures, experiences a huge amount of trauma, loss and adversity – more than any human has evolved to cope with. While our ancient ancestors no doubt saw some pretty horrific things, there simply weren't enough members in a tribe for them to see the volume of people experiencing sickness and injury hour upon hour, day upon day, to rival that of today's medics. On the other hand, we're far more protected from it in our daily lives than our ancestors were. In the developed world we don't grow up seeing people with open wounds, major disease tends to be treated in hospitals rather than in the home and even death has become removed from everyday life. I was recently speaking about this to Dr Fearnly, a consultant paediatrician from Accident and Emergency in a busy London hospital. She described how as a junior doctor you suddenly encounter an onslaught of despair like nothing you've ever known before. She also explained how she believes that empathy is 'banged out' of student doctors during training. She described being given a cadaver to study very early on in medical school, which she felt was a deliberate way of trying to desensitise students – to see the body as a body, not a person. There is research that points to the same thing, reporting an increase in cynicism and a stunting of ethical and moral development as students become 'immunised' against the more humanistic elements of healthcare. At a neurological level this is like numbing emotions, which diminishes our ability to make effective decisions. This is not healthy or helpful to the caring professions, not only with regard to levels of empathy, but also to patient diagnosis where consideration of emotional factors should form part of the decision-making. While

shutting down emotions may seem 'strong', in reality it encourages a brittle existence and increases the chances of burnout.

Dr Fearnly also explained how she believed some medical schools are now beginning to place greater emphasis on not desensitising students, but the issue is that they don't know how to go about training them to respond and cope in the most effective way. She described a young medic who, having remained 'sensitised', really struggled. He diligently went about developing his bedside manner, but ended up 'over identifying' with his patients and their relatives' distress. It was not long before doing this caused him to burn out.

This is where there is an ironic twist when it comes to what the evidence is telling us. On the one hand research says too much empathy causes burnout[30] – as displayed by this young medic – but on the other hand there's also research to suggest that empathy can protect healthcare workers against exhaustion.[31] This research isn't referring to healthcare professionals who are desensitised or downregulating emotion, but actually being empathic and working more effectively as a result.

Why do we see these conflicting messages from studies? Does empathy protect some people from the effects of stress but cause others to become exhausted? And, more broadly speaking, how can we protect against empathy being trained out of people, either as the result of culture or through individuals protecting themselves? I believe that the answer to all of this lies in the brain mechanisms that are behind empathy. Our understanding of those mechanisms, together with how empathy is used, could help to address all three of the above: culture, stress and individual responses. It could also help you to be more empathic in whatever role you play in life.

Emotional vs cognitive empathy

Earlier we defined empathy as 'understanding another person's experience by imagining oneself in that person's situation'. This is a broadly held understanding of what empathy is. However, there is also a second component to empathy that is extremely important. *The Encyclopedia of Social Psychology* explains that: 'One understands the other person's experience as if it were being experienced by the self, but without the self actually experiencing it. A distinction is maintained between self and other.' It's understanding the mechanism associated with this point that is absolutely critical to using empathy in the most constructive way. The first type of empathy is called 'emotional empathy'[32] and involves being in tune with another person's emotions, actually feeling (although to a slightly lesser extent) what they are feeling. Emotional empathy is something that we share with animals and is a system that develops early on in life. A simple example would be when one child starts crying and the other one also starts for no apparent reason. Learning empathy begins when we're babies. It's not a sudden occurrence, but an iterative process that happens through millions of interactions. Evidence shows that as an infant our mother or main caregiver is more likely to imitate our emotional facial expressions than other movements we make, including smiles, looks of surprise, anger and sadness. This mirroring time and again forms the basis from which empathy develops, gradually building the capability of our mirror neurons. Initially we just feel the emotion ourselves, but gradually our brain begins to synchronise the emotion with our caregiver, then we start to understand that emotion and are able to perceive it in others. The areas of the brain all connect up, which means that our mirror

neurons are activated both when we feel something and also when others feel it.[33]

The second type is called 'cognitive empathy' and involves understanding the emotion and what another person is feeling, but not being engulfed by it. This is different from becoming immunised against emotion, which involves shutting that feeling down as a protective mechanism. Cognitive empathy in contrast illustrates a more developed capability than either emotional empathy or emotional immunity.

A doctor needs to understand the causes and symptoms of a disease, but not catch it. They have to get close enough to the disease to understand it but ward against becoming infected with every virus that comes their way. In the same way, a doctor or nurse needs to understand the emotions and concerns of patients (*i.e.* showing cognitive empathy) so that they can fully diagnose and treat them, but neither 'catch' their emotions (*i.e.* showing too high a level of emotional empathy) nor ignore them, which would prevent understanding (immunisation). If a doctor or nurse caught every disease they would become too sick to work. The same is true if a medical professional catches every emotion through emotional empathy. It wears down and burns out the person on the receiving end. It's critical to understand where one stops and another starts.

Let me give you a personal example of using emotional rather than cognitive empathy due to a lack of understanding. When I first started working as an occupational psychologist I was assigned to a project that involved assessing people for their own jobs, with the likelihood that they would be made redundant. This isn't something anyone relishes. I would spend four hours profiling each individual and then write up a report, which, following calibration, was shared with them in a face-to-face feedback session. One lady, who

I knew was going to lose her job – it had been discussed with me by the client – was so distraught when I shared her report that I was struggling to hold back my own tears. I sat there with a hugely heavy heart, desperately wanting to make her pain and distress go away. I gave her my personal phone number and told her she could speak to me if she was struggling. This was a major rookie mistake.

She called me incessantly at all hours of the night for days on end. I was terrified that she would commit suicide so kept speaking to her, but it was not something I was trained to deal with. Together with more experienced psychologists from my firm we got her the help she needed, but I clearly hadn't understood the boundaries nor the difference between emotional and cognitive empathy, despite being a psychologist. I'd always thought I was empathic because I could 'feel into' people's pain. If I saw someone crying on the street, I'd feel like crying myself, and go and check they were OK. Whenever I saw someone was upset I would sit for hours just listening and reassuring them, whether I knew them or not. This, however, is not the type of empathy needed by psychologists or healthcare professionals, nor many other roles that require you to understand others' feelings and perspectives without becoming entwined in them. It's far more helpful, sustainable, effective and healthy to understand and help others when you don't 'catch' their emotions. That doesn't mean being immune to them, rather making use of the more complex and developed form of cognitive empathy.

Cecilia Heyes, an eminent British psychologist and senior research fellow at the University of Oxford, has examined empathy and the mirror neurons in depth. Heyes explains that there are two steps involved in empathy related to these two different forms. The first

step involves a simpler mechanism: for example, we see someone who is sad and think, 'I feel sad because you feel sad'. This is emotional empathy; you are feeling something on behalf of someone else. The cost of this is that we are mirroring so closely that we experience, to a lesser extent, the pain of the other person. Beyond this simpler process of emotional empathy there is the more complex form of cognitive empathy – 'I understand that you feel sad and feel sorry for you, but I don't feel sad myself'. Heyes believes that emotional and cognitive empathy occur as two different functions in the brain, and that emotional empathy has to happen first in order for cognitive empathy to take place.[34]

We can liken this to everyday emotions that we experience without mirroring. Imagine that someone really annoyed you at work or even at home, and that you are so angry that you want to shout and scream at them. But you don't: you stop yourself, assessing that feeling instead of giving in to it, and decide that shouting wouldn't be helpful in the long run. Your reacting brain elicits the initial emotion and your more advanced observing brain then decides what to do with it. This is in effect what happens with emotional and cognitive empathy. Emotional contagion is a primitive response that happens through being human. We can give in to it and feel the emotion (emotional empathy), block it by compartmentalising the emotion (limiting information available to our decision-making processes) or experience it and then assess it at a cognitive level (cognitive empathy). From this we can see how constantly feeling others' distress through only exhibiting emotional empathy leads to burnout.

Moving to a state of cognitive empathy protects from exhaustion. It enables us to help others and to be prosocial (which itself has a positive impact on the mental and

physical well-being of the person 'helping'), but not to get overwhelmed by emotions, maintaining a healthy distance. Those who are overly stressed, have soaked up too much of the problem-solving approach or have become overwhelmed by what they see may switch off their empathy. Others may have been trained or train themselves not to consider the emotional information, problem-solving purely from a rational viewpoint. What's most helpful is the continuous interactions between emotional and cognitive empathy, with a level of skill that enables more time spent in the latter.

A brain-imaging study carried out in 2010 by Eva Greimel, professor of psychology at Karl Franzens University, scanned the brains of boys and men aged between 8 and 27 years, showing that the neural mechanisms of empathy, specifically the mirror neuron system, continue to develop with age. The authors suggest that maturation of the pre-frontal cortex (part of the observing brain) is likely to facilitate this change.[35] The reason this is interesting is that other recent advances in our understanding of the brain show us that it continues to develop between the ages of 18 and 29 in a phase known as 'emerging adulthood'. The parts of the brain developing at this time relate to strengthening a connection between the observing brain and the emotional connections of the reacting brain, improving our ability to manage emotional responses. Before emerging into adulthood we find it more difficult to manage our emotions, so it makes sense that we would also find it more difficult to manage the emotions we experience as a result of seeing someone else in pain through emotional empathy. This suggests that cognitive empathy and the mirror neurons associated with it develop as our brain and our ability to manage our own emotions develops.

In order to really enable cognitive empathy in a way described by experts as 'top-down control'[36] – a conscious awareness and management of the empathy we are feeling – we need to process the emotions of the other person and then decide how we are going to respond given the context. Our ability to appraise an empathically elicited emotion can depend on a number of factors such as our relationship with the other person, our motivations and priorities, and how our responses have played out in the past. For example, now, following my experience with the distraught client, if I'm with someone who is upset within my professional capacity I will express sorrow for them, be open and hopefully come across as caring and considerate, but I won't actually take on their emotion for more than a fleeting moment. To be empathic in a way that is helpful to our lives we need to understand not only how to take a 'conscious, cognitive view' of what we're picking up from someone else, but also how to appraise their emotions in order to make the most effective decisions. We shouldn't completely suppress our own emotions as they give us useful information about the situation and guide the level of support we provide. As you can see, cognitive empathy is not a straightforward 'have or have not' skill; it takes understanding and practice to develop. You may have learnt this skill without having an explicit understanding of how it works, or how you learnt it, or how to use it effectively all of the time. It's a skill we learn through experience, interaction with others and observation of people who display it. It's learnt most effectively from a role model who understands the mechanisms involved and are able to explicitly explain how they are behaving and why, so that the observer can understand what the role model is experiencing on the inside as well as clearly demonstrating their response on the outside. When skilled

in cognitive empathy it provides a tool by which to deliver better care of others and more effective relationship building, and can also be a tool that helps to protect from burnout. If empathy is linked to the mirror neuron it makes sense that mirroring through observation will help to build it.

While researching this book I found more examples within medical literature of how role-modelling can and should be used in the healthcare profession than in any other area. As many as 90 per cent of medical graduates remember role models who shaped their professional attitudes[37], and it is seen as something that is imperative for medicine worldwide.[38] The titles of papers on the topic range from 'Role-modelling: A missing link in medical education' to 'The hidden process of positive doctor role-modelling', reflecting both the need for and the lack of understanding. Role-modelling is also often massively underutilised or even forgotten. While there is recognition that it can help, it's still not well understood, frequently being described as an enigmatic process[39] – something mysterious and inexplicable. But if we think about it within the context of mirror thinking it's neither mysterious nor inexplicable.

What does role modelling look like in medicine? In the literature, role models are described as being excellent at what they do with a great deal of experience, which is hardly unprecedented given the whole concept of role models. They show empathy and have a positive impact on patients and their families, as well as co-workers. These characteristics, according to various areas of medicine, are something that all experienced professionals should be sharing with more junior staff. For example, the British Medical Association states that: 'All doctors have a professional obligation to contribute to the education and

training of other doctors, medical students and non–medical healthcare professionals.[40]

An article in *Nursing2019* states 'as a nurse, you teach people every day'.[41] Another paper went so far as to say that students themselves are role models to fellow medical students, to other health professionals staff and to faculty. They suggest that medical schools should encourage students to comment on role models in order to really leverage the opportunity that role-modelling affords.[42]

Dr Fearnly is a fantastic role model for empathy. While sometimes things do become too much for her and she goes home and sobs – having to diagnose a child as terminally ill or tell parents that their child has been in an accident that will cause them major life limitations is never going to be easy – she is able to maintain a healthy balance. She wouldn't ever cry in front of the parents of a child. This is cognitive empathy: the ability to step back from what she is feeling and from her patients' pain to give them the messages she needs to, while knowing how to consider their needs and feelings, to see things from their perspective and sometimes to feel it too. Her patients come from all walks of life and a wide range of cultural backgrounds, and by all accounts she carries out her work in a way that gives them the consideration, warmth and empathy they need, taking into account the different needs or concerns they may have. She is recognised as an outstanding teacher and role model, yet until I pointed out the role of cognitive empathy and how she was using it she was unaware that this was something she was modelling. To really help others learn we need to start by telling those who are already role-modelling empathy and other skills what they are doing. Without an explicit awareness they can't optimise their role-modelling or know to explain their responses and behaviours to colleagues, which limits the opportunity for passing on that learning.

Learning how to be empathic is arguably a core part of learning how to be human. We learn this from others and the mechanisms needs to be better understood, modelled and shared. While that may begin with the healthcare professions it is most definitely not where it should end. Empathy is a phenomenon that it is critical across all areas of life and essential to emotional connection. We are gaining a greater understanding of how this type of connection is a central component of mental health and well-being. Empathy is also critical to success. Without it we are simply not as adept at relationships – and relationships underpin all aspects of life, from work to play, spanning beyond healthcare, within the working environment from customer services to leadership, friendships and home life.

Our Social and Emotional Mirrors

At 16, Raul Sanchero was heavily involved in street crime. At a similar age Emilio Ramirez looked like a fully fledged adult, oozing a menacing persona that shouted, 'Don't mess with me'. Ramirez was also deeply entrenched in gang warfare. Living in a rough area of Belmont, California, the two boys were in a high school class of 32 kids who were nearly all mixed up with guns, gangs and an environment that nurtured crime. Each had street cred of their own that was more important to preserve than any grade in school. This was a class of tough, disengaged, 'at-risk' teenagers that education had given up on. The various teachers they went through could be described as 'instructors in attendance' of the class rather than someone sent to actually help them learn. It was wholeheartedly believed by all those in charge that these students, despite every effort, would come to nothing and more than anything were simply a drain on the system.

This describes the opening of the film *Dangerous Minds*, in which Michelle Pfeiffer plays LouAnne Johnson, the newly appointed teacher assigned to the class. It's not what she'd expected for her first job. In that initial encounter with the rowdy teens, the colour drains from her face and a look of terror fills her eyes. However adamantly she tries, she cannot even get her voice heard above the commotion. She leaves the class in a state of desperation, worn down by the relentless backlash, but in true Hollywood style it

doesn't end there. She returns, dressed in clothes that look like theirs; she teaches them karate that she learnt during her time as a Marine; she even goes to Raul's house to speak to his parents about what a wonderful student he is. Echoing the drama and grandiosity of many a film, she operates against school policy and despite being pulled up on her approach numerous times keeps on going. There are moments when she wavers, leaving us wondering whether she'll see it through, but ultimately she doggedly sticks with her methods. By the end of the year she has achieved success that no one had dreamed possible.

In truth, this isn't just a Hollywood tale, but a genuine story based on the autobiography *My Posse Don't Do Homework* by LouAnne Johnson herself. She achieved success through her unconventional methods, which was all the more significant given the respect and encouragement she provided to each and every pupil. Someone who knew Johnson said: 'Her constant support and unorthodox teaching strategies instituted a phenomenal success rate in her students ... simultaneously increasing student self-esteem, academic achievement and class retention.'[1]

Johnson gave the teens hope and stood as a positive role model. Someone they could see following through on promises, who didn't falter in her support, who lived by her commitments. One of her pupils, Oscar Guerra, who later went on to become a technician in a science lab, said: 'She showed me you shouldn't be afraid to try.'[2] In doing so, Johnson went beyond the boundaries of conventional teaching, focusing less on curriculum content and more on the social and emotional learning that would enable her students to believe they could participate in class. Beyond that, she showed them that they actually wanted to do so – they wanted to learn, they wanted to be a part of society and they could be valued as such. This emphasis on social

and emotional learning as a gateway into all learning is often overlooked, to the detriment of fostering emerging generations worldwide. Even as adults we need the opportunity to continue to evolve and develop our skills, adapting to the world around us as it constantly shifts and changes. Social and emotional learning occurs constantly throughout our lives in a multiplicity of settings – through interactions with peers, siblings, colleagues and friends. But it starts with children and teachers, both in and outside the classroom.

Life lessons

For most of the day, every day of the week, teachers are the guardians of our mind when it is at its most malleable. We spend an average of 15,000 hours at school. In the context of what we've learnt about the mirror system so far, the impact of teachers must surely be immense. As the American historian Henry Brooks Adams once famously said: 'A teacher affects eternity; he can never tell where his influence stops.'

This unfortunately, however, doesn't reflect my own reality; teachers did not have a huge impact on my life besides reinforcing how much I disliked school. There was one, not particularly profound, exception and that was my physics teacher. Mrs Maslin was a tall, slim lady with kind eyes, short white hair and always, in my memory at least, adorned in a white lab coat buttoned from top to bottom. I didn't become passionate about physics, but her belief in me and the personal interest she took in who I was made a lasting impression. I felt seen, heard and appreciated. She was perhaps the only teacher who really reinforced a conviction given by my parents – that I could achieve whatever I put my mind to in life. By the time she taught me I had been

through a list of career choices: fighter pilot, architect and clothes designer among them. But my obsessive interest in my own thoughts and trying to understand those of other people meant that at 15 I wanted to be a psychologist. She understood and agreed it was along the right lines, but she wasn't convinced psychology was the right degree and recommended that I do medicine and psychiatry instead. Perhaps this was her own commitment to working hard, perhaps a societal belief that one is better than the other. Regardless, it felt great that someone had faith in me. I chose my A level subjects with the aim of pursuing medicine, diligently seeking out part-time work in hospitals and medical centres. Although I later returned to psychology, Mrs Maslin still influenced the path I took at a critical juncture of life. But this was the only vaguely impactful experience for me with teachers, which made me question if this is the norm. My experiences in profiling have led me to continue to question this from all aspects.

I met Lara a couple of years ago. When she walked in the room I was immediately struck by her appearance: tall and willowy, with beautiful auburn hair, pale freckled skin and deep-green eyes. She carried herself with poise and confidence. As she began to tell me her story she described being fairly disengaged by school until the age of 14. She did OK, but really wasn't that bothered about any particular subject. What she might do when she left school wasn't something that had crossed her mind. She didn't feel like any of the teachers took much notice of her, possibly confounded by the fact that she was always very quiet. This, however, all changed when her art teacher, Mrs Hudson, began to take a real interest in her work. As she described this experience it was clear that it wasn't just the attention that Mrs Hudson gave her artwork that mattered, but that she saw Lara as a 'real' person. She suddenly felt seen and

heard, and her interest in school picked up. Mrs Hudson encouraged Lara to spend more time at the weekends and out of hours experimenting with different art and design, taking photos, making models, drawing, painting. Lara went on to become a top fashion designer with a strong belief that her art teacher had not only influenced her choices, but given her hope in the future, opened her eyes to opportunity and unlocked her potential. This is surely the impact we'd hope every teacher has or at least wants to have on their pupils. Lara's parents were loving and encouraging, but it was what she referred to as a 'lifeline' from the outside that made a significant difference.

Lara's experience was immensely positive and echoes LouAnne's pupil when he said: 'She showed me you shouldn't be afraid to try.' However, reviewing what I've heard as a psychologist, Lara and LouAnne's whole class stand out as more of an exception than a rule. It's more commonplace for the influence of teachers to be relatively neutral, beyond perhaps affecting a subject choice; or worse, still negative, with the impact lasting well into adulthood.

Kirke Olson, a psychologist who specialises in education and the brain, said 'Teaching changes the brain in far more complex ways than any brain surgeon's scalpel,'[3] which brings the significance starkly into focus. What's more, we're now understanding how so much of this, both good and bad, is dependent on the mirror neuron.

The most typical negative impact is leaving someone with the ingrained belief that they're 'not very good with numbers', were 'never any good at English' so their 'communication skills are terrible' or worse still are 'just not very bright'. Take, for example, another person I profiled. When I met Amir he came across as a very self-assured, grounded man, who had a stable inner confidence in his capabilities, with no whiff of superiority or arrogance.

Amir had an impressive track record of success across a range of companies in various countries; at the time he was working as managing director for a well-known brand, which under his tenure had done exceptionally well. When he shared his story he described an experience at school in which he was publicly shamed by a teacher for being so bad at maths. The class had been told to revise for a test on a topic that Amir had found confusing. No one did well, resulting in his teacher being furious with the whole class, presumably because this would reflect badly on him. Amir came bottom and described how the teacher pulled him to the front, shouting at him and using him as an example of someone who shouldn't be in the class, making him feel deeply ashamed. Amir could rationalise this as a bad experience with a poor teacher, yet his lack of confidence with numbers had never left him. He could read the financials and easily spot errors, but would freeze up in meetings with shareholders, leaving him completely dependent on having a good, trusting relationship with his finance director. On testing his cognitive aptitude, it was clear that he had the capability to be good at maths, but that self-doubt had remained with him through life in spite of his other successes. A similar kick to the self-esteem of many would have left them with a more overarching belief that they just weren't worth it, couldn't do it or shouldn't try. It doesn't take much to send a child off course for life.

So, even though we may expect our teachers to have a profound impact on us as role models, do they? Do students in education today consider teachers to be significant role models in their lives? The answer, it seems, is not really. Take, for example, a 2016 study interviewing 220 teenagers from the states of Massachusetts and Connecticut in the US.[4] Of all the people these teenagers came into contact with, family members were nominated most frequently as role models,

including parents, aunts, uncles, grandparents, siblings and cousins. This was followed closely by friends. Teachers fell within the last category, lost somewhere among 'other adults'. Yet what the research tells us is that when teachers do positively role-model, the impact on students is phenomenal. A 2018 study that demonstrates the broader impact of positive role-modelling was published by Kirabo Jackson, a professor of economics at Northwestern University in Illinois.[5] The study of more than 570,000 pupils from high schools in North Carolina showed that beyond test scores, the teachers who improved their students' ability to adapt to new situations, their ability to self-regulate and who were able to engage the pupils' overall motivation had a significant impact on a range of outcomes including attendance, whether or not pupils graduated and whether they went on to further education. The author of the report said, 'The results support an idea that many believe to be intuitively true, *i.e.* that teacher's effects on test scores capture only a fraction of their effect on human capital.'[6] From this, together with the scant anecdotal evidence, it's clear that teachers as good role models make a huge difference. Not making use of this is an opportunity missed, as it has an incredible impact on individuals and society. So, what is it that those, seemingly few positive role models do differently from all of the other teachers? How do they have this effect on children? What's the difference between having no impact and changing a life? If we knew that, not only could we help more teachers to role-model effectively, but we could also learn from it ourselves, whatever our job title or role in life.

The connection, trust and exposure model

Returning to LouAnne Johnson, my own experiences and Mrs Hudson, there are themes emerging that we introduced

right at the beginning – connection, trust and exposure. So, what does this look like? To illustrate, imagine you are going on holiday. You walk into a hotel lobby, relieved to arrive having travelled for several hours. You're tired, it is an expensive hotel – a real treat that you've been looking forward to for a long time, but at the moment you just want to get to your room and have a shower. However, the person on reception won't look at you, won't listen to you saying excuse me, they are too busy doing other things. When they do eventually engage, they hand over a pile of forms for you to fill in and then leave the desk to do something else without giving you a room key. How do you feel? Probably exasperated, frustrated, annoyed, fed up, upset, even. In short, not great. A few days into your holiday you travel from one country to another. Your flight is delayed, once again you're tired and desperate to get to your room when you arrive. This time you're booked into a smaller family-run hotel, not the luxury one you had to start off. When you arrive, you are greeted by a smiling owner who looks you straight in the eyes; it feels like they can read your thoughts as they express how tired you must be having had such bad delays. They offer to take your bags and suggest you just go straight up to your room because everything else can be sorted in the morning. It may be an obvious question, but do you think you'd feel any different to how you felt at the first hotel? This is clearly a far cry from being a child at school, but the disparity between these small interactions illustrates a number of simple but significant disparities between good role models in teaching and those that have no impact. At its most basic level the first interaction involves no connection and very little empathy, the second scenario prompts a genuine connection and a level of empathic concern. The other elements we know are critical for good role-modelling are trust and

exposure, which take more than this simple scenario to explain. We will, however, also explore those below.

Empathy enables the connection in this example. As we discussed in the previous chapter, empathy is powerful even when it's just expressed for a moment in time. The nurse who understands how much pain you're in; the doctor who gently explains what's wrong with your loved one; in the previous example, the hotelier who understands you're tired after a long journey. When empathy is stretched out over the course of time it can have a profound impact. Johnson's approach demonstrates a relentless empathy: she doesn't let her pupils doubt her commitment to them. She gets to know them, to understand their individual situations, to make them feel valued and worthwhile as individuals, and as a result understands how they feel and why they behave in the way they do. Johnson herself once said: 'People forget what it feels like to be a teenager ... I guess I just never grew up.'[7] This empathy is, as we discussed, enabled by the mirror system. Research shows that the most helpful type of teacher–pupil relationship is based on compassion – warmth, nurturance and openness, which increases the quality of the relationship.[89] A teacher who role-models the social and emotional aspects of learning also connects. Children who report better relationships with their teachers based on these behaviours also demonstrate greater motivational, emotional and behavioural engagement in school.[10]

Relationship quality is also based on trust. In a superficial interaction as a customer visiting a hotel we needn't worry about how authentic the empathy is: we just want to feel better at that moment in time. When we are a patient or a pupil, we need to trust that the empathy is authentic – what the health professional or teacher is doing is going to have a long-lasting impact on us. Johnson's pupils trusted her;

she never gave up on them however hard they pushed her, because her empathy was real. As an adult, trust is essential to most, if not all, of our relationships – at work, at home, in friendships and with family. The difficulty is that trust between a teacher and a pupil is not only critical, but as a child gets older is also far harder to generate.

In elementary-level education a child is immersed among their peers for the very first time. Although they are probably still not conscious of mirroring, they suddenly have a huge choice over who to mirror for the first time. It's no longer just parents, siblings or relations. At this point a child tends to trust their teacher and they can even do so in heroic proportions. A small child may come home from school parroting everything that Mr Brown or Ms Pierce said. Attention can make them feel elated, but undermining trust, connection or empathy at this point by showing little interest in one particular child can dramatically deflate self-esteem.

When children hit adolescence, their brain structure and the effect of physiological factors such as hormones create a hugely complex maelstrom of influences on behaviours, emotions and how they respond to others in their environment. There are also evolutionary and developmental factors that lead teenagers to make poor decisions and mirror peers who are not necessarily beneficial to them. And at this age that's what it's all about – being social. A pupil is more likely to trust their parents who love and care for them, their relatives who they've known all of their lives and their friends who they have chosen. This is one of the many factors that plays into teachers being listed lower down as role models than relatives or peers. Trust becomes tricky. To enable trust a teacher must connect and show empathy. Remember this is not sympathy, nor giving in to

whims, but being able to take a cognitive understanding of a teenager's viewpoint.

Another factor that causes difficulty for teachers in terms of being 'good role models' is exposure. Not only do many teachers lead a class of teenagers for merely two to three lessons a week and possibly just for a year, but they are competing for exposure because of the class size. Even those who do teach the same class of pupils for several years often have to contend with pupil numbers, which undermines their opportunities to connect. The teacher is usually one of 30 other individuals in that classroom, but most of the others will be the pupil's peers, who they are with all day every day and are far more important to impress. Their attention is more likely to be focused on their peers than on their teacher. Jean Rhodes, professor of psychology at Massachusetts University, and her colleague Professor David DuBois showed how important exposure, together with connection and trust, is when it comes to the relationship between young people and adults. Their research shows that to be able to establish trust there is a certain reliance on a long-standing relationship.[11] The positive effect that a relationship has on the life outcomes for young people becomes stronger the longer the relationship lasts.

If these are the factors that are once again essential to role-modelling – connection, trust, empathy and exposure – we can see that it's not simply a matter of a teacher having an impact by standing in front of a class. It's dependent on a complex set of interrelated factors. To really get under the skin of how role-modelling – essentially passing on social and emotional skills – does or doesn't work in schools, there is another important question we need to address. It's not just about why some

teachers are having a positive impact, but why others, with all the will in the world, are not.

Stress: the social and emotional blocker

It's no secret that across much of the Western world – with the exception of a number of Scandinavian countries – heavy workloads, lack of support and the increasing pressures faced via testing is hugely impacting the levels of stress and burnout of teachers.[12] Stress makes it difficult for any of us to function at our best. It not only clouds our judgement, but also prevents certain areas of our brain from working effectively. We all experience daily stressors, whether we're teachers or not. This is a natural state of being alive, resulting from the way our brain has evolved to function. Stress is in effect our reacting, more primitive brain keeping us safe. We see a threat and it fires off chemical signals as a warning even though many of today's daily stresses don't appear threatening, such as finding someone sitting in our chair, a person bumping into us on a train, a car pulling out in front of us, not being invited to a meeting, being left off an email, feeling compared with someone else. These are all stressors and they add up in our brain. Every day, hundreds of situations cause our brain to release chemicals that would in our ancestors' time have been dispersed through action, but in our modern world they get trapped. Once these chemicals have been released there is no pressure relief: we don't turn around and fight a person who is sitting in our chair, or flee when someone bumps into us on a train.

A moderate level of stress actually helps us to accomplish more. As stress increases, so does our physiological and psychological arousal until it reaches an optimal level, enabling improved performance – for example, doing

better in a presentation or exam, finding it easier to concentrate or being more able to think on our feet.[13] There is also evidence that acute stress can increase certain aspects of empathy such as prosocial behaviour,[14] which actually help aid the development of those positive teacher–pupil relationships that are so essential. Moderate stress may therefore facilitate social and emotional learning.

However, with too much stress, when demands on the brain become excessive, we quickly tip into overload. Our performance follows a downward trajectory, leading to negative emotions and overall cognitive decline. Once we're snowballing downhill, our observing brain is flooded by stress hormones (*e.g.* cortisol, adrenaline) from our reacting brain, and we lose sight of how to get ourselves back into a more positive position. While short bursts of stress are not damaging, when stress occurs unremittingly it begins to wear us out mentally and physically. This is not only an issue for teachers because it can then lead to a plethora of illnesses (*e.g.* heart disease, headaches, digestive problems, insomnia, depression) and over the longer term damage the immune system[15]; it is also an issue for modelling positive social and emotional behaviour. Research using fMRI has shown that when people are stressed they show stronger and inappropriate 'other-related responses' – in other words their ability to mirror what another person is feeling is diminished. Our capacity to regulate compassion also declines.[16] This reduces the ability to display cognitive empathy, which alongside emotional empathy is essential for a positive teacher–pupil relationship, and therefore critical to enabling social and emotional learning. Added to this we all know that when we're stressed we become distracted and it's difficult to think through how to do things 'the right way'. Again, this limits the opportunity for helpful role-modelling. Think about when you're stressed. If your child,

partner or friend starts demanding your attention, how patient are you? It's hard to give to someone else when you're struggling to keep your head above water yourself. Whatever type of stress we experience, as soon as it becomes prolonged and unrelenting it's really hard to care about what the people around us are feeling. As a result, ongoing stress interferes with a teacher's ability to empathise and therefore to teach. The same is true in any walk of life. Stress, for example, interferes with a parent or line manager's ability to pass on the essential elements of social and emotional learning. This could very well explain why some teachers are having 'no' lasting impact on students; disrupting a teacher's ability to connect and show empathy impacts their capacity to engender trust. Worse still, another mechanism enabled through the mirror system passes stress from teachers on to students.

Imagine that you get a message from your partner to say that they're nearly home from work. You're excited because you've got some news you can't wait to share. You wait impatiently for the front door to open, but then it doesn't just shut – it slams. You rush to see your partner, but can tell from their face that your news is going to have to wait. They launch into a tirade about what a crappy day they've had, recounting everything that's gone wrong and all the people they hate without drawing breath. Are you still excited to share your news? Probably not. In fact, it's hard not to catch their mood. Within a matter of moments, you go from elated to feeling fed up and angry at the world. The very same thing happens when a teacher is stressed, except the impact is on their pupils. This was demonstrated by Eva Oberle, assistant professor of population and public health at the University of British Columbia, who led a groundbreaking study showing the direct impact of teachers' stress on pupils. Oberle and her team looked at

406 pupils from 13 elementary schools across an urban area of Vancouver, Canada, recording their cortisol levels at 9 a.m., 11.30 a.m. and 2 p.m. within the actual classroom setting. This provided an indisputable biological measure of stress in the children. Oberle also looked at teacher burnout levels and found that even after adjusting for differences in cortisol levels due to age, gender and time of waking, higher morning cortisol levels in students could be significantly predicted from higher burnout levels in classroom teacher. The more stressed the teachers, the more stressed the pupils.[17]

How does a teacher connect and build trust when they are stressed? As we explored in the previous chapter, it becomes incredibly hard. Worse still, a teacher's stress can actually have a detrimental effect on their pupils. On the other hand, when stress is removed, the factors relating to effective role-modelling, connection, empathy and trust are far easier to access. This means the likelihood of a child viewing their teacher as a role model and mirroring their behaviour, values and attitude increases dramatically. In fact, engaging and connecting with pupils as individuals opens the door to far more than this, as reflected in Jackson's study – it enables social and emotional learning to naturally take place. This is learning that can have a positive life-long impact on children. Impactful role-modelling by teachers forms a virtuous circle because it is helping to develop the mirror system of pupils.

Young people, particularly those in at-risk environments, need as many opportunities as they can get to see how to behave in a way that will support their passage through life. This includes prosocial behaviour – showing empathy and respect for others, helping, working through emotions, understanding and learning how to regulate emotions and how to communicate effectively. A study that looked at high

school students who had someone to positively role-model social and emotional skills from found they engaged in less risky behaviour such as gang affiliation and violence, had higher psychological well-being, and engaged in more positive health behaviours such as being physically active and using contraceptives.[18] In turn, this positive role-modelling of social and emotional skills, as we saw in Jackson's study, which has been repeated in other research, has been shown to improve academic results. It has also been shown to improve relationships with parents, peers and other adults in a child's social network,[19] reinforcing the positive impact and virtuous circle.

Increasingly, there is a worldwide recognition of the need for greater emphasis on social and emotional skills, due to an understanding of the broader societal outcomes. In 2015, a study commissioned by the UK government looked at the longer-term effects of social and emotional learning in schools. They found that the impact of neglecting these skills cost the government around £17 billion annually – a result of 'picking up the pieces of damaging social issues affecting young people'.[20] These issues could be effectively addressed through placing more emphasis on positive role-modelling by teachers, but first the stress needs to be removed from the system.

Embedding emotional intelligence

Positive teacher role-modelling is not just helpful for underprivileged populations. I see the importance of the social and emotional skills, which can be transferred as a hugely significant by-product of teacher role-modelling within much of the work I do.

Social and emotional skills overlap considerably with what was termed by psychologist Daniel Goleman as

'emotional intelligence'.[21] It is now widely accepted that high emotional intelligence (EQ) is as important, if not more so, than IQ in leaders. I have worked with underprivileged kids and will continue to do so, but the leaders I see tend to come from middle-class or privileged backgrounds. Many Cambridge graduates, Harvard alumni and leading medics, who have sailed through life on the back of outstanding test scores and track records of success, yet suddenly reach a ceiling, tripped up by their lack of social and emotional capability. In a similar way to those Gregory House-like medics, these people typically have the right intentions. They want to be effective at navigating the social and emotional world, but have come to this realisation later in life when the nuances begin to matter more and they find they are left wanting. A personal experience, a partner who's left them, a dispute at work or an inability to close a deal may have made them realise they could be and do so much more in life with a more developed EQ. While they have often attended some of the 'best' schools, where academic learning was the core focus, other softer aspects such as 'making sure we do the best for your child and develop their moral compass', was often left to chance, with academic achievement taking centre stage. In other words, there is a gap for how these skills are taught across every socio-economic background.

These social and emotional skills impact performance across a whole host of jobs beyond leadership. For example, two studies have looked at how EQ impacts performance in the military, in these cases the US Air Force and the Israeli Defence Forces, finding that higher levels of EQ related to higher performance. A study in the UK looked at 100 managers in Beefeater restaurants and found that the higher a manager's EQ, the better guest satisfaction and annual profits. EQ has also been linked to better

performance in account officers, head teachers, clerical employees and project managers.[22] Beyond the workplace, more highly developed social and emotional skills impact a number of longer-term life outcomes including well-being, life satisfaction and mental health. Someone with good social and emotional skills is also less likely to become obese, smoke or drink excessively.[23] In short, as the government report looking at this states, 'The evidence gathered makes it clear that social and emotional skills matter for the things people care about in life, including adult mental health and life satisfaction, socio-economic, labour market, health and health-related outcomes.'[24]

An emotionally intelligent leader can develop these skills later in life. They have a priveledged opportunity to focus on this and seek help in how to do it. Not all of those people who are busy slogging away in a 'normal' job have the time or inclination to improve their social and emotional skills, but it can make a huge difference in their lives. A friend of mine, David Sole, who captained the Scotland rugby team in an historic 1990 match, learnt that lesson throughout his career. The game was held at Murrayfield in Edinburgh, the Grand Slam decider against the 'bookies' favourite' – England. The English side were described by the media in the lead-up to the match as arrogant. They believed that they already had the game 'in the bag' before they even played and Will Carling, the England captain, was even televised telling his team that they were better than the Scots.[25] To add insult to injury, some of the England supporters had arrived in Edinburgh prior to the match wearing 'England 1990 Grand Slam' T-shirts.[26]

Sole is a quietly confident and thoughtful man. Whenever I am in conversation with him I feel he is actively listening to every word and considering it with a genuine respect.

When he's with other people he does exactly the same – not saying a great deal in a group situation, but getting whatever his message is across with clarity and impact. When he talks, people listen. As captain he projected this persona, his calm self-assurance, on to the whole team, leading them on to the pitch in a slow march.[27] The Scotland team defeated England 13–7 that day, against all the odds,[28] calmly and confidently. Sports journalist Richard Bath wrote:

> *David Sole is another of those players who is remembered and virtually defined by one moment: in this case it was when he made the decision for his side to take the now famous walk onto the pitch for the Grand Slam decider against England at Murrayfield in 1990. As a statement of resolve, it was a masterstroke from which the English never recovered as they lost the most high-profile game in Five Nations Rugby history. It also cemented Sole's name in Scottish folklore ...* [29]

It doesn't matter that David is quiet because his assurance, lack of arrogance and settled confidence – his own emotional intelligence – meant that his mood was positively magnified on to those around him, mirrored in the way they behaved, their attitude and their approach. And in the 1990 Grand Slam final, that secured Scotland's win.

In the same way David set the tone for that match, we set the tone for the entire day for our family, work colleagues, all the people we come into contact with; teachers set the tone for children. It may be a subtle influence, they may not be conscious of it, but it's there. As a parent in a family, an angry mood can ruin our child or partner's whole day. They become upset because you are and then fall out with a friend at school or work, get in trouble with the teacher or their boss, or don't concentrate on a critical task. As captain of a sports team, whether it's a confident, calm

manner or an angry war cry, the tone is reflected by teammates throughout a match. Certain factors can intensify this impact. A child, for example, finds it hard to shake their parent's mood because it matters so deeply to who they are and how they live. They look to a parent for guidance on what to do and how to be. A teacher may not always have a positive impact on the children in their class, but their stress will be contagious. A friend could hurt us deeply, but also make us happy with one kind comment.

Mirroring the mood and emotion of others through social interaction enables us to learn these skills throughout life, but positive and constructive expression of emotion is far more helpful than 'out of control' moods. Louis Cozolino, a professor of psychology at Pepperdine University in California, specialises in the evolution of the brain as a social organ. He explains that the brain is not static, but rather continually changes and adapts throughout our life in response to the interactions we have and the emotions we encounter both in ourselves and others. Our neural networks are constantly adapting and reforming based on the interactions we have and we are recurrently learning social and emotional skills.

So there is no doubt that these skills are critical. What's worrying is that we're learning them less and less on a day-to-day basis, due to increased interactions with screens as opposed to people. This is something that impacts each and every one of us as it is in effect starving our brain of the opportunity to grow and evolve. Children not only have the barrier of a fast-paced, technologically saturated world, but within the school environment an increased emphasis on test scores and a corresponding increase of stress in the system exacerbates the problem further.

One of the main reasons that we don't focus on these skills in schools is that although governments,

organisations and individuals are beginning to acknowledge their importance, they are still unclear as to what their exact impact is or how to pass them on. We don't have processes and methodologies in place to understand, let alone learn, these skills, so policymakers tend to stumble. We can't measure these aspects so we can't point to the successes. It's easier to say that we have higher grades as a school so we're doing better. Ironically, the focus on higher grades creates stress in the system, undermines the capability of teachers to role-model social and emotional skills, and actually limits academic achievement. This means where there is achievement it's often force-fed and the social and emotional skills are neglected. We could create a positive cycle yet we are focused in the main on going the other way.

Yet it's not hard to leverage social and emotional learning given the right conditions. The most natural way to do it, the way in which our brain has evolved to do it, is through role-modelling. Now that we're learning more and more about how mirroring happens in the brain and how essential it is to see and hear these behaviours in order to learn them. This is something we perhaps always intuitively knew, but it has now been proven through neuroscientific research, and we need to use these skills in order to develop them. What better place than the 15,000 hours spent at school?

What are the solutions? At a policy-led level there are some fundamental changes that need to happen. Firstly, the most obvious thing to do is aim to remove at least some of the stress. It's impractical to think we can remove it completely as we are humans living in a busy modern world, however we can minimise it. A straightforward way to do that is to change the focus purely on grades as a measure of success. This may seem unfeasible or unrealistic, yet it's already done in Finland.

In Finland teachers are free to teach students in whatever way they believe will help them. The schools have no mandated standardised tests, except for one at the very end of senior school. Schools are not ranked against each other, and students, schools and regions are not in competition with one another. Every school has a focus on national goals and the teachers all come from the top 10 per cent of graduates who are then chosen to complete a master's degree in education. In 2000 an international standardised test was given to 15-year-olds across 40 global locations. Finland took part and the results revealed that it had the best readers in the world. In 2003 it came out top in maths and by 2006 it also topped the rankings in science, across 57 countries. Another impressive and significant finding is that the difference between the strongest and weakest students is the smallest in the world.[30] Marjanna Manninen, a Finnish school principal from Helsinki, explained in an interview that one of the core principles of teaching is that children encounter learning everywhere they go: 'The whole of Helsinki is the classroom. We have the park, the city centre, the zoo – it's ideal for this kind of approach.'[31] In other words, children learn best by using the brain we have all been given in the environment it has evolved to respond best to. This is the same environment in which our ancient ancestors learnt – the natural world – through observational learning and good communication or storytelling. Taking away testing and pressure, and providing teachers with the freedom to teach how they see fit, removes a huge amount of stress for both teachers and pupils, and also frees the teacher up to be a good role model. Providing teachers with a greater level of autonomy has also been shown to increase their levels of motivation.[32] The Finnish system gives a far more effective platform from which to pass on social and emotional learning as

well as academic. It's already done and done well. It may need to be adapted for the cultural needs and socio-economic environment of different countries, but surely this should be where our focus lies.

Secondly, role-modelling and mirror thinking need to be moved up the agenda. Providing evidence for why these approaches to teaching work for both improving academic results and social and emotional learning. With this information in mind other approaches can also be introduced to improve a teachers' ability to connect in spite of potentially limited exposure. One of these approaches is storytelling, which we'll explore in more depth in the next chapter because of its fundamental link to the mirror system and internal role-modelling.

Another way in which the knowledge of the mirror system and role-modelling could be used to help teachers is to provide them with better role models. In the same way health professionals need strong examples to follow, so do teachers. Dr Mieke Lunenberg, professor at the VU University Centre for Educational Training, Assessment and Research in Amsterdam, is passionate about how to enable the best professional development of teacher educators – those who teach teachers. Dr Lunenberg says, 'Teacher educators not only have the role of supporting student teachers' learning about teaching, but in so doing, through their own teaching, model the role of the teacher.'[33] Yet she has found that this primary source of role-modelling is widely overlooked both in research and in its practical application. Lunenberg recommends making role-modelling explicit by encouraging practices such as observations and discussions, which can help both the teachers of teachers to more effectively role-model and also help teachers learn how to positively role-model themselves.

Thirdly, something that has been a large focus of my profession is to help people with their personal development. Doing this, specifically in the context of teaching, has a number of positive outcomes: it improves our ability to role-model effective social and emotional skills and protects us against stress. Teachers should have access to the type of personal development available in corporate organisations. This would give them the opportunity to really explore who they are, what they are about, their strengths, blind spots, what makes them stressed, what relieves their stress, when they are at their best and when they are at their worst. This is a critical foundational layer to being a good role model. To really speak with passion, to authentically connect, we have to know who we are, what we stand for and how we come across. That understanding needs to continue to evolve and adapt as we do, and as our environment and the people around us continually change.

Focusing on personal development is something we can all benefit from hugely. Self-awareness is something we all 'think' we have, but in reality probably don't – in fact a hugely significant 95 per cent of us think that we're self-aware, but the reality bears a stark contrast with 10–15 per cent actually knowing who we really are.[34] Having better self-awareness improves our social skills, decision-making capabilities, and our ability to deal with pressure, resolve conflict and deal with stress.[35] The psychologist Daniel Goleman who has studied emotional intelligence in depth describes self-awareness as the cornerstone of emotional intelligence and if we want teachers to help pupils gain higher EQ, then they need to have it themselves and to be supported in using and developing it. While governments may be reluctant to invest in the same way as corporations when it comes to personal development of teachers, there are other methods that could be used. For example, there's

potential to make use of what's known as 'peer-group mentoring', which has proven to be very successful in Finland. In effect it's peer role-modelling, and providing a mirror of feedback and also a vehicle for support. It's been shown to improve teachers' ability to cope, to strengthen their personal identity, to motivate them, give them confidence and to support them in more effectively using their skills and capabilities.[36]

More than that, if we want to continue to develop our mirror thinking and emotional intelligence throughout life it's something we should all pursue.

There are obviously a multitude of factors involved but, put simply, the current expectations on teachers and schools to produce outstanding academic results is putting huge pressure on the system. The pressure is undermining teachers' ability to role-model and teach in a way that inspires, unlocks potential and creates a love of learning. The stress undermines their ability to connect, build trust and show cognitive empathy towards pupils. It can also prevent teachers from transmitting the capabilities that are not learnt through instruction yet are essential to life and society – social and emotional skills. Teaching the syllabus is only one aspect of education. Teachers should also be able to communicate effectively, engage with pupils, enable them to feel seen and heard as individuals, valued, inspired about learning and about their future – that's surely what we want for our kids. This may seem unrealistic yet we've also seen how in Finland, where the focus is not purely on academic outcomes, teachers are able to exercise their own judgement in how to help pupils achieve in a rounded way through these means. Really this is making use of mirror thinking in the way nature intended. Within our modern world, Finnish schooling supports – rather than creates a barrier to – evolutionary mechanisms. Teachers are invested

in having an important and respected role to play in society, with comparable status to that of a lawyer or doctor.[37] If we consider the latent impact that a teacher can have, this should surely be the case everywhere in the world. To make use of what we are learning about the mirror system we could provide evidence-based mechanisms to enable positive changes. If we were to switch emphasis and place it on supporting teachers and an expectation that they become positive role models who build connections with their pupils, instil trust and show empathy, rather than to purely focus on grades, then the positive outcomes would be multifarious. They would include better academic outcomes to happier, healthier and more fulfilled teachers, but most importantly pupils would be equipped not only with the grades to achieve in life but the social and emotional skills to do so in a way that is rewarding and enables them to really reach their true potential.

Storytelling and Daydreams

As history has unfolded, it is the storytellers who have been prevalent across cultures and centuries. The tribal elders who told tales around a village fire, the philosophers such as Plato and Aristotle whose words we still quote today, the mythmakers of every continent, the clergymen and the pastors of the past, the writers who underpin our global literary canon, right through to the vloggers and bloggers of today – their stories have shaped humanity. These great communicators weave words together in a way that tells an authentic, emotive and captivating story, which causes the brains of those around them to fall into synchronicity not just with the storytelling, but with each other. The story is imagined in their own brain, with its own personal meaning, tapping into the emotions and motivations of the listener via the mirror system.

Within the US, pastors are recognised as leaders who stir emotion among huge swathes of the population using powerful narrative. For example, Barbara Brown Taylor, an Episcopal priest, was named in *Time* magazine's Time 100 list of the most influential people in the world[1]; Rick Warren, an American evangelical Christian pastor, has sold more than 32 million copies of his book *A Purpose-Driven Life* in 85 languages. Warren has addressed audiences of more than 80,000 people in locations such as the Los Angeles Rose Bowl.[2] They seem like natural communicators, but their capability has been carved from many years of mirroring and experience.

One boy, who grew up the son and grandson of such leaders and communicators, we all know well. We know him because of his beliefs. Many of us have strong beliefs and feel injustice in one walk of life or another, but it was not just his deep commitment to his beliefs and his willingness to take the helm that made him a global household name: it was his ability to tell a story in a way that made those around him stop and listen.

Martin Luther King Jr was born on 15 January 1929 in Atlanta, Georgia, his father a Baptist preacher and outspoken advocate of the civil rights movement, and his mother a schoolteacher. His maternal grandfather was also a Baptist preacher. An African American, King had a dear friend who was a white boy, but at the age of six they were sent to separate schools due to state segregation laws and the white boy's father no longer let them play together. The injustice of this never left King. During his high school years, he became adept at public speaking, joined his school's debating team and was known for his oratory skills. He was bright and went on to study hard with a preference for medicine and law. During his time at college, he would regularly go listen to the preaching of his teacher and mentor, Benjamin Mays, a Baptist minister, civil rights leader and president of the college. He later reflected in his biography on the influence Mays and his father had on him:

> I guess the influence of my father also had a great deal to do with my going in the ministry. This is not to say that he ever spoke to me in terms of being a minister, but that my admiration for him was the great moving factor; he set forth a noble example that I didn't mind following.[3]

King and Mays were clearly very close and he was no doubt a huge influence on him – so much so that King was known as his 'spiritual son'.[4] Learning from his father, grandfather, spiritual father and many other great black orators who he

grew up around, King himself delivered one of history's most memorable speeches. His call to end racism in the United States was delivered to more than 250,000 civil rights supporters on the steps of the Lincoln Memorial in Washington DC on August 28 1963. It has been heralded as one of the most iconic speeches in American history.[5] His passion and focus for this movement was clearly influenced by the role models that surrounded him.

Within the context of mirroring we can see where King's values, beliefs, attitudes, skills and aspirations came from. He witnessed incredible speakers throughout his life and began mirroring and shaping his own capabilities from a young age. He heard how stories were told from Mays, who in turn had been inspired by Ghandi, and thus he refined his approach to be respectful and non-violent, while still powerful and inspiring to millions then and now. The words he spoke from the Lincoln Memorial that day have reverberated through the decades:

I have a dream that one day on the red hills of Georgia the sons of former slaves and the sons of former slave owners will be able to sit together at the table of brotherhood.

I have a dream that one day even the state of Mississippi, a state sweltering with the heat of injustice, sweltering with the heat of oppression, will be transformed into an oasis of freedom and justice.

I have a dream that my four little children will one day live in a nation where they will not be judged by the color of their skin but by the content of their character.

I have a dream today.[6]

Even in this short snippet of his speech, we are transported via our imagination to the red hills of Georgia, the sweltering heat of Mississippi and are propelled forward to

a hopeful future of an oasis of freedom and equality, where men sit together in brotherhood and children are, unlike King was himself, able to play with whom they choose. He paints a picture of what is and what could be with powerful imagery that carries the listener with him, away from the hatred of slavery and towards a unified America. There is emotion in the language: he empathises and relates to his audience, speaking of his own little children who are unfairly judged. His authenticity is clear: his words come from the heart and from his experience of being separated all those years ago from his childhood friend. For his white audience there is a message not to judge the innocent without knowing 'the content of their character', rousing their conscience, but in a gentle way that would not turn them against him.

According to present-day civil rights leader John Lewis, 'By speaking the way he did, he educated, he inspired, he informed not just the people there, but people throughout America and unborn generations.'[7]

King's gift for storytelling was undoubtedly passed down to him through the generations and this is frequently the case for all of us. From the earliest days of humankind, each generation has told stories to the next. Most often these stories are not from books, but told aloud – stories about life, their own life, their parents' life, their parents' parents' life. Stories are magical, they engage, and we remember and pass on values, morals and ideas through them, despite perhaps forgetting a name or a place. My own grandmother, Ruby, would tell me stories of her youth – stories from her unhappy childhood; her time as nanny to a wealthy London family; the days on which she was whisked off by various suitors. In one tale she described a ball at Knole Park, a Jacobean manor, and in my childish mind it became the palace of Cinderella. The stories were

told to me with so much detail, clarity and emotion that I could imagine myself there standing alongside a younger version of my grandmother as she described the colour of the fabrics, the feel of the gowns, the arrival at stately homes, the romantic endeavours. Just like King, my grandmother was lighting up multiple areas of my brain by engaging my sensory receptors and deepening my sense of empathy via the mirror neuron.

We are all made of stories

Every family has a story and this human ability to pass on messages provides a different sort of opportunity for mirroring, and is a huge contributor in shaping the culture and society we see across the world. From an evolutionary perspective storytelling was absolutely critical. Thousands of years ago there was no formal education or books; storytelling was a key means by which information and learning were passed on. While during the day children would have followed their parents on a hunt, observing their every move, or walked with them to learn about the berries that were safe to pick and which to avoid, those that would heal and those that would poison, it was around the fire at night that stories were told. These would be fables about people who came before them, their history, tales of mistakes made, customs, values and principles that made up the culture of the society they lived in. This continued for thousands of years right up until today. Although we may not be explicit aware of the values and beliefs of our family, they tend to live on from one generation to another. Not many of the family stories are written down either, unless we happen to be related to someone notable. So how do we remember these things? Through photos, yes, but also by hearing the narrative that goes with those photos; the memories

transmitted and shared in our own minds and storing its meaning to pass on again and again.

A story well told can mesmerise children and adults alike, and plays a crucial role in passing on those intangible necessities of life such as morals and values. Storytelling is definitely relevant for early on in childhood, but what about later? Beyond drama and literature does it play a role? And how is this relevant to the mirror neuron? Something that makes us unique as a species is our ability to, as psychologist Jean Decety puts it, 'consciously use our imagination to simulate reality as well as fictional worlds'.[8] We are equally able to listen to or create a story, and to imagine what has happened in our own or others' lives and what is yet to happen. This not only provides us with a critical social capability and vehicle for passing on knowledge, but also a massively important channel for communication, connection and learning. A large part of the responsibility for this lies in mirror thinking. Stories are powerful, not simply because they are engaging and entertaining, but because of the parts of the brain that they activate in the listener. Mirror neurons allow what has been described as 'embodied simulation' of the actions, thoughts and feelings of others.

How does it work? If something is explained to us using facts it engages the parts of our brain associated with language, which helps us to understand the words being said and process their meaning. It doesn't, however, engage much more of the brain or connect with the audience emotionally. In a classroom, for example, if a teacher is expected to explain through instruction they are not connecting with a pupil in a way that forms an effective foundation for role-modelling.

When the same information is conveyed via a story, not only are the language-processing areas of the brain engaged, but so are areas of the brain that relate to various aspects in

the narrative. Research carried out by Véronique Boulenger, a neuropsychologist at the Laboratory of Language Dynamics in France, used brain imaging to show the impact of storytelling. Boulenger found that when participants heard sentences such as 'John grasped the object' and 'Pablo kicked the ball', scans of the participants' brains showed activity in the motor cortex relating specifically to that same grasping or leg movement. Other imaging studies have shown that when we hear words associated with smells such as cinnamon, ammonia or lavender, our olfactory cortex lights up;[9] when we hear metaphors relating to texture, the part of our sensory cortex that perceives texture when we are touching something becomes active;[10] the same is true for the visual cortex in terms of colour and shape and the auditory cortex for sound.[11] This shows that at a neurological level stories engage more areas of the brain than those which process facts alone, by creating a colourful and emotive simulation of reality as if the listener is actually experiencing what they are being told. The brain of the listener mirrors that of the story or storyteller. When listening to a narrative our imagination is engaged for us and our emotions are switched on. We not only understand what we're being told, but we also have an emotional connection with what is being said. The use of analogies and metaphors are seen in all of the best storytelling – Martin Luther King's speech is just one example.

A team of neuroscientists at Princeton University led by Uri Hasson, professor of psychology at the Neuroscience Institute, went as far as to show that the brains of storytellers and listeners actually synchronise when stories are being told. In 2010 Hasson and his colleagues used fMRI to record brain activity in both the speaker and listener during storytelling and found that the activity was both

spatially and temporally coupled.[12] In other words, the same areas of the brain were activated in both the speaker and the listener and there was also a synchronisation in time, albeit with a slight delay. While the speaker and the listener's brain activity mirrors each other, there are 'temporal' differences. The researchers found that these delays can be explained by the time it takes a listener to process the information from the speaker.[13] Hasson has explained how, incredibly, the process is equivalent to a person 'perceiving' and experiencing an event themselves, but rather than it coming from the physical environment it comes from another brain and body.[14] They mirror what they hear in their own brain, thus replicating what's happening in the brain of the storyteller. Consequently, a massively strong connection is formed between storyteller and listener. Engaging the brain of the listener means that important messages are passed on and remembered as if they've been lived through a shared experience. This is powerful stuff, as it shows us the mirror neuron is in action when it comes to passing on vital learning. Before the written word, this was the basis by which culture and society was not only maintained, but also learnt and progressed.

When it comes to the details of storytelling, a study carried out in 2018 showed that it is the characters rather than the plot that we engage with first. In other words, when we are listening to someone telling a story it is the storyteller and the people they encounter that capture our attention most, followed by what actually happens. Once again, this illustrates the influence of other people on our brain. When we're listening to any story it triggers neural networks relating to very people-driven factors. For example, when someone is depicted as scared and desperate, the corresponding areas of our brain simulate

that feeling in us as the listener. This phenomena was demonstrated in 2018 by neuroscientists at McMaster University in Ontario, Canada, also using fMRI to examine the brains of participants. While being scanned, they were presented with headlines such as 'Surgeon finds scissors inside patient' or 'Fisherman rescues boy from freezing lake'. They were then asked to generate a representation or story of the event by describing it verbally, by pantomiming using gestures or by drawing it. They found that whichever form of retelling the narrative people used, the brain networks that were activated were strongly character-centred, looking at intention, motivations, beliefs, emotions and actions of those at the centre of the story.[15]

It's therefore not surprising that new research by Dr Paul Zak, director of the Center for Neuroeconomics Studies at Claremont Graduate University, suggests that stories not only shape our brains, but also change our attitudes, opinions and behaviours, inspire us, tie strangers together, and move us to be more empathic and generous.[16] Our sociability and, in fact, our social dependence as humans mean that we use stories as a way to pass on important information and values from person to person, generation to generation and community to community. Using fMRI, Zak and his team found that personal and emotionally compelling stories engage more of the brain, which in turn means that they are better remembered than factual information conveyed in isolation of a narrative. Zak and his team used two films of the same child with cancer, but conveyed in a different way, to explore which aspects would make it more likely for people to connect with a story and therefore donate money. They used the following narrative of 'Ben's story' played out in a video, which is described by Zak as follows:

'Ben's dying.'

That's what Ben's father says to the camera as we see Ben play in the background. He is two years old and doesn't know that a brain tumor will take his life in a matter of months.

Ben's father tells us how difficult it is to be joyful around Ben because the father knows what is coming. But in the end he resolves to find the strength to be genuinely happy for his son's sake, right up to Ben's last breath.'[17]

Participants were also shown a video of Ben, with no hair due to chemotherapy, going around a zoo with his father. The first film stimulated cortisol, associated with stress, presumably triggered by mirror neurons and oxytocin, linked to our bonding capability as humans. It appears that this was simulating what the father and child were going through reflected in the brain of the listener. The second, which showed far less about the characters of Ben and his father, resulted in less interest and didn't hold the attention of viewers. Unsurprisingly, people donated more to a childhood cancer charity after seeing the first video than the second. Fascinatingly, Zak was able to show that the levels of each of the hormones released predicted donations with an 80 per cent accuracy.[18] This one simple example shows how storytelling influences people at the molecular level, shaping their brain and impacting attitudes, opinions and behaviours.

Often we are unaware that this is happening to us when we hear a story, this allows us to be transported, entertained and educated. It also allows us to fall prey to those who would seek to manipulate our brain functioning for their own ends unless we are conscious of these reactions. As we have seen, storytelling can be and is used across all walks of life: for charities to raise funds, educators to share knowledge, documentary-makers to get important points

across to viewers, film-makers to startle, amaze and enthral audiences, and advertisers to sell. The advertisers and marketers of the world know how our brain chemistry works and use our unconsciousness to persuade us to buy into their products. How, for example, do you make a sanitary product emotionally engaging or something people even want to think about? #LikeAGirl tapped into the knowledge that puberty is a time when confidence is a real issue for girls. The brand managers for the sanitary product manufacturer Always found that this is due in large part to gender stereotypes, with the message that men are more powerful and stronger than women. They picked up in particular on the fact that in Western culture boys are raised to be anything but a girl, as if being a girl isn't good enough. In a case study of the brand proposition the marketeers explain: 'The expression "like a girl", in fact, is often used as an insult to tease somebody who is weak, over-emotional or useless.'[19] This is what they used to command the emotional engagement of their audience. Using a real-life social experiment they, unbeknownst to participants (who believed they were simply on a casting call) were asked to do things 'like a girl'. To run, hit a ball, throw a ball, fight. Men, boys and women acted in a feeble, half-hearted or pathetic way. Pre-pubescent girls, however, were feisty, confident and strong. The message – that before society reaches these girls they believe in themselves. This campaign was so emotive and shared a story that resonated so strongly with the population that the video was shared more than 90 million times, the hashtag #LikeAGirl was used more than 177,000 in the first three months of the campaign and in March 2015 it was even recognised by the United Nations. Always claimed that it has 'changed the meaning of "like a girl" from an insult to the ultimate compliment it really is!' and while

unfortunately that may not be entirely true, it certainly boosted sales with an increase in purchase intent of 50 per cent. It may not have changed cultural views for good, but it certainly made a positive impact.

A good friend of my husband's, who has made his way through various unbelievably interesting marketing roles, has a deep passion for telling a story, something he learnt from listening to his grandmother growing up. He has successfully weaved narratives across products ranging from cigars to aeroplanes, online hotels to the music industry. At Adidas he played a significant role in the 'Impossible is Nothing' campaign involving boxing legend Muhammad Ali, long-distance runner Haile Gebrselassie, football icon David Beckham and NBA star Tracy McGrady. The listener's imagination is captured by a shared understanding: they have all faced setbacks and been given hope; despite their challenges they have mastered the impossible by taking risks, setting new records and changing conventions.[20] His stories have created cultural shifts with games such as Candy Crush, which at one point was played by one in seven people in the Netherlands, through to creating playgrounds across the UK to support the Olympics. The playgrounds increased sports participation by 110 per cent in deprived areas, the knock-on effect being an increase in well-being and decrease in crime in the youth involved. Being able to tell stories provides us with such a strong currency and enables each of us to be a leader and to role-model and convey our values, beliefs and ideals within the mind of the listener. These are examples of where, alongside seeking to gain market share or sales, there is some good intent and a broader positive outcome. However, that is not always the case.

These images and stories, and many more portrayed by the media, politicians and advertisers around the world,

have an impact on each and every one of us every day. We play the film role of what we see in our mind, the story comes to life in our own neural networks, we rehearse and unwittingly prepare to respond, we make decisions without thinking and we live our life blind in too many instances. All too often this means that the skilled communicator, however poor they may be as a leader or politician, can manipulate simply through their ability to tell a good story, and we end up unable to see past that to the truth of the issue. One that comes to mind is Hitler, who during his time in prison read the work of French Polymath Gustave LeBon. In 1895 LeBon published a book titled *The Crowd: A Study of the Popular Mind*, which Hitler referred to in his manifesto *Mein Kampf*. The understanding he gained from this work is widely believed to have influenced the way in which he went about convincing the population of Germany that his hateful ideas were in their best interests. Hitler mirrored the propaganda techniques laid out by LeBon and used them to draw others in via mirror thinking. Unfortunately, there a number of individuals in any given population who are able to consciously manipulate others. If, however, we are all educated about the potential for these influences it provides at least some protection against being unwittingly pulled in. While we thankfully do not have a modern-day equivalent to Hitler, unfortunately the ability to manipulate has been amplified by the power of videos and soundbites on social media. How can you counteract this in your own life by understanding these manipulations? What can you do differently given not every story you hear is the truth?

Leaders can, however, consciously use their influence to role-model in a positive way. A good leader using a story can evoke emotions and understanding in their followers in a way that makes their core message clearer and more

meaningful. This helps people to know what to believe in, what to truly value and what the path ahead looks like. When a story is told well, the information is more likely to be remembered clearly, accurately and for longer periods of time than fact-based information.[21]

The power of daydreams

When we listen to a story we imagine what we hear within our own mind. We can also use our imagination in immensely powerful ways without anything being said by in effect telling ourselves stories. Within the area of psychological research this is referred to as 'daydreaming'. It is also a well-used technique by athletes, referred to as 'visualisation'. Significantly self-storytelling, daydreaming and visualisation are another key facet of mirror thinking.

A lot of the people I advise are immensely driven and time-poor, so feel that they don't have the mental space for daydreaming; the leaders, surgeons or consultants are intent on delivering their next goal with no capacity to let their mind wander. But I encourage them all to try. Among those I work with, the most obvious group of people to use imagination are the fashion designers and creative directors whose goals depend upon inspired 'flights of fancy'. And yet daydreaming is not just for creatives, or for letting our minds wander with no specific outcomes. The most eminent researcher in the area of daydreaming is Jerome L. Singer, now professor emeritus of psychology at the Yale School of Medicine. Singer distinguished between unhelpful daydreaming, where for example we obsess over worries, therefore losing concentration, with what he terms 'positive constructive daydreaming'.[22] Singer explains that this positive form of daydreaming involves

playful, wishful imagery, playful creative thought, imagination and fantasy, which are all believed to be essential elements of a healthy mental life. Positive constructive daydreaming is also associated with future planning – being able to imagine what tomorrow will be like, next year and decades ahead. This type of daydreaming also allow us to problem solve and reflect – looking back on what's already happened and what that means.[23] It is this form of daydreaming that enables creatives to create and athletes to visualise, but it also forms the basis of many other successful life outcomes.

The majority of the time this form of inner role-modelling, mirroring events as they may be, is done unconsciously. Examples of this are not uncommon to any of us. You will have had situations, maybe while reading this book, when you're suddenly a couple of pages on and you don't actually know what you've just read; or when you're in the shower and completely lose track of time; or perhaps when you're driving and you don't actually recall the journey because you were thinking of other things. Sometimes you may have been worrying – did I lock the door, have I got my phone? And other times when you are simply not paying attention, you may find that you've worked through a problem or scenario. It's estimated that we daydream for up to 50 per cent of the time. That's a lot, so imagine how helpful it would be to take more control of that.

You will, perhaps without realising it, also use daydreaming and imagination intentionally. Examples include thinking through what you need to pack for a holiday, to take to work or buy for a dinner party; or distracting yourself from a bad day with the thought of your plans for the weekend; or fantasy indulgence in your favourite food. The ability to constructively daydream, to allow mind-wandering in a way that enables creative

possibilities, is not something we can all easily switch on. It's a skill that some may find easier than others and one that some people have developed more effectively. Nevertheless, it's also a skill worth developing, and one way to do that is through breaking down the different ways in which daydreaming actually works within the functioning of the mirror system.

A powerful illustration of what happens if we lose control of imagination and its associated brain mechanisms can be seen in schizophrenia. Nearly 70 per cent of people with schizophrenia have hallucinations,[24] which are internal experiences and the detection of sensations that other people don't experience. These are described by some scholars as 'degenerate kinds of imagination – degenerate because they are episodes of imagining over which [sufferers] lack direct voluntary control'.[25] While I don't like the derogatory language inferred in this, the point is that imagination plays a huge role in the mind of people suffering from this disease. Even more relevant is the fact that this has been linked specifically to faulty functioning in the mirror neuron system. When, for example, people are suffering from more severe auditory hallucinations, the activity in the mirror neurons increases.[26] It's believed to be so strongly linked to the mirror neuron that certain scholars have gone as far as to say that the various impacts of other symptoms even trigger 'a pathological metaplastic reorganisation' of the mirror neuron system.[27] And that is unfortunately as dramatic as it sounds: in plain English it means an extreme reorganisation of the tissue relating to the mirror neurons. Our brains are truly powerful in helping to manifest our realities and unfortunately – in the case of those suffering from various mental illnesses – our unreality. If we are lucky enough to have control then it's certainly something we should use.

Using daydreaming constructively – futurecasting

As I have already mentioned, one useful way in which we can use imagination is to see into the future, to project our thinking into a realm of possibility that hasn't yet happened. This is incredibly important for mental well-being and achievement, to enable us to hope and envisage positive outcomes. It is also vital for goal-setting, allowing us to decide on what we want to do, by when. One of the powerful elements of this inner 'futurecasting' is that it teaches us how to hold complex information in our mind in order to problem-solve and create alternate realities. The latter sounds fantastical, but it's what many of the most pioneering leaders, inventors and scientists of all time have done through using their imagination.[28] Leonardo da Vinci was able to imagine a future with a parachute, helicopter and even a tank 500 years before they existed. Einstein projected his thinking beyond Newtonian mechanics in order to propose the special theory of relativity. Emmeline Pankhurst believed in a world where women could play a full part in the political process. Rosa Parks imagined a life where African Americans could sit where they wanted on a bus and Martin Luther King envisioned one where 'my four little children will one day live in a nation where they will not be judged by the color of their skin but by the content of their character'.[29] In the world of business, Henry Ford had the vision to develop an automobile and Bill Gates dreamt of a personal computer in every home.

Imagination can be powerfully used to solve conceptual problems. Leaders are typically required to be strategic, and that means looking ahead and thinking through what's not yet happened or what's not even considered possible. There are a whole range of definitions for what 'strategic thinking' really means, but broadly speaking it's the ability to think ahead by a defined number of years to consider

what the goals are for an organisation. It's not that simple, though, as it also has to take into consideration potential changes in the marketplace, possible threats and opportunities, financial limitations, investment and many other factors. In other words, it requires juggling a lot of information at once, in your head, and that's done via imagination. We can imagine different possibilities, working through how they may play out and then deciding on a plan of action. Of course, it's also put on paper and discussed with others and then socialised, but the imagination phase even when underpinned by financial goals is critical. We all use imagination in this way to make plans, set goals and consider different possibilities. It's also something that we can all enhance. Imagine we were all like the pioneers mentioned above. That may not be realistic, but we can at least put our ability to think forward to its most effective use. Those little mirror neurons are immensely helpful.

Using daydreaming constructively – creativity

An element of our imagination that often seems mysterious, impossible to define and even out of reach for those who believe they don't have it, is in reality available to us all: creativity. It adds depth and colour to our lives through art, music, literature and fashion. In business innovation this is essential to stay a step ahead of the competition, the current buzzwords talk of failing fast, providing employees with the space to experiment and make mistakes. This gives a clue to how creativity works.

Psychologists looking at the link between creativity and the brain recently defined creative cognition as 'a set of mental processes that support the generation of novel and useful ideas ... Self-generated thoughts [which] arise from

internally focused mental activity.'[30] Creativity involves multiple brain networks and cannot be isolated to the mirror neuron or any other specific elements of the brain. However, the basic elements of creativity are believed to depend in part on observational learning, which is directly related to the mirror neuron, together with memory, cognitive flexibility and novelty seeking.[31] In addition, the 'internally focused mental activity' is also hypothesised to depend on mirror neurons.

One person who brought pleasure, escapism and enjoyment to millions through what would widely be heralded as both novel and useful ideas was born on 7 June 1958 in Minneapolis. Prince Rogers Nelson, known to his friends as Skipper, was born to jazz singer and pianist mother Mattie Della and songwriter and pianist father John Lewis Nelson, who was quiet and softly spoken.[32] Growing up around music must have flooded this young boy's mirror neurons with examples to observe, hear and repeat. He first saw his father play at age five. He said: 'It was great, I couldn't believe it. People were screaming. From then on I think I wanted to be a musician.'[33] By the time he was seven he was teaching himself the piano and writing music. He went on to learn how to play an astounding twenty-seven instruments.[34]

Using his first name, he released his debut album in 1978 and went on to have one of the most influential and prolific music careers of all time. His determined obsession to teach himself music he was exposed to as a child shone through in an artist who took his music, dress and dance to a level beyond what was expected. He explored and wasn't afraid to try and keep trying with a no–holds–barred approach. He once said to one of his performers 'dance like it's a higher calling,'[35] showing how he pushed the limits on this like so many other aspects of his life. He broke the rules of

gender, wearing high heels and stockings, yet also displaying masculinity at the same time. This openness to experience is one area that is frequently cited as necessary for creative capability.[36] He was confident enough to resist conforming throughout his life, enabling his creativity to flourish. He wrote all his own music – writing something completely different, a new song every day – and he often played every instrument on his albums. He refused to let Warner, his first record label, take creative control and would only sign if he could do his own music production. He was focused and always curious, always learning.

Prince was a leader in the music industry and beyond. He embodied creativity and a boundary-free approach, enabled by a mind operating on imagination, courtesy of the mirror neuron. But mirror thinking has more to do with it than just that. It begins with the influences on Prince while he was growing up. He was surrounded by music, and even though he created his own distinctive sound, that initial learning came from mirroring, in a similar way to how all children imitate their parents and unconsciously absorb from the environment around them.

Interestingly, the initial findings surrounding the mirror neuron related to movement. This also applies to all of the elements of music, from drumming and singing to wind chimes and woodblocks – all instruments played by Prince. The 'well-coordinated motor actions that produce the physical vibrations of the sound'[37] engage the mirror neuron in order for the watcher to see how the sound is created and how to replicate it. A 2006 study led by neuroscientist Istvan Molnar-Szakacs at the McGill University Health Centre suggests that this use of the mirror neuron goes beyond the person learning and playing music to actually synchronising the brains of the listener and the musician. Invoking a comparable mechanism to when our brains synchronise during storytelling: 'This

shared musical representation has a similar potential for communication as shared language or action.'[38] Molnar-Szakacs explains how the association between music, movement and synchronisation is evident not only when producing sound and listening to music, but also when dancing. Both music and dancing are related to the frontoparietal mirror neuron system – the more advanced part of the brain. As such, musical genius is something not based on IQ alone, but comes down to a highly advanced mirror neuron system. This sense of synchronisation between artist and listener or fan also touches on another key part of the mirror neuron system, one which is exemplified by the outpouring of emotions that often surrounds this relationship, particularly when much-loved musicians pass away, such as we saw in recent years with Bowie, George Michael and Prince himself.

I was lucky enough to see Prince at the Hammersmith Apollo in 2002. I'd grown up with his music and always loved it and bought it, but wouldn't have described myself as an avid fan. I then met my husband who knew everything there was to know about Prince and was passionate about his capabilities. I could understand, but still didn't get overly excited. But that concert moved me. His emotional connection with the audience to me was immense and unique. When I heard he had died I was shocked by how upset I was. Even the President of the US at that time, Barack Obama commented: 'Today, the world lost a creative icon. Few artists have influenced the sound and trajectory of popular music more distinctly, or touched quite so many people with their talent. As one of the most gifted and prolific musicians of our time, Prince did it all.'

Why did he touch so many so deeply? There are multiple reasons: admiration for his creativity, his individuality, his courage and curiosity. But one thing that I believe connected people so strongly with Prince was what he gave

of himself in his music. Molnar-Szakacs argues that the expression of music conveys a message about the emotional state of the musician. Each element plays its part – the words express semantic meaning, while the melody, dance and different tones in the many different instruments convey more meaning still. The complex and subtle qualities of our emotions, or in this case Prince's emotions, are conveyed allowing 'empathy that requires no intermediary cognitive process, but rather, is our automatic and immediate "motor identification" or inner imitation of the actions of others'.[39] Such responses allow us to feel connected to musicians and to each other in a similar way as people do when they hear the same story using creativity. As such, musicians are good examples of role models whose creativity connects to our emotions via mirror thinking. They can also teach us how to use our imagination for creativity. In Prince's case, he let his imagination know no bounds. However, many of us associate creativity as being far from our own reach, but we can all harness the way in which the mirror neuron works to tap into it.

This is where the development of 'metacognitive' skills – a more deliberate and conscious control over being able to switch in and out of daydreaming – is helpful and through practice gradually enhances our capability to make use of it. I've seen this in the creatives I've worked with: although they may not have set out to have this level of meta-cognitive control, they do and they make use of it all of the time. In a similar way we can learn to use cognitive empathy to modify how we experience emotional empathy. The impact of this level of control was shown in a 2019 study looking at 228 students from eight Chilean high schools in Santiago, and which measured creativity using something called Guilford's Alternative Uses Test. The results showed that the students who were better able to control their attention while also making conscious use of

daydreaming were more creative. The lead author on this study, associate professor of psychology David Preiss, suggested that 'creativity may depend upon a particular combination of controlled and spontaneous thought processes'.[40] Although some students in this study had this skill and some did not, it is a skill that can be enhanced with practice. This would involve developing the metacognitive skills associated with being able to fluidly switch from conscious to unconscious, through deliberate practice or methods such as mindfulness meditation.

Using daydreaming constructively – reflection

Another component of imagination commonly used by leaders in all sorts of fields is reflection. This may not feel like a natural fit under the heading of daydreaming, yet Singer considers it a critical component. More significantly, it's a mental activity that while not yet tested we can assume entails mirror thinking – in effect reliving via the mental reconstruction of past events. As with schizophrenia, such reconstruction can be negative, when we no longer have control over it and are locked into the events. This also often happens with those suffering from PTSD, but for most of us it can be a powerful tool.

Reflection may well happen subconsciously: for example, when you find yourself dreamily reliving the holiday you just had while you're sat back at your desk, or when you're trying to work out what something someone said to you early on that day meant. This is helpful as it provides meaning to past events and experiences. For example, if you were blindsided by a colleague shouting at you during the day, this 'mental reconstruction' might help you to remember that they had mentioned being particularly tired and stressed earlier on in the day – and so your brain places their uncharacteristic response in context and allows you to

make sense of it. This type of daydreaming is also critical for a wide range of social and emotional skills, including compassion, moral reasoning, understanding our own and others' behaviours and emotional responses, and considering other people's perspectives.[41] You will be using these skills, although you may not even be aware of it – they are essential in any social interaction. They are especially significant for leaders to enable them to influence, engage and negotiate, and when used consciously they can become an even more powerful tool.

When I profile people, I am in effect asking them to relive their past in order for me to predict their future berhaviour. We all reflect on our past – what happened yesterday, last week, last year – but when we're busy that can get lost under a to-do list, tiredness and a need to focus on just getting to the end of the week. Going through a biography requires conscious reflection in a way that many of the people I see have not experienced for some time, but that reflection inevitably provides insights and revelations. I consider myself to simply be a facilitator. Often those insights come from our own re-evaluation and we just need to be given the time and space to do that constructively.

Once I was doing some work for a global oil company, helping them to restructure a section of their business that employed several thousand people. One person I saw in Houston, Texas, was clearly not a good fit for his role, which he'd been doing for 15 years. I had to write a report on who he was and how he matched with the shape of the organisation moving forward. The problem was, whichever way I looked at it, he just didn't match. I absolutely hate doing something like this. I doubt anyone enjoys it, but I agonise over it to the point that I start losing sleep. When it came to flying back to the US to deliver his report, I was dreading it. I sat down opposite him, handed him the document and waited for him to read it. He started crying.

This big burly man was sobbing in front of me. My heart was in my mouth. I took a deep breath and asked him if he was OK and what he was thinking. And he simply replied: 'I'm so so relieved.' I was taken aback, but he quickly went on to say: 'I've been in the wrong job for so many years and just going through the motions without even realising it and finally I feel like I'm free to look for something I could really enjoy.' Most of us feel like this through at least some part of our life – going through the motions as time passes us by. Not everyone has the financial or pragmatic freedom to enable them to follow their dreams, yet being stuck in a job or a life that we're not suited to is not actually what we evolved to do. While the days of our ancient ancestors were spent hunting, gathering and remaining safe, the nights were spent around the fire, not just telling stories but spending time reflecting on the day, staring into the fire and thinking, learning what mistakes had been made and what they could do differently next time.

It's easy to think of reflection as simply reminiscing over what has already happened in life, whether that's yesterday or years ago. Something that may be 'nice' to do, but that doesn't really have any consequences. However, around the turn of the last century American philosopher John Dewey described it as more of a purposeful activity, a 'dynamic and intentional process that profoundly influences one's experiences'. He said: 'We do not learn from experience. We learn from reflecting on experience.'[42] This point of view has now been backed by decades of research showing that there's far more to reflection than mere unconscious daydreaming and that when done with intention, it significantly improves learning and performance.[43] In fact, reflection has been shown to be as important – if not more important – to learning than action or experience once we already have some knowledge in an area. One research study described the phenomena using the example of a surgeon:

Consider for an instance a cardiac surgeon in training. She has completed ten operations under the eye of an instructor. It is in everyone's interest for the cardiac surgeon to get better as fast as possible. Imagine she was given a choice in planning her agenda for the next two weeks. She could spend that time doing ten additional surgeries, or she could take the same amount of time alternating between a few additional surgeries and time spent reflecting on them to better understand what she did right or wrong.[44]

While time spent reflecting takes her away from actually 'doing' surgery and helping the unit she works in, research shows that it is more effective to reflect than working the additional hours in the operating theatre. Time spent in deliberate reflection will make her a better surgeon, ultimately having a positive impact on her patients. It's an example of slowing down to speed up and using mirror thinking to do so.

Scientists have shown that this works with the way our brain naturally functions. If we engage in deliberate reflection, the brain has an enhanced ability to develop our cognitive (*i.e.* thinking and problem-solving) abilities.[45] We begin to understand the task better and we also improve our confidence in being able to carry out the task. If you look at some of the world's greatest leaders, reflection was part of their daily or at least weekly routine. Take, for example, Benjamin Franklin who would conclude every day with reflection, or Nelson Mandela, Albert Einstein, Maya Angelou or Tchaikovsky, to name but a few. And reflection requires imagination to relive events, to replay them, contemplate and consolidate the emotions and meaning, the highs and lows, the lessons learnt.

Making the time to reflect – to consciously daydream – regardless of where we are in life therefore has a very powerful effect. But beyond using this as a learning tool, this form of mirror thinking also has a positive effect on our mental health

and well-being by helping us to process worries and concerns in a constructive way. It allows us to become more self-aware, so that we're able to notice what's draining us or causing us problems, and recognise how to keep things in perspective: to appreciate what we have and to remember happy moments or kind things that have been said or done. It also provides us with a greater level of clarity over who we are and what we're about, allowing us to work out where we thrive, what we're good at and what we love most – meaning we can plan to spend more time focused on those aspects of our life. Without pausing to reflect we can, like the man in the oil company, unintentionally let life pass us by.

Despite these clear benefits, reflection is not something that society proactively encourages. In fact, some experts worry that the high attentional demands that we're placing on people via technology and social media are depriving us of the opportunity to daydream and to reflect. This is especially concerning when it comes to children. The fast pace of technology risks depriving kids not only of learning opportunities relating to academic education, adding additional strain to an already crammed curriculum, but also threatens to rob them of very basic social and emotional learning, as we explored earlier.[46] It limits face-to-face interaction and creates an obstacle to reflection that typically allows us to create personal meaning from experiences and relationships.[47] One Canadian study, which looked at 2,300 college students aged 18–22, found that over a five-year period increases in texting were related to decreases in reflectivity. They also found that higher levels of texting were significantly related to lower levels of moral reflectiveness, such as a motivation to promote social equality or justice in the community, and a much lower belief in the importance of living with integrity.[48] This makes sense as texting and social media engage the reacting

brain, not the observing brain, which is more meaning driven. Considering that the level of social and emotional education we give children in schools is already below where it should be, this is something that surely we should proactively address. Guided reflection alongside overt role-modelling provides another pathway for improving social-emotional skills across life. For example, nursing students are often encouraged to engage in journaling, writing down thoughts and feelings, capturing what they are going through following a traumatic event to help create understanding, insight and self-awareness. Simply the act of sitting and writing things down has been found to help make sense of traumatic experiences and improve well-being. This is something that we can all do with very little guidance and could very easily be encouraged within the school environment with little training or cost.

We can also take advantage of the natural mechanisms of storytelling to communicate with those around us more powerfully, to role-model effectively and pass on messages at a level that resonates like no other. Added to this we are all capable of using our own storytelling more effectively via the mirror neuron's powerful facilitation of daydreaming and imagination. Being able to envisage a different future and seeing how to get there, being able to solve problems by holding multiple elements of the world in our mind at once and being able to bring creativity to the world are vital if we are to build a better future. Similarly, giving ourselves the opportunity to reflect on who we are, what we are and why will enable us to understand and learn, and then inspire others to do so too.

The Art of Observing

On 1 October 1975 at 10 a.m. one of the most-watched events in history was about to take place. Viewers in 68 countries around the world waited excitedly. There was a murmur of anticipation hanging in the packed auditorium of the Araneta Coliseum in the Philippines. The capacity was officially 60,000, but many more crammed into spaces in the aisles. Sports reporter Ken Jones was there and said, 'It seemed pointless to announce an attendance figure, since by the time the contestants reached their corners people filled every inch of floor space. There was no aisle space, just a wall-to-wall sweep of sweating bodies. More daring spectators had even crawled out on to rafters.'[1]

No air-conditioning, packed bodies and spotlights added to the already sweltering heat of the Philippines, the sun beating down on the aluminium roof. It was estimated that temperatures reached more than 49°C (120°F).[2]

The fight, which had been dubbed the 'Thrilla in Manilla' by contender Muhammad Ali, was about to begin. The hype leading up to the final in a trilogy of matches between Joe Frazier and Ali had been immense, raising the stakes and expectations of people worldwide for weeks beforehand. The murmur became louder as commentator Don Dunphy, anchorman for HBO, said, 'I understand that Joe Frazier is on his way from the dressing room towards the ring.' White lines flickered across the screen as a spotlight and camera tracked Frazier's walk out. But it was difficult to see, as he was hidden from view by the

crowd. The noise from the audience grew ever more excited as Frazier approached and ducked through the ropes into the ring, coming into full view.

In the weeks before the fight, Ali had courted the media and taunted Frazier relentlessly. In one interview he made fun of his opponent with provocative childlike taunts over and over: 'It will be a killer, and a chiller, and a thriller, when I get the gorilla in Manilla.' He laughed and punched a toy gorilla; the media laughed too. He put the toy gorilla in his pocket and patted it, indicating to Frazier that's where he belonged. Frazier already felt betrayed by Ali, who he'd supported through his refusal to join the US Army for the Vietnam draft. This took things too far for him and it wasn't until just before his death 36 years later that he forgave Ali for the insults. Still, all of this drama just added to the suspense of the upcoming fight.

'A roar goes up as Ali comes into view,' said Dunphy. Camera flashes lit up the path of Ali. Clapping, cheering, whistling, chanting. 'Muhammad Ali approaching the ring rather deliberately. This is how you go in, it's how you go out that's the important thing. Muhammad Ali for this epic moment.'[3] Ali's face suddenly came into full view almost filling the screen, lit by the bright spotlight. His silver dressing gown, with turquoise collar contrasting against his skin. The man who was most typically shown joking around, having fun, stared hauntingly, deadly serious into the distance. As he climbed into the ring the already riotous crowd grew even louder, a deafening roar filling the stadium.

The two men came face to face in the centre of the ring, eyes locked. These giants towered over the tiny referee in his 1970s-style turquoise shirt and navy bow tie. Before they even began Ali kept up the taunts: 'You don't have it Joe, you don't have it. I'm going to put you away.'

Ali came out fast, faster than Frazier was expecting. This meant that he was in control in the early rounds, but Frazier didn't give up or give in. He continued to battle, cornering Ali, backing him up against the ropes. In an article for the *Independent* Ken Jones wrote:

> *By the fourth round Ali's punches had lost zip. He was tiring. The heat, the bright lights, the muggy, oxygen-deprived atmosphere and Frazier's toughness were wearing him down. The exchanges proceeded with such brutal intensity that questions hung in the air. How much more could Frazier take? How much more did Ali have left? By round six Frazier was still there in front of him and, worse, now coming at him, unleashing damaging hooks to the body.*[4]

Why was this so engaging to watch? Think about what this would do in the brain of an observer. Imagine the activity of mirror neurons. What do you feel when you see someone being hit? Excitement, adrenaline, do you wince, do you duck? A sporting event is a story unfurling live in front of your eyes. Ken Jones said:

> *Both men continued to batter each other with such relentless savagery that you began to fear for their lives, marvel at their courage, the extent of their will to win. In round 12 Ali regained the initiative, staggering Frazier again. In round 13, a jolting left hand sent Frazier's gumshield spinning into the crowd. He was spitting blood ... He could no longer block or evade Ali's blows.*[5]

By the fourteenth round both Ali and Frazier were stumbling, struggling to stay upright. Ali had hit Frazier so hard at one point that his right eye was now swollen almost completely shut. Frazier was virtually blind in his left eye as the result of an accident a decade earlier. They refused to stop trying. It was painful to watch.

Eddie Futch, Frazier's trainer, stopped the fight before the fifteenth round. He genuinely feared for Frazier's life. But Frazier responded by shouting, 'Don't you dare stop this motherfucking fight!' When Futch asked Frazier how many fingers he was holding up, he couldn't tell him. Ali later said: 'It was like death. Closest thing to dyin' that I know of.' When the towel was thrown in, Ali dropped to his knees, nothing left.

This has been hailed as the greatest heavyweight fight that has ever taken place. Back in 1975 when not every house had a television, and no one had the electronic devices to stream it live, it was watched by 1 billion viewers.[6] The vast majority of those people would never have boxed in their life. Today, it's estimated that global audiences of football matches total 4 billion people, cricket 2.5 billion and tennis 1 billion. Yet we don't have 4 billion footballers, 2.5 billion cricketers and 1 billion tennis players worldwide.[7] Why is it that so many people find sport so engaging even if they don't take part themselves?

Watching sport is exciting, engaging, visceral. A huge proportion of any population connects with sport in a way that feels quite natural. If you are a football fan, for example, you may travel miles every month in order to watch matches played by the team you support, you probably spend a great deal of time socialising with people who support the same team, you buy merchandise, read about the players in the media, follow the profession more broadly and encourage your kids to do the same. It's so natural that it becomes an integral part of your identity. Watching sport is also key to learning and performance, improving our own capability. Sport brings together observing, learning and doing. The natural and emotive connection that is enabled via sport is a vehicle to improved health, a means

from which to learn how to do things that are mentally and physically valuable.

Sport takes us back to the very basic principles of the mirror neuron – the first findings of neuroscientists Giacomo Rizzolatti and his team in Italy. When the researchers saw what are now known as the mirror neurons firing in response to an observation of one of the team picking up his lunch and putting it up to his own mouth, they were uncovering what happens when we observe sport, and how we engage with and learn to execute an action for ourselves.

The eminent neuroscientist Marco Iacoboni explains how seeing a sport being played, such as a baseball game, replicates many aspects of how our brain responds when we actually play it:

> *Some of the same neurons that fire when we watch a player catch a ball also fire when we catch a ball ourselves. It is as if by watching, we are also playing the game. We understand the player's actions because we have a template in our brains for that action, a template based on our own movements.*[8]

Even if we haven't learnt or participated in an activity, we can still relate to it and get fired up by watching something like the Thrilla in Manilla. At some point in our life most of us have probably reached out to hit someone or something, even if only as a toddler claiming back a toy; it's an action and movement that is familiar to our brain. We've all darted around, whether play fighting, dancing or even hopping on the spot when we're desperate for the loo! Many of the movements boxers make share what Iacoboni calls 'similar movement properties', activating similar muscles to those involved in actions we've all made. We know what it's like to stare someone in the eyes when we're angry and have them stare right back at us. We've all

experienced and felt the excitement of being in a crowd, whether at a concert, football match or party. We know what it's like to push ourselves to our limit, to feel we have nothing left to give. We are living the storytelling of the sport, the competition and the anticipation, so we become totally and utterly engaged. Not knowing the outcome and watching it unfurl in front of us only adds to the excitement and reality as our mirror neurons are firing.

Sometimes it's not just about what we actually see, but what senses are at play that engage the mirror neuron at a heightened level and feed into a deeper type of observational learning. Many would-be spectators were unable to actually watch the Thrilla in Manila as it wasn't available for normal TV viewing in the US. Spectators had to hold off seeing the fight, pay to go and watch it live in one of many cinemas across the States or listen to it on the radio. Tom Boswell, a *Washington Post* sports columnist, was one of the many people who, rather than going to watch the fight, heard it translated by a commentator, retelling the story as it unfolded. Tom recalls:

> *Neither before, nor since, have I been as tense during a sports event as I always was when Frazier fought Ali … And, depending on whom you rooted for – and everybody cared deeply, because Frazier and Ali were symbols of the time on several levels – your heart jumped and you thought, 'How badly is he hurt?' It was awful not to know. And it was better, too. The mystery added another layer of tension.*[9]

Why was listening even better? The mirror neurons were fully in play; the listener wasn't only hearing what was happening – the crowd roaring, the announcer explaining – but also had to imagine and replay the fight in their own mind, which for some will have heightened the sense of 'being in the crowd's shoes'. The auditory mirror neurons

specifically trigger when we hear sounds relating to actions performed by other people rather than non-action sounds and are believed to be related to empathy, allowing us to imagine what that person is feeling.[10] When listening to what is in effect a story, not only are the language processing areas of the brain relating to different parts of what is being said engaged, but the sensory areas are, too. Recall the research by Véronique Boulenger, which found that parts of the brain – such as the motor cortex and the sensory cortex – are triggered when people hear words associated with movement and texture respectively. The radio commentary will have engaged all of these senses with the detailed description of what was going on, potentially offering more areas of brain stimulation than watching without such a detailed description.

The mirror neuron also plays a critical role in the anticipation process.[11] We know that people actually derive happiness from anticipation – expectation is in itself entertaining.[12] Many areas of the brain are engaged in this type of situation – we're not just watching and predicting, but we're also connecting the dots on the overall narrative. Knowing the participants' backgrounds and stories creates a sense of personal connection between viewer/listener and player. The spectators feel like they are rooting for a friend, a character, an individual – perhaps even someone who they want to be.

The super mirror neuron

But how do we move from this role of being the observer of sports to actually learning sport ourselves, either at school, in a club or at a professional level? And once we've learnt the basics how do we improve? Again, it is mirror thinking that enable us to learn how to execute different actions relating

to sports – our brain mirroring what we see is the crucial underpinning to developing our capabilities. This raises a very important question about the mirror neuron and how it works – one you may already have asked yourself as you've been reading! How can we watch, as we do in order to learn, without actually doing it ourselves? How can our brain be active and send messages to our muscles, yet we don't throw a serve when we're watching tennis or thump the person sitting next to us when we're watching a boxing match? There must be some sort of mechanism in the brain that controls all of this. So what is it?

The answer, or at least a proposed mechanism, can be found by returning to the work of Iacoboni. After much head-scratching and a lot of detailed research and investigation Iacoboni came to the same conclusion – that there must be something controlling our more basic mirror neuron function. At least controlling in the sense of supressing the activity while we observe, preventing us from throwing a ball when we watch someone else do it, for example. This is an aspect of brain activity that not only subdues neuronal firing, but then essentially 'stands back' in order to organise all of the actions that, for example, make up a tennis serve, into one coherent piece. This enables the brain to make sense of what's going on, ordering it and modulating it.[13]

In 2010, Iacoboni attributed responsibility for this mastery of mirroring to what he called the super mirror neuron – cells in the frontal lobe that inhabit the more advanced, slower, observing areas of the brain. These neurons have a 'super' ability – they are, if you like, the leaders or facilitators of the other mirror neurons. However convincing this hypothesis was, Iacoboni had no way to prove it. To do so would mean recording single neuron activity, which as we've discussed before just isn't possible

in humans. While Iacoboni was mulling over this conundrum he bumped into an old colleague, world-renowned neurosurgeon Dr Itzhak Fried, who was about to perform complex neurosurgery, which serendipitously could provide an opportunity to test the hypothesis. Fried gained consent from his group of patients to carry out research while their brains were uniquely accessible. The areas he would be operating on and therefore accessing for research were those very same areas where Iacoboni believed the super mirror neurons to be.

The purpose of the surgery was to try to ease the symptoms of severe epilepsy in 21 patients. The research involved Fried inserting microelectrodes into the frontal lobes of the patients' brains, making it possible to record extra-cellular activity from an astounding 1,177 cells. In collaboration with Iacoboni, this was used as a remarkable opportunity to see which areas of the brain were active when people were observing, but not carrying out an action. During this study the patients were asked to simply watch someone's hand grasping an object (to provide a control and comparison) and then also to grasp that object with their own hand. The results revealed what Iacoboni had proposed was in fact correct: that a smaller subset of mirror neurons, which he dubbed the super mirror neurons, inhibited the action during observation of movement.

Iacoboni believed this evidence showed that the super mirror neurons organise the simple imitative actions into more complex combinations of actions, behaviour and emotions. This therefore provides the mechanism by which we are able to watch someone throwing the ball without throwing it ourselves and also to arrange the different aspects of throwing it into a more complex pattern. So, in order to learn how to execute a move in sport we need the mirror neuron system. For example, if we were watching a

tennis coach who is demonstrating the serve in tennis it would follow something along the lines of this:

1. Set your feet in the correct serve stance (notice this first assumes that you've seen and know how to do this step).
2. With your weight slightly forward on your front foot bounce the ball a few times in front of you and release any tension from your hands, arm and body.
3. Hold a tennis ball lightly in your fingertips and move your hands into the ready position (again there is an assumption you already know what the ready position looks like) with the ball lightly touching your tennis racquet in front of you.
4. Begin transferring your weight slowly towards your back foot.
5. As your weight reaches your back foot start to move into your trophy pose (another example of needing to see it first to know what they are referring to).
6. Drop your hands down together and then lift your throwing arm towards the sky using your shoulder. Lead with your elbow and keep your arm straight. Once your arm reaches the top of your head open your hand wide to release the ball.
7. As your throwing arm moves upwards, allow your dominant arm, which is holding your racquet, to swing back like a pendulum behind you and then continue up behind your head.
8. Bend your knees so that you've achieved a full bend by the time your arms complete their motion.[14]

It would be very difficult to understand, let alone perfect, a tennis serve by simply following these written instructions.

We need to see it role-modelled in order to learn how to do it and thus engage the mirror neurons. Not only that, the instructions alone miss many more aspects – how to hold your wrist and elbow, where there should be tension in your arm, which part of the arm to lead the throw with, how exactly to hold the ball with your fingers and where in your hand, how tightly you should hold the ball, when to release the ball, how high you should throw the ball and how to carry out different types of serve. We need both the instruction and observation to get it just right. Indeed, in 2002 Dr Eleni Zetou, associate professor in the Department of Physical Education and Sports Sciences at Democritus University in Greece, found that the 'most ideal' way of improving skills in volleyball players was through a combination of observing 'model' behaviour with a verbal description.[15] And this all needs to be organised so that we do it in the right order, with the right levels of intensity and nuances even when we're at the novice stage. How? By piecing together thousands of bits of information and ordering it courtesy of the super mirror neuron. They, or an equivalent mechanism, organise all of this complex information gleaned by the mirror neurons into something we can make sense of.

Super mirror neurons are not just responsible for sports and motor activity, but are also hypothesised to help organise the complexity of our social world – the interactions between you and someone else and between you and a group of people. In a community or workplace this allows us to remember who said what to whom, who is well-meaning, who is unkind, who to speak to in confidence and who is the key influencer. The super-mirroring function enables us to keep track of the context of what we're observing, hearing and feeling.[16] This is of course also relevant in sport where there is a need to

understand and anticipate the behaviour of an opponent or a team member, to manage and understand the dynamics of a team we are playing against and to keep track of our own thoughts and emotions.

Once we've learnt the basics of any sport and become more practised there's always more to understand, fine-tune, refine and perfect. We need to watch so that we can improve our capability. In order to get the split-second advantages, we have to employ that sensorimotor fine tuning to anticipate to the millisecond. A large part of what we're doing with this is developing our mirror neuron system so that we're not only able to work out how to improve our own performance, but to improve our ability to forsee our opponent's next move. Or when it comes to my sport of choice, snowboarding, we need the ability to anticipate, predict and decide how to respond to the slopes, rocks, different terrains and changing snow conditions.

I have skied since I was a child, but I didn't start to snowboard until I travelled in my 20s. Surfing my way around Australia I met some fellow surfers who I went across to New Zealand with for the winter season. My friends thought that rather than ski I should snowboard – a sport that has much in common with surfing (and of course they were snowboarders themselves!) So off we went to hire the gear. They then left me on my own halfway down a slope to teach myself while they went on up the mountain. I became a pretty competent snowboarder that season, from watching, trying, falling and getting up over and over and over again.

A close friend who I met during my time in New Zealand has been running a snowboarding school in the French Alps for many years. She has guys coming out from the UK frequently who try to show off to her how good they are. She is also a phenomenal snowboarder and while

she doesn't compete, she boards with some of the best in the world. Her little joke with the more cocky 'punters', as she calls them, is to let them show off for a bit and then fly past them effortlessly. However hard they struggle to catch up they can't and they usually snowball down the slope. The funny thing with snowboarding is that a lot of people think they can do it and to some extent they can – they get down the mountain, but they don't know how to do it optimally. In fact, people often think that because it's such a laidback kind of sport there isn't a 'proper' way of doing it. I regrettably fell into this mode of thought for some time. Then I trained to be an instructor and I saw everything that I was doing wrong.

One of the key turning points in my snowboarding career was actually watching myself on video during that coaching. I was able to see for myself where I was placing my weight on the board and when I was disengaging to go into a turn. This was a mirror of my own boarding, an opportunity to see my own reflection, which I was then able to dissect, once I'd been given the knowledge of what good snowboarding really should look like. This is not possible without the super mirror neurons, which prevent action while we watch and make sense of what we see. For sports professionals, video analysis has become common-place; playing back parts of a football match, a tennis game or a sprint start both at normal speed and in slow motion allows a detailed visual breakdown of technique. When athletes are shown where they can improve, they are able to learn and apply that far more effectively. Learning sport properly, as opposed to teaching ourselves to do a sport in a fun way, gives a clear example of being conscious and of knowingly giving it our attention. Consciously watching, consciously practising, consciously doing something and consciously counter-mirroring are all part of the process

of perfecting technique. I'd spent many years watching snowboarders from the lift as a skier, but that was just for entertainment. I'd seen my friends snowboard, but it took that conscious and deliberate breakdown of each step to turn it from something that I wasn't just doing, to something that gave me a far better grasp of the sport. I'd learnt without instruction in the way observational learning happens incidentally all the time across the many different settings in life. But when I had instruction the conscious observation became far more focused and intense, deliberate and worthwhile. For elite athletes this becomes part and parcel of training: constantly fine-tuning the nuances of their performance. So many of the things we encounter in life, especially the social and emotional, require us to carry out the same sort of detailed analysis. However, most of the time we are unaware, it's unconscious. For example, reading someone's facial expression requires a detailed analysis in our brain. Each interaction shapes our neural networks. If we neglect to keep using them we miss out on fully developing our mirror neuron system. Our social and emotional skills will wither in the same way as an athlete who stops paying attention to the details. If, however, we at least some of the time remain conscious of these skills it affords us a much better opportunity to keep refining them.

Visualising success

Sporting professionals also use the mirror neuron in one other significant way to improve their performance – visualisation. Albert Bandura, professor emeritus of social sciences and psychology at Stanford University, was the originator of much of the research on observational learning. He proposed that people who take what they

hear in words or through instructions and explanations, and then transform this into visual images, achieve higher levels of performance than those who don't.[17] This has been backed up by research into the mirror neuron. When we're learning our mirror neurons divide the observed action into individual pieces, which are then reassembled into a sequence that allows the overall series of actions to be reproduced,[18] mapping the activity to specific areas of the brain. Those mirror neurons then activate the same neural substrates, or behavioural pathways, in the brain, whether that action is actually performed, observed in someone else or imagined.[19] Tapping into this ability to imagine or visualise has been shown to actually improve performance of the action in 'real life',[20] which is one of the key factors that gives elite athletes the edge in their technique. They can practise their technique, but with a controlled, positive outcome, even when they're resting or injured. And this has a measurable impact on performance.

Before qualifying, Formula 1 drivers often sit, eyes closed, visualising the lap they are about to do, thinking about every braking point, every apex they must hit making decisions at a thousandths of a second. Over a lap several miles long this can make the difference between several positions on the grid. Prior to the London 2012 Olympics, in which Jessica Ennis-Hill won Gold in the heptathlon, she used visualisation 'to think about the perfect technique. If I can get that perfect image in my head, then hopefully it'll affect my physical performance.' In preparation for Wimbledon, British tennis champion Andy Murray has been known to go to an empty court in order to prepare. He said, 'I have sat on Centre Court with no one there and thought a bit about the court, the matches I have played there,' projecting that forward he

gets himself into the right mindset. He added: 'I want to make sure I feel as good as possible so I have a good tournament.'[21]

In an interview with the *Independent* newspaper, sports psychologist Dr Steve Bull said, 'The most important thing with imagery is using multiple senses, like sound, sight and smell.' Referring to footballer Wayne Rooney, also known to heavily rely on imagery, he said:

> *What makes (a player like) Rooney unique is his imagination. When he visualises scoring a goal, he can feel his foot hitting the ball, the smell of the grass under his foot and the sound of the crowd. This incredibly vivid imagery helps an athlete to prepare mentally, by improving their confidence, focus, clarity and speed of thought. It helps them prepare for any scenario: how will I react to the crowd? What if we go 1-0 down? What shot will I take in a certain situation? But it also fires impulses to the muscles, therefore priming them for action. The more vivid the mental image, the more effectively your brain primes your muscles to complete the same physical and technical action in a real game.*[22]

Using mirror neurons in this way, accessing the senses – auditory, olfactory, visual and touch – during visualisation enhances performance even more. Stimulating and practising with those same sights, sounds and smells while carrying out the perfect kick, pole vault or backhand can only reinforce those patterns in the brain.

Supporting the working hypothesis put forward by Iacoboni, visualisation, by nature of pursuing an action over and over again without actually enacting it physically, must also be dependent on the super mirror neuron. They are controlling and modulating the activity of certain areas of the brain, for example, those different senses and muscle activation, in order to let the visualisation play out.

When the brain goes wrong

Across every aspect of life, while there are those myriad ways in which we observe and imitate without being conscious – the crossed legs in a conversation, the influence of peers on what we say and how we dress – there are an equal number of, if not more, situations in which we observe but do not react. We also process the detailed complexity at a level we are not even aware; we respond in a socially, context-specific manner.

It's not yet possible to directly measure these brain mechanisms. One way in which academics try to get to the bottom of how these complex aspects of our brain work, when there is a lack of clarity over the exact mechanism, is to combine data such as that found by Iacoboni, with research into where brain functionality has gone wrong. When someone has a brain injury or some form of psychological dysfunction, their atypical behaviours and way in which they view the world provides neuroscientists with valuable information. What they don't understand or can't do, mapped to which bits of their brain don't work, tells us about the functionality of how that part of the brain typically works in healthy individuals.

The most historic and oft-cited example of this from long before we knew much about the brain is the case of Phineas Gage, a railroad worker in nineteenth-century America. Gage was a foreman for a team of workers whose job it was to use explosives to clear rock in order for a new railway to be laid. On 13 September 1848, they were preparing to blast rock, which involved creating a bore hole and packing explosives deep inside with an iron rod. Typically, this was then filled with an inert substance, such as clay or sand, so that the force would be directed towards the rock, not outwards. But Gage's iron rod somehow sparked on the rock and the powder exploded, sending the

metre-long rod through his left cheek bone, behind his eye and out through the left side of his frontal skull bone. The force of the blast was so immense that the iron landed 10m away. Incredibly, he survived this horrendous accident, literally walking away from the scene to be patched up by a doctor named Harlow. Gage was left blind in one eye, but once his wound had healed seemed otherwise healthy.[23] However, Harlow continued to treat Gage's wounds for a number of months and was struck by his behaviour. He describes Gage as using the

> ... *grossest profanity (which was not previously his custom), manifesting but little deference for his fellows, impatient of restraint or advice when it conflicts with his desires, at times pertinaciously obstinate, yet capricious and vacillating, devising many plans of future operations, which are no sooner arranged than they are abandoned in turn for others appearing more feasible. A child in his intellectual capacity and manifestations, he has the animal passions of a strong man.*[24]

Before the accident Gage had been a popular, warm, reliable individual who was 'persistent in executing all his plans'.[25] The case of Gage gave early insight into the functions carried out by the frontal lobe of the brain, planning and emotional regulation being the most obvious. While we now know this to be true, this case is used more for illustration than as a factual account, happening at a time when accurate records were not as meticulously collated as they are currently. However, it is a clear demonstration of how damage or dysfunction to areas of the brain can help us understand what those areas are responsible for. Notably, Gage's damage in the same area of the brain that Iacoboni investigated when testing for super mirror neuron functionality.

Today the level of information obtained is far more accurate, and we can combine it with a body of existing

knowledge and use extremely sophisticated imaging techniques to pinpoint more specific areas of the brain. We largely know what the general aspects of the brain do and in some instances we have gained a clearer understanding of the more detailed functions, such as the mirror neuron. However, there is a lot we still don't know for sure. While we are broadly aware of areas that the super mirror neuron or their equivalent must be responsible for, the exact detail of how and where has yet to be confirmed.

Beyond sport, another area that is believed to rely on both the mirror neuron and some sort of control mechanism is how we maintain a distinction between ourselves and others. Like being able to watch or visualise yet not carry out an action, there must be something that enables us to understand someone else's intentions and feelings while knowing that they are not our own. If we are for example empathising with someone's loss, if they are grieving, to an extent our brain may mirror their emotion, but we don't necessarily burst into tears just because they do. How do we mirror their emotion without taking it on ourselves? And how do we understand that it is their feeling and not our own? Our understanding of what is known by academics as 'self-other' is immensely complex. It must therefore rely on some form of management and control.

In everyday interactions we are endlessly trying to make sense of other people's goals using factors such as facial expressions, speech, gestures, body posture and mood to deduce their intentions. Simultaneously we are trying to predict how this will impact what they will say or do next and why. This largely relates to empathy. Claus Lamm, professor of biological psychology at the University of Vienna, and his colleagues published a paper for the Royal Society in 2016 that explores the possible mechanisms behind this – the functionality that enables us to detect,

select and keep track of these complex social cues.[26] The focus of one part of their discussion is on clinical populations who are lacking in empathy. Identifying which part of their brain does not activate during a typically empathic experience helps researchers to identify which parts of the brain are involved in healthy individuals. They examine perhaps the most striking example for self-other impairment – psychopaths.

Psychopathy is a disorder that relates to a lack of remorse or guilt. When the majority of us come into contact with someone who is in physical or emotional pain we feel or mirror a degree of that pain ourselves. Psychopaths, in short, do not. Lamm refers to a study by Jean Decety, professor of psychology and neuroscience at University of Chicago, who investigated this in 2013 by looking at 121 male prisoners varying in their level of psychopathy. Using fMRI, Decety and his colleagues scanned the inmates' brains while they looked at photos involving a painful scenario: for example, a foot stepping on a nail or finger being trapped in a drawer. They used fMRI to scan the brains of participants simply looking at the pictures imaging the painful experience happening to them, and then also happening to another person. This is known as a perspective-switching technique, which taps into the self-other distinction we've been referring to. In healthy adults this will typically provoke an empathic response.

The brains of the inmates responded in the same way as any healthy individual when they imagined themselves in pain. However, the prisoners who had the highest psychopathic tendencies showed far lower levels of brain activity when imagining someone else in pain.[27] The specific areas that this related to in the brain were the amygdala, where fear is processed, and the ventromedial prefrontal cortex, which as

we anecdotally saw for Gage is critical for the regulation of emotion, empathy and morality.[28]

Lamm explains that what is 'somewhat contradictory' about the evidence is that while psychopaths in studies such as Decety's did not display normal brain activity, other research has shown that psychopaths are able to empathise when instructed to do so. This, he believes, points to some form of 'top-down' mechanism that compensates for the lack of an automatic empathic response, which brings us back to Iacoboni's hypothesis: 'The higher order of mirror neurons may be called super mirror neurons, not because they have superpowers, but because they may be conceptualised as a functional neuronal layer "on top" of the classical mirror neurons, controlling and modulating their activity.'[29]

But while the super mirror neurons are a very feasible hypothesis as to how this critical neuro-cognitive mechanism works, we do not yet know for sure. The question remaining over these neural processes has even been dubbed the 'dark matter' of social neuroscience.[30] There is still a huge amount to explore and understand moving forward.

What we do know, although research has not yet replicated it, is that some form of the super mirror neurons identified by Iacoboni and Fried resides in the frontal cortex of the brain. These are areas responsible for the regulation of emotion, empathy and morality, with connectivity being abnormal in psychopathic inmates. It makes sense that this is where neural networks reside that allow us to distinguish between self and other when it comes to emotion, intention and prediction of behaviour.

Are we really selfish or selfless?

A recent study[31] carried out by Iacoboni and his colleagues could indicate another function that may in future research be

attributed directly to the super mirror neuron. Regardless of the exact mechanisms and labelling, the implications of this study are truly groundbreaking and worth exploring in the context of role-modelling. He examines whether we are innately good or bad. Do we naturally model prosocial or selfish behaviour?

The debate over whether we are born moral or depraved has been raging for centuries. Aristotle claimed that we are born into the world amoral, that morality is learned. St Augustine proclaimed that humans are constantly attracted to evil. Seventeenth-century English philosopher Thomas Hobbes proposed that we are wicked and that good only comes from us avoiding or controlling that. In equal measure, others such as philosopher Jean-Jacques Rousseau claimed that we are by nature gentle and pure, and corrupted by society. But now, with advances in neuroscientific, biological and psychological knowledge we are able to look for more clear-cut answers to this question. Iacoboni and his team are responsible for intruiging evidence that helps unravel the truth.

Led by neuroscientist Leonardo Christov-Moore, Iacoboni's team used a cutting-edge technique to examine what happens when the function in a specific area of the frontal lobe is disrupted.[32] When I met Iacoboni he animatedly described this study, which used something called 'theta burst stimulation' (cTBS) to interrupt activity in two areas within the observing brain – specifically the right dorsolateral prefrontal cortex and dorsomedial prefrontal cortex. Participants were asked to divide $10 with another player at their discretion using an economic game called the 'Dictator Game'. The other player was presented to the participant as a headshot photo, with their yearly salary displayed. Their income was either low or high. These pictures were of real people living in Los Angeles who would actually receive the money given. The

research question – would generosity vary depending on the other players' socio-economic status and their perceived need? Given five seconds to look at the picture of the person, participants were then given a further five seconds in which to decide how much they would give by pressing a number between zero and ten on a keyboard. The experiment was designed in such a way that their decision remained anonymous, which prevented decision-making based on a need to 'impress' or 'conform to expectations'.

Iacoboni and his team found that when the signals in the prefrontal areas were interrupted, thus limiting the capability of the brain to carry out slow, rational thinking with what we have dubbed the observing brain, levels of generosity increased. The participants unable to use their observing brain, relying on reacting brain impulses, were therefore more prosocial, cooperative and helpful to their fellow players. This happened when sharing the money with people of both low and high socio-economic status. Iacoboni and his colleagues concluded that this illustrates humans' natural tendency is to be prosocial, which explains that while we are young the self-maximising and prosocial tendencies co-exist, but this changes as we move into adulthood. Hence when asking whether humans are primarily selfish or selfless, this together with a building body of evidence suggests that we are in fact born selfless, which is great news. I returned to Iacoboni to ask him if he thought that the control of whether or not we are typically generous is the responsibility of super mirror neurons. He replied:

> It's hard to say whether what I call super mirror neurons in my book have been disrupted by the mirror system in our study on increasing generosity at the dictator game. The reality of it is, we don't need to posit their involvement. 'Regular' prefrontal neurons in those areas may suffice to reduce generosity and may have been the ones whose activity got disrupted by the mirror system.

Whatever the mechanism and exact functionality in the brain, this research is incredibly exciting and hopeful for the human race, if we make use of it and don't let our advanced world get in the way. Iacoboni's research also accords with current evolutionary psychology which emphasises that we are a deeply social species and our survival is hugely intertwined with others. While this is just one study it is also backed by a growing body of evidence from studies carried out by others at, for example, Yale University,[33] Duke University in North Carolina[34] and the Max Planck Institute for Human Cognitive and Brain Sciences in Leipzig, Germany.[35] Adding further weight to this concept, a cross-discipline study published in *Nature* carried out by specialists from Harvard and Yale in developmental psychology, moral philosophy and biology also came to the same conclusion. Our first instinct is to act cooperatively rather than selfishly.[36]

The mirror neuron system illustrates this in that we are uniquely inter-connected with other humans – our own behaviour, intentions and beliefs being mirrored on to others' brains and vice versa. We want to protect ourselves and we also want a good outcome for ourselves, so it makes sense that we should, intuitively want that for others, too. Indeed, Iacoboni and his colleagues conclude that our primary driver to be prosocial may be as a result of 'reflexive forms of empathy that blur the boundaries between individuals'.[37] He finished my last conversation with him saying that regardless of the name of these neurons 'what we think these neurons do is to preserve a sense of self and control unwanted imitation'. That may be for actions, such as watching someone throw a ball without throwing one ourselves, through to complex emotions. Understanding that boundary between self and other becomes even more crucial now we are aware of the mirror neuron system and our propensity to pick up on everything, including the emotions of everyone we come into contact with.

GOOD AND BAD MIRRORING

Bad Role Models

On the morning of 7 November 2007, 18-year-old Pekka-Eric Auvinen should have been at school. Auvinen grew up in a town called Jokela in Tuusula, Finland, where he'd been born and raised. He attended the local secondary school, with 400 other pupils between the ages of 12 and 18.

Auvinen lived with his father Ismo, an amateur musician who worked on the Finnish railways, his mother Mikaela and his younger brother.[1, 2] Ismo, so passionate about music, had named his son after the Finnish guitarist Pekka Järvinen and the English rock and blues guitarist Eric Clapton. Auvinen was an average student at school, had friends and didn't get into any trouble. But on that morning he skipped his first lessons. Instead he sat at home on the internet uploading videos to YouTube. At 11.28am he turned his computer off and rode his bike the 1.7km from his home to school. It was a cold, grey, overcast day.

When he arrived at school he didn't go through the main entrance, but through a door to the basement below the canteen where some of the students were having lunch. From there he made his way up to one of the corridors of classrooms where Joni Aaltonen and Nurmi Sameli waited for their English lesson to begin, busy chatting.[3] In an interview with the *Guardian* newspaper, Joni recalled what happened next:

'He walked towards us calmly and slowly. We didn't really pay him any attention. Then he stopped about two metres away from me and my friend. I looked up. He was watching us. He lifted his arm. He pointed the gun at me and started shooting.'[4]

Joni fled, but his best friend Nurmi didn't manage to escape and was killed. Auvinen massacred five more students within the next six minutes before the headteacher had been able to make an announcement on the PA system: 'Get into your classrooms immediately, lock the doors, and hide.' Auvinen then carried on through the corridors shouting: 'I'll kill all of you.' In total, he fired 69 bullets, killing eight people – five boys, two girls and the headteacher. He saved the final shot for himself.

A policeman described utter chaos at the scene, with students jumping from windows and scrambling for shelter.[5] One of Auvinen's teachers said: 'It felt unreal – a pupil I have taught myself was running towards me, screaming, a pistol in his hand.' He called the video he had uploaded on the morning of 7 November the 'Jokela High School Massacre'.

How could this happen? This was a boy from a seemingly normal, stable family in Finland, a country known to be peaceful, with one of the best schooling systems in the world. He wasn't behaving like this as a mirror to his friends, teachers or anyone else in his immediate environment. Was he mirroring anyone at all? And if so who and why?

The Ministry of Justice compiled a report following the massacre looking at the lead-up to the attack. It stated that Auvinen had found it increasingly difficult to make friends as he moved through school, becoming more isolated and withdrawn. It's believed that his parents' behaviour could have played a role as it was discovered they had values that were 'no longer current with young people'. They went as far as to contact the parents of other pupils to tell them that they weren't doing a good job and that their children behaved badly. Although we don't know how much, to some extent Auvinen would have been mirroring the

beliefs and attitudes of his parents. In turn, this would only have intensified his differences from schoolfriends. The teachers interviewed believed that the outlook encouraged at home made it harder for him to get along with other boys and led to him being bullied and taunted for his extreme interests.[6]

The connections we choose

As we have discovered, we are a prosocial species driven by a deep desire to connect. If we can't find what we need in one environment we look for it elsewhere or suffer the consequences of loneliness with major repercussions on both mental and physical health. Auvinen's search for belonging saw him turn to the internet where he took part in discussions about school killings in web communities and chatted to people he met online. This was a place where he felt he belonged. This combined with influences from home will have led to the pupils at Auvinen's school interpreting him as an outsider, part of the out-group. Earlier in the book we discussed the dramatic impact on how we treat people. Neuroscientist Grit Hein showed that we feel more empathy towards and are more likely to help people in pain if they are part of our own in-group. On the other hand, Hein showed that not only are we less likely to feel empathy for those who are not part of our in-group, but we also actually derive pleasure from seeing them in pain. While we can't directly link these effects to a killing spree, this is one of the psychological factors that built up in a vicious cycle over time to contribute to the extreme outcome.

Auvinen's understanding would have been directed toward people he met online because they became part of his in-group; he trusted them and also spent many hours

exposed to his online friends. All of the ingredients for role-modelling were apparently present. Added to this, adolescent brains have a heightened sensitivity to social needs, group membership and influence from their in-group, making them highly susceptible to mirroring.

Maren Strenziok, research collaborator at George Mason University in Virginia, led a research paper looking at the impact of viewing aggressive media material on the brain of adolescents. Using fMRI, Strenziok and her colleagues exposed participants to increasingly violent videos. They found that the more content the participants were shown, the more desensitised they became to the content, with those who had been exposed repeatedly to aggressive media in their daily life showing the greatest level of desensitisation. This translates to lower levels of sympathy and empathy towards victims of violence and motivates them toward situations that present hostile cues. It also leads to them responding more violently to different circumstances. The more advanced areas of the brain, specifically the left lateral orbitofrontal cortex (LOFC) typically notices violations in social norms causing someone to readjust their behaviour to align with what's expected of the group. However, over time the perceptions of what is normal changes, with the LOFC in adolescents exposed to the most violence responding less and less. In other words, what they perceive to be normal changes.[7] The more violent material or aggressive role models that adolescents are exposed to, the more brutality becomes normal and the less conscious they are to its impact.

The new groups that Auvinen began to associate with shifted the behavioural norms that his mirror system was emulating, moving away from those aligned with his peers to associate with the more risky attitudes and beliefs of these new friends. This could also have desensitised him to more

and more extreme violence, creating a vicious negative cycle. This will have made him increasingly different from his contemporaries and pulling him gradually in line with the extreme groups he had begun to connect with. As Auvinen became more removed from the 'rules of engagement' of his peers, this also potentially removed one of the natural mechanisms (*i.e.* the LOFC) of keeping violence in check.

Jaap Koolhaas at the University of Groningen in the Netherlands researches the effect of aggression in rats and explains that typically the expression of hostility is controlled or modified by social norms.[8] Among humans 'social norms' comprise cultures, customs, moral values, beliefs and laws. However, when taken out of context these behavioural controls no longer operate in the same way, and in effect the pressure valve that normally keeps violence in check disappears, as shown by Strenziok's research. Auvinen had removed himself from the norms of his peers and aggression was no longer modified; in fact it was glorified by his newfound friends. As a consequence we can assume that Auvinen may have even been using the massacre violence as a means of social communication, displaying his despair at being excluded.

When investigators looked back over his interactions on the internet it became clear that he was enthralled by US school shootings. He looked up to the Unabomber Theodore John Kaczynski and posted videos online about Hitler, Nazis and the Columbine High School killers, Eric Harris and Dylan Klebold.[9] Peter Langman, an American psychologist and expert on school shooters, notes that much of Auvinen's writings were modelled on the prose of these individuals saying: 'The parallels between the writings of Auvinen and Harris are too numerous to include them all.'[10] This, we can only assume, shows direct mirroring of their behaviour enabled via the mirror system in Auvinen's brain.

Langman also explains that Jokela and other massacres cannot simply be described as 'copycat' killings in the way that is often portrayed by the media. Multiple other complex factors are involved: infatuation with a killer, casual reference to a previous massacre, sympathy with a cause, carrying out the will of others, seeking fame and leading a revolution with killers.[11] However, one commonality is that a large proportion involve some form of mirroring and imitation; according to Langman, the killers are 'drawn to the prior perpetrators for a variety of personal reasons'.[12] As we've discussed throughout the book, this connection with a role model makes it far more likely that someone will mirror their behaviour. Combined with this we can see other complex social and neurobiological factors at play: group membership, age and vulnerability of the brain to peer influences and the expression of aggression.

Kaj Björkqvist, professor of developmental psychology at Turku University in Finland, has also written about the shootings at Jokela, raising concerns over the increased threat of school shootings in normally peaceful Finland. For example, during the two months following the Kauhajoki shooting at Seinajoki University on 23 September 2008, which by all accounts was itself inspired by Jokela, the police reported 200 threats.[13] This, Björkqvist proposes, is exacerbated by not only having seen these examples, but also an increase in media violence more broadly. Iacoboni, one of the world's leading experts in exploring the function of the mirror neuron, states that the results of numerous studies are 'unequivocal: exposure to media violence has a strong effect on imitative violence'[14] and that this applies to children across all age groups and races. The link is so strong that it outweighs the strength of the relationship between passive smoking and lung cancer, bone mass and calcium intake, or exposure to asbestos and cancer.[15] Iacoboni explains that the

evidence of these underlying neurological mechanisms of this violent imitation is now emerging, giving more weight to the links than ever before. While some of the hypotheses that we have proposed regarding Auvinen's behaviour cannot be proved – after all we cannot interview him or look at his brain using fMRI – the broader evidence linking media violence and the neurobiological underpinning to mirroring only add weight to this being the result of mirror thinking.

Extreme corners of society

Not far from the actions of a lone killer are those of terrorists. While their motivation is different, their behavioural mechanisms share many striking similarities. A solitary individual, not really part of any social group within a real-life setting, starts looking for a sense of belonging and connection, which they find on the internet. Indeed, research has found that these young recruits want to be part of the in-group even more than they associate with the ideology itself.[16] Jean Decety and his colleague Clifford Workman[17] explain how, as for isolated shootings, the factors involved in radicalisation are complex. Decety and Workman explain that terrorist activity needs to be examined through evolutionary theory, social, personality and cognitive psychology, political science and neuroscience. We need to look specifically at areas including group dynamics, interpersonal processes, values and personal narratives, as well as microsociological processes, as we have for Auvinen.

What is frightening is how the recruitment of youngsters to terrorist cells is more deliberate and carefully thought through than the process for other groups of extremists. While their techniques may not directly draw on the evidence, it nevertheless leverages many of the mechanisms

we've explored. Take, for example, the case of the so-called Islamic State of Iraq and Syria (ISIS), where the 'cause' is delivered through a carefully constructed process of gradual social influence. The group initially downplays the overt association with violence, which could turn people off as it's against 'accepted' social norms. They lure young recruits in by providing broad and compelling stories about the terrorist movement and of course storytelling is a powerful mechanism by which to engage via the mirror system. Gradually recruits are exposed to more and more extreme and violent content, which is filmed in a way that makes it look 'cool' and worth emulating. This begins to realign their view of social norms and the 'cool' factor raises social standing within a group. Direct mirroring is encouraged by providing leaders for recruits to look up to all adding to the social desireability and lure. Dr Rosanna Guadagno[18] from Stanford University, who specialises in internet behaviour and social influence, explains that the individuals who already belong and are considered most honourable are overtly celebrated as leaders. Their biographies are shared with potential recruits, providing inspiration and a direct route to understanding how, if they mirror that pathway through life, they too can be revered. This is highly motivating for young people at an age when what their peers think of them is of such critical importance. They therefore mirror the behaviour at a neurological level, literally mapping the actions of the person they venerate[19] on to their own brain. Over time potential recruits begin to strongly identify with the terrorists. They not only become part of their in-group, but the aspirations, goals, beliefs and attitudes turn into internally represented models in their own minds. While recruitment of young radicals cannot be explained by simply looking at one specific area of the brain, we know that the mirror neuron plays a part in many of the complex factors involved.

When it comes to the broader population, the internet and its influence as a role-modelling platform pulls in other waifs and strays in a way that negates geographical constraints. In the time of our ancient ancestors people with extreme beliefs, unless held by a very influential person, would tend to realign their views with the tribal norms in order to belong, or would be removed by natural group processes. The latter would inevitably lead to death, giving strong incentive to assimilate or at least keep extreme opinions to themselves. As a result, everyone mirrors the same accepted way of behaving. New members to the group align to that behaviour. Think about it this way: if you've always worked in an office where people wear suits, you will typically wear a suit. If you then go and work for a company that has a dress-down policy where people come to work in jeans and T-shirts, will you continue to wear your suit? The likelihood is that you won't, you'll align to the group you've joined. You are normal and you want to belong.

Today those with more fanatical ideas can turn to other like-minded people thousands of miles away via the internet, creating their own in-group. It doesn't matter if the rest of society disagrees – it is not a threat to their survival. These communities, rather than providing a social 'stop' point to unreasonable beliefs, instead reinforce them, creating new 'norms'. As a result, large swathes of extreme behaviour are enabled across dispersed populations. While in the case of corporate dress this may be no bad thing – if you want to keep wearing a suit you may find people in another division of the company you've joined doing the same – when it comes to extreme behaviour the consequences are more serious. Angela Nagle, author of *Kill All Normies*,[20] talks about the escalating social and political divide that is arising. 'Normies' are people like you and me. People who have everyday tastes, opinions, political views, refer to everyday

news sources and live in the real world. It's us who the far-right and other radical subcultures congregating online call 'normies' – we are the ones who they believe it's 'impossible to explain things to' because 'we are ignorant and unenlightened'. 'Normal' in the real world is not 'normal' online. Nagle points to a world of adults, not just disenfranchised youths, who live within these online worlds. In an interview with the *Economist* she says: 'Ruthless competitive individualism is being applied to the romantic and private realm and it's deeply antisocial.'[21] This is just one example of 'bad' role models mirroring and exacerbating each other's behaviour, beliefs and attitudes aided by the internet.

Bad influences

'Bad' role models can also wreak havoc on populations offline, especially when influenced by a strong and persuasive leader. Many believe President Donald Trump to be a 'bad' influence on followers. For example, the US Center for Investigative Reporting showed that almost every metric of intolerance in the US surged after Trump came to power – from reported anti-semitism and Islamophobia to violent hate crimes based on skin colour, nationality and sexual orientation.[22] One study used time series analysis (a series of data points listed in time order) to demonstrate the 'Trump effect' hypothesis. Trump's election was linked to a statistically significant surge in reported hate crimes across the United States, even when controlling for alternative explanations,[23] with more than 150 reports of Trump-themed taunts and attacks spanning 39 states following the first 18 months of his time in office.

Trump is a powerful influencer. He follows a president who many believed was liberal and fair-minded, instead

representing opposing values via suggestions that certain
Democratic congresswomen should 'go back' to the 'totally
broken and crime infested places from which they came'[24]
and calling Mexican immigrants criminals and 'rapists'[25]
who 'infest' America,[26] as well as saying that there should
be a 'total and complete shutdown of Muslims coming into
the US'. These attitudes inevitably become mirrored in
society. We know that imitation, underpinned by the
functionality of the mirror neuron, is key to the acquisition
of culture[27] and that people are more likely to imitate
someone demonstrating rank, prestige or success – all
aspects that are strongly associated with being President of
the United States.

We are also more likely to mirror people who are similar
to us in terms of race, which may well exacerbate the
'Trump effect'. A 2012 study carried out by Elizabeth
Reynolds Losin,[28] assistant professor of social neuroscience
at UCLA, and her colleagues, looked at how race modulates
neural activity during imitation. The study used fMRI to
examine neural activity of participants copying gestures
performed by actors of their own race and two 'racial
out-groups' – people from a different racial background to
themselves. The participants were all European-American
and watched videos of actors from three different ethnicities:
European-American, African-American and Chinese-
American. The actors performed hand gestures and
participants were asked to imitate the actions, observe
without imitating, look at 'still' images of the actors or
look at a white screen with a black cross in the centre. The
researchers found different levels of neural activity when
participants were viewing actors of their own race in
comparison to out-groups. The specific areas of the brain
stimulated in each condition suggests that a 'race-processing'
region may modulate activity within the imitation system.

The findings also showed participants' brains were more active viewing Chinese-American than African-American actors. The neuroscientists concluded that this could relate to social status – Chinese-Americans are regarded more highly within American culture than African-Americans, therefore the participants would be more likely to mirror the Chinese-Americans than the African-Americans. This study provides empirical evidence to show how race may shape biases of how we learn through imitation and mirroring.

Played out within the 'real-life' environment following the election of Trump as a prestigious European-American President, the racial effects of mirroring were rapidly transmitted. Due to the speed of connectivity between and across individuals in our technologically advanced world, this can happen fast and on a large scale. Although we don't know for sure, the study discussed suggests that European-Americans, who form the majority of the population within the US, would more strongly identify and imitate Trump's beliefs, behaviours and attitudes; one of the most worrying factors is that this pattern of hate spread beyond the far-right, beyond adults and into the classrooms, with online news platform BuzzFeed finding dozens of cases of children using Trump's words to bully their Latino, Middle Eastern, African-American, Asian and Jewish classmates.[29]

Gangs fill the void

Regardless of who is in power, every society has clusters of the population that are less fortunate or well-off. In the UK, areas such as Hackney (London), Handsworth (Birmingham) and Moss Side (Manchester) are parallel to Belmont, California, where LouAnne Johnson taught. When you and your family are battling with poverty,

surviving in a community struggling with excessive unemployment and holding mental health issues at bay, gangs – just like terrorist groups – provide somewhere to belong. Youths growing up in these areas, like Johnson's pupils Raul Sanchero and Emilio Ramirez, see gang membership as a way of gaining respect and power: a route to escaping the poverty that surrounds them and rising above the demeaning position of unemployment. The strongest influence over children who become entangled in gangs is their peers. If a young person becomes entangled with 'antisocial' friends it naturally limits their involvement with more prosocial contacts. Direct exposure to violence being role-modelled also has a mirrored effect within the community. For example, exposure to gun violence is strongly associated with aggression.[30] Those presented with these behaviours begin to learn different norms of operating – their antisocial beliefs and attitudes are reinforced. What the research calls 'deviant role models' are the most strongly associated risk factor of someone joining a gang.[31] However, there is hope. A fascinating piece of research carried out in 2015 involving over 26,000 students taking part in the California Healthy Kids Survey showed that empathy mitigated the detrimental effects of being around other peers who were members of gangs. The authors attribute this to youngsters, who have high levels of empathy, being more able to build social bonds outside of gangs, decreasing the need for gang membership for companionship and support.[32] The empathy that Johnson showed is an anecdotal example of how a teacher can have this effect, but research has also shown that this empathy frequently comes from family members.[33] So while the mirror system can operate to negative effect absorbing the behaviours of negative role models, another aspect of the same system can serve to mitigate those adverse effects.

Beyond world leaders and gangs, prominent figures in the media can also exacerbate racism, hatred and aggression, serving to reinforce stereotypes and norms that may otherwise not be prominent. Tyson Fury, O. J. Simpson, Plaxico Burress, Ray Rice, Luis Suarez and Stan Collymore are all examples of high-profile athletes who sensationalise violent behaviour. We've discussed how powerful athletes are as role models, so it should come as no surprise that this reinforces an acceptance of aggression in young boys and normalises it. Children exposed to more media violence show more imitative violence.

What about young girls?

While some we know join terrorist groups, females have repeatedly been found to be less likely to join gangs or to be influenced by violence. Adolescent girls are more likely to rate pop stars as their second most favoured role models after family members. More recent research has also added social influencers into the mix. Do female celebrities have an impact on their audience? In 2015 researchers in New Zealand carried out a study looking at girls and 'tween' popular culture in everyday life, researching what is described as the early sexualisation of pre-teen and younger girls. They suggest that it courts the risk of child abuse and sexual assault, and launches girls into 'premature sexuality under the influence of their idols'. This is not simply a matter of worrying about youngsters wearing short skirts and make-up, and has moved so far up the public agenda that in 2013 a series of policy papers were published in the UK, US and Australia highlighting the sexualisation of girls and 'corporate paedophilia'[34] as a pressing social problem.

This premature sexualisation is not driven by the parents of young girls strutting their stuff at home – it is believed

to come directly from the celebrities that they see in the media. It is the medium of pop music that is more saturated by what associate professor of psychology Sue Jackson at Victoria University in New Zealand[35] calls the 'expressions of gendered, "sexualised" porno-chic' than other mediums. There has been an increase in the amount of sexually explicit material since the millennium. For example, Miley Cyrus, whose career started at age 11 in the Disney series *Hannah Montana*, jumped straight over into the music scene at 17 years old with a video called 'Can't be Tamed' in which she pole dances wearing a skimpy black leotard and leather straps that bear a resemblance to S&M gear. Although exploited herself by a male-dominated entertainment industry – something she later explains as having been psychologically damaging – her presence nevertheless had an impact.[36] Young girls watching a role model that they have connected with, trusted and been exposed to over years through what amounts to hours of television viewing will absorb what they see. The mirror system in their brains will repeat the movements observed. Mirror neurons also enable young viewers to understand the intention of sexual allure. Many kids will not consciously look to imitate, as we all make inferences about others' behaviours spontaneously, unconsciously and continuously, and then evaluate them before incorporating them into our own mental model. Such inferences are part and parcel of everyday social understanding.[37] However, other girls may overtly copy. Either way, the majority who pay attention will to some extent be influenced. Professor Ap Dijksterhuis, a social psychologist at Radboud University in the Netherlands, explains that while we may not deliberately imitate others' behaviour, the perception of what someone is doing leads to an unconscious series of behavioural adjustments in which the patterns of others' behaviour are

subtly brought into line with their existing view of the world and way they behave.[38] In the case of young girls this in essence leads them to incorporate sexualised behaviour into their own repertoire, while also normalising it as a socially accepted way of acting. At a collective level this means that girls are learning from their role model, whether Cyrus or another celebrity, and in turn transmitting the behaviours into the culture of their generation as they repeat them at school and with friends. Young brains, specifically those of adolescents, are particularly malleable and responsive to social interaction. For example, researchers at the Institute of Cognitive Neuroscience at University College London[39] explain how the 'social brain' – areas that relate to 'social perceptual processes including reading facial expressions, detecting biological motions and making inferences about others' mental state – undergoes significant changes during adolescence. Referencing numerous neuroimaging and behavioural studies the authors show the myriad behavioural and cognitive changes that occur at a neurological level as children develop into teenagers before transitioning into emerging adulthood. The changes lead to an increase in exploration and novelty-seeking, emotional lability (rapid changes in mood) and social salience (increased sensitivity to social and emotional information).[40] Brain imaging suggests that children in early adolescence are especially sensitive to the emotional expression of others, which can lead to higher levels of vulnerability, but also – one could assume when directed toward positive role-models and peers – may enable the development of more adaptive behaviours and brain development. For example, psychologists at the University of Washington found that greater activation in these regions was associated with lower social anxiety and fewer social problems.[41] The

researchers at UCL argue that increasing our understanding of the development of these social abilities, and the way in which they interact with each other within the brain, could give insight as to why some adolescents are successful in making the transition to adulthood, while others experience difficulties. One key factor in this could be the extent to which their role models are positive or negative; neurological processing of social information and the context in which it is available is particularly relevant in understanding adolescent mental health risks.

Despite not having direct neurological evidence for exactly how the mirror system works, the understanding we have to date from neuroscience and social psychology enables us to infer that celebrities have a huge influence. Not only when it comes to feminism and sexuality, but also to the choices we all make about lifestyle, health, what we do with our bodies, what we buy and many other factors in our daily lives. One article in the *New York Post* claimed that a decade of the Kardashians had 'radically changed America', creating a generation of 'oversexualised tween and teenage girls, sexting and oversharing online, and "social media influencer" is now a viable career option'.[42] The results of a 2014 study carried out at the University of Pretoria in South Africa revealed two common themes resulting from exposure to such role models. Firstly, women more frequently believe using their body for profit is normal and secondly their bodies can be used as a means of power.

Kim Kardashian entered the limelight as stylist to Paris Hilton. In 2007 Kim Kardashian's career as a media starlet and influencer was launched via a leaked sex tape of her with former boyfriend rapper Ray J – widely believed to have been a publicity stunt. Whether or not this is true, it definitely drew attention to the reality TV show that launched later that year *Keeping Up with the Kardashians*,

featuring her and her family. Momentum continued and in 2009 she appeared nude in *Playboy* and also released a fitness video – *Fit in Your Jeans by Friday*. This shows her moving at a snail's pace, while claiming that copying her moves will 'melt away the flab' and help you fit in your jeans by Friday.

To an adult this may seem unrealistic and not carry great weight. However, for a teenage girl who is desperate to fit in and is searching for anything that will allow her to be part of the in-crowd, she can get swept up with believing that this person who is wealthy, good-looking and has social prestige is worth emulating. So if Kim Kardashian says you have to look good and you have to stay in shape, that is taken at its word. At the time of writing Kim Kardashian has 147 million followers on Instagram – that's a lot of people who are being influenced. Yet what she is portraying is unrealistic; not everyone can be a celebrity, nor can they have her figure, especially given the claims that she has spent £70,000 on surgery to change her body shape.

One academic believes images of women like Kim Kardashian promote 'that women should look a certain way in order to be accepted, admired, praised, successful and happy'.[43] And this gets to the nub of the issue. Regardless of whether or not you or I agree with the Kardashians' values, everyone wants to be happy; that is fundamentally what we strive for in life, together with health. Even success is ultimately a route to being happy. We know from extensive research that a fundamental factor in happiness and mental well-being comes from having meaning and purpose in life – depth of understanding of who we are, what we truly believe in and how we can contribute to the world. However, such campaigns as those described above pull in the other direction. They say that happiness and success are built on a) the unattainable, b) selling ways of getting there that will not work and c) promoting the

superficial aspects in life. The media furore around these women sees less emphasis placed on 'empowering themselves through education and knowledge, and more emphasis on their beauty and sexuality in order to attain success'.[44]

Screen mirroring

Research shows that children spend on average more than seven hours[45] a day looking at a screen – and the remainder of their school and leisure time is spent with peers who are also looking at the same images on their screen – so it is not surprising that celebrities and influencers are impacting social and cultural norms. The problem is that when girls and women internalise these ideals of appearance, which happens because of the way in which the mirror system works, it has been shown to have a significant impact on self-esteem, self-image[46] and dissatisfaction with their own body.[47] In turn this leads to a dangerous cycle with an increased desire to be thin and increase in symptoms of eating disorders such as bulimia.[48] The same is even true with men, which has been explained as resulting from the more prominent and ever-present images of male perfection.[49]

However, it isn't just children and adolescents who get scooped up by celebrity. To an extent we all do. Advertisers and marketeers know this and frequently use celebrities to endorse products for very good reason. It helps them sell. But why? Anthropologist Dr Jamie Tehrani at Durham University, whose focus is cultural evolution,[50] believes that our fascination with and desire to emulate celebrity comes down to the uniquely human feature of prestige. Prestige is dependent on enabling a form of social learning that allowed for survival thousands of years ago – and social learning is dependent on the mirror neuron.

Imagine being alive in the time of our ancient ancestors. Out on the plains of Africa your main concerns are staying alive and reproducing. You've been trying to hunt a particular type of wildebeest for some time, but you just can't seem to throw your spear in a way that captures them. They get away every time. One fellow in your tribe, let's call him Fred, is particularly good at hunting. He has 'prestige' within the group and one day he comes back to camp with the very type of wildebeest you've been trying to catch unsuccessfully. The next day you ask if you can go with him to hunt and watch very carefully how he throws his spear, not just at this particular type of wildebeest, but in general. What does he do when he's hunting? How does he approach, stand and throw? What type of spearhead is he using? How long does he observe his prey before he chases? What does he observe? You go with him for several days, over the course of several weeks, and you mirror what he does. Then, bingo, you manage to kill that very species of wildebeest that has been eluding you for so long. Your friends who know that you've been trying for some time ask you how you did it. You tell them. This gives Fred more prestige and leads to more of the tribe joining him when he hunts with the specific intention of learning from him. It gives you some prowess with the women, too – a successful hunter is admired and seen as a strong potential partner. You also show other people what you've learnt – your nephews, your friends' children. The other people who have learnt from him do the same. This enables the successful hunting techniques to be spread among the tribe and shared with future generations. Each generation then builds on that learning and adapts it, improving the skills and capabilities as time passes. This is a fantastic way of passing on knowledge and expertise. However, Tehrani explains that 'because this strategy is somewhat indiscriminate, it can lead to people adopting

all kinds of behaviours exhibited by a role model, including ones that have nothing to do with their success'.[51]

For example, Fred may also have hopped on one leg for several minutes before he went out hunting each day. It's difficult to know whether this does or does not add to the success of his hunting technique, but because he does it, it would be risky to exclude it from your own approach. You have no evidence to say that it's not related, you don't have access to the internet to check up, nor were you educated in a way that enabled you to figure out the reasoning. Hence you copy that, too, and so does everyone else. This, then, over the course of generations, becomes an intricate dance that it's unlucky to exclude before any hunting expedition. Today we could look at a lucky dance or charm and say it makes no logical sense, but how would our ancestors have known that? In the same way, future generations may look at our generation and wonder why we filled our faces with Botox even though it looks very peculiar.

Tehrani posits that prestige-based learning – following and emulating someone because they are successful – is a broad strategy looking at the whole role model rather than the specific elements that make them successful. Today, although we may have the knowledge to help us differentiate the elements that enable success from those that don't, our core drivers, from an evolutionary perspective, are focused on the person as a whole – mirroring every behaviour. If David Beckham wears a particular cologne then, even though it makes no sense and it doesn't mean that wearing that cologne will make you an incredible footballer, good-looking or wealthy, a young man who admires him will look to emulate anything he can of him. We're more likely to buy something if it's endorsed by someone we admire.

In our ancestors' time the good aspects of mirroring behaviour will most probably have outweighed the bad in terms of what we learnt. The learning was associated with

adaptive behaviours. However, today we copy more of those behaviours 'that are of no use in themselves', says Tehrani, such as having plastic surgery. Because of this, it's not hard to see why big brands sponsor celebrities to endorse their products. Celebrities are highly visible via extensive media attention and people copy them indiscriminately – the clothes they wear, the things they do. Celebrities knowingly accept sponsorship from brands, or agree to wear an outfit designed by a certain fashion house. This I see first hand as some of the designers I work with slave away to get garments right for the Oscars, Golden Globes or their latest gig. They know that thousands of people will do what that star does and want to wear what they wear. But in many cases those thousands of people who are mirroring them do so without consciously deciding to. What affects sales at a surface level has an impact at a far deeper level psychologically in fans and followers. This makes an impression on their self-esteem, their happiness, what they strive for in life and how they go about living it. Don't all celebrities have a responsibility to be aware of this, and don't those who want to be good rather than bad role models need to look for ways of breaking the cycles and norms rather than reinforcing the more negative ones? Tehrani asks: 'We gorge ourselves on images of wealth and success because they appeal to our appetite for prestige, but are celebrities actually good role models?'[52]

They are not good hunters or gatherers, they have not reached their position through being effective at storing food or protecting territory. They may be more socially adept and better at attracting a mate, but we don't interact with them first hand, so cannot see the nuances of their behaviour that may enable our own success in these areas. Yet we still mirror their behaviour unconsciously, playing

into the hands of marketeers and advertisers because that is what our brains have evolved to do. So, where does the responsibility lie? Products are one thing, but entire behaviours, values and attitude choices are another. While parents and caregivers undoubtably shape children and teens more than anyone else in their life, their eyes quickly fall upon athletes, pop stars and social media icons. These people have the opportunity to be a massively positive influence, which we'll look at in the next chapter. They may just be there for fun and light entertainment, but they also play a part in perpetuating violence, aggression, sexism, racism and have a profound effect on individuals and the shaping of culture.

It's for this reason that media channels carry a huge responsibility as they have become the mouthpiece of society. It's no longer the church, the school or family values that are broadcast and reinforced, rather the values of terrorist groups, people lacking their own meaning and purpose, and glamourising that life for others to chase, along with some incredibly well-meaning individuals. But as a child, or even as an adult, it's difficult to know who to follow, who to listen to, what's right and what's wrong.

Outlets themselves are aware and many of those who are most prominent fully understand the responsibility and what to do with that. It's also up to parents and the personal role models who are actually in youngsters' lives to explain what should and shouldn't be mirrored and why. They should discuss what it means, whether it is something they really want to aspire to and why.

In the absence of someone to follow or somewhere to belong, disaffected youths may join gangs, turn to radicalisation or even carry out violent attacks. Celebrity takes the place of people who would have once been respected for their values and capabilities – not the number

of followers they have, which has little meaning. The online world offers more opportunity to access people who traditional society would not have respected or given prominence to, yet today anyone can take centre stage on the internet. Because our brains are set up to mirror, we need someone to mirror at the vulnerable and impressionable stage of life from our teens to emerging adulthood – with the lack of someone positive, something or someone bad will take its place.

Good Role Models

The transformative power of mirroring

Jameela was born in 1986 in Hampstead, London, to an Indian father and Pakistani mother. She was harassed at school, both physically and verbally, for being from a minority and less privileged background than her peers.[1] In an interview Jameela said: 'I was very chubby on and off at school. I didn't look like the other girls. I was much taller than everyone else. I had bad skin, and braces. I was bullied about appearance, but I was mostly bullied for my race as a child, and very violently.'[2]

She developed an eating disorder, struggling with anorexia between the ages of 14 and 17. As an adult she describes how the relentless victimisation became internalised, making her feel shame about her background and appearance.[3]

In an interview with Krishnan Guru-Murthy on Channel 4, Jameela said that as a child she felt she was 'bombarded with a narrative that had no alternative. There were never any women who were celebrated for their intellect ... and all of my magazines were selling me weight loss products or telling me to be thin. Otherwise, I wasn't worth anything.'[4] She had no positive constructive role models and found no one in a prominent position to mirror or saying that it was OK to be different.

Jameela Jamil has grown up to be a television presenter for Channel 4, DJ on BBC Radio 1 and most recently a

Hollywood star in the hit NBC show *The Good Place*. Owning her celebrity status, she has become overt about her responsibility as a role model, passionately embracing the opportunity the position offers her. She stands up for the things she believes in, representing minority women and providing the mirror to others that she herself was lacking.

Jamil speaks up on social media about issues ranging from body positivity and feminism, through to race and LGBTQ rights. She's not afraid to call out others, from journalists to high-profile celebrities – people who could have a very negative impact on her career if they chose to. For example, in the interview with Guru-Murthy she refers to Kim Kardashian as 'a wolf in sheep's clothing', going on to say: 'Just because you look like a woman, we trust you and we think you're on our side, but you are selling us something that really doesn't make us feel good … You're selling us self-consciousness.' She's breaking the evolving social norms to create an alternative attitude and approach for people to mirror.

In March 2019, Jamil saw one particular post on Instagram which tipped her over the edge. It showed a line of women who all had digits on their image in the photograph and those numbers it turned out were what each of the women weighed. She wrote in her blog: 'This is how women are taught to value themselves. She went on to say:

> *I couldn't believe what I was seeing … the post asking what we think of their weights and then asking its followers, 'What do you weigh?' … What kind of crazed toxic nonsense is this? What is this post trying to achieve other than to induce anxiety into young women about something so entirely irrelevant? What are we teaching women about our value?*

In response, Jamil launched an Instagram account called *I Weigh*, with the aim of measuring a person's weight not

by pounds and ounces but by attributes and accomplishments. She wants to encourage people to see that their self-worth goes far beyond a media image of perfection or how much they weigh. At the time of writing *I Weigh* has a million followers, with posts from women and men across the world. The attitude this role-models is for people to value who they are inside, not just how they appear, nor to feel pressure to look like unrealistic images on social media. The mirror neurons will pick up and assimilate this as a mental model, alongside existing ideas about how to view their self-worth. In some it may even take the place of what were formerly more negative mental models.

We could say that Jamil is a good role model. She stands up for large swathes of the population in a positive way, but she swears a lot, which may make some parents take issue with their children following her. People have also questioned whether she is the best person to represent the body-positive community, given that she was formerly a model. But that begs the question of what actually is a good role model. Is being a good or bad role model subjective? Who decides? We could after all pull anyone apart for one aspect or another of what they stand for, who they are and what they say.

An area where there are great expectations around role models – something that is incredibly intertwined with lifestyle and beliefs from childhood through to adulthood in many families – is sport. Arguably this is a vehicle for incredible opportunities. Take, for example, John McAvoy, who began life as a high-profile armed robber locked in the most secure prison in the UK and is now a professional triathlete represented by Nike. During his jail sentence, McAvoy began using the gym so avidly that, together with one particularly supportive prison officer who himself played the 'good role model' and encouraged him to fulfil

his potential, he changed his whole outlook on life. This not only led him away from crime, but towards becoming a professional athlete when he was released. McAvoy now wants to spread the message of how powerful sport can be, saying in an interview with the *Telegraph*: 'If I'd carried on as I was I'd be dead. Or they'd have banged me up and thrown away the key, which is the same thing. Sport saved my life.'[5]

In an interview he described how his life of crime was totally immersed in a world that he mirrored. He absorbed the attitudes, values, beliefs and actions within the community he lived, mirroring his stepfather and uncle in particular who were both hardened criminals. It's all his brain knew. His personality is that of someone who is determined, curious and headstrong, and in that environment it led him to become a 'successful' criminal. When a healthier alternative presented itself that same personality began to mirror a different set of values, beliefs and actions.

McAvoy frequently speaks at schools and encourages children to become involved with sport. If a school PE teacher engages a child as their role model, unlocking their skill and capability can be transformational, not only to self-esteem and confidence but also to what they go on to achieve. Dame Kelly Holmes grew up on a council estate in Kent with a single mum and is open about having struggled at school. She had little belief in herself, feeling like she wasn't very good at anything. That is, until a PE teacher took an interest in her. Seeing her talent for running, her teacher encouraged her to focus, to work hard and to believe in herself, building her self-esteem. This was a turning point in Holmes' life and the ensuing hard work and commitment saw her become the first ever British female athlete to win both the Olympic 800m and 1500m,

in 2004 in Athens. It doesn't mean that all children have to have the talent that Holmes did, but realising potential shows up in other ways. Simply having an adult who is not a parent or relative show interest and belief in a child is often enough to help send them on a more positive trajectory through life. It directs them and what their brain mirrors towards a constructive outcome. If where they end up is in a position like Holmes did, once they are there they also hold a huge responsibility as a role model. Sports role models inspire thousands of people who follow their quest to achieve, win and overcome obstacles, hence the vehicle for incredible opportunities. But is it fair that they shoulder this accountability? Is this what a sports professional should take on when they become the best in their profession?

The pressure of being the mirror

In a 1993 Nike ad, professional NBA basketball player Charles Barkley famously balked against this saying: 'I am not a role model ... I'm not paid to be a role model. I'm paid to wreak havoc on the basketball court. Parents should be role models. Just because I dunk a basketball, doesn't mean I should raise your kids.'[6] His point at the time was that being a great athlete has nothing to do with being a role model. It is, however, a reality, whether or not a professional sportsperson wants to accept it. While on the whole both boys and girls rank their parents as their primary role models,[7] beyond that athletes come quite high up the list, especially for boys.[8] In the UK this tends to fall into the camp of footballers who are perhaps the most overt role models in the public domain. They inspire because children can see and understand what they do. It's much harder to work out what a business leader or politician actually does or to relate to it. They can see the route to success for an

athlete and will frequently find a clear path from any background or beginning in life through to stardom. They can imagine themselves doing the same. Added to this there is the excitement associated with winning, competing, being watched by thousands, and with the huge wages also come the glamour and the bling. This is heightened by media attention telling the whole story, covering multiple aspects of their personalities and personal lives. But being held on a pedestal is not always good and it does involve taking on an immense responsibility.

An article published in 2019 on football website Prost International titled 'Why every female athlete is under pressure to be a role model' points out that 'The problem with role models is that they are expected to be perfect and flawless when the rest of us are not.' This is to an extent true when it comes to 'aspirational ' role models. Although sometimes we may blame our parents for things, we don't in reality expect them to perfect, nor do we expect that of our teachers, relations or healthcare workers, so is it fair to expect professional athletes to be? The article specifically refers to the England and Saracens women's flanker and World Cup champion Marlie Packer, who was found guilty of drink-driving in 2018 for the second time. This is something that will then potentially have negatively influenced the behaviour or attitude of young followers. Packer of course is not alone. While those in the spotlight are outstanding at sport, it doesn't mean to say that they are perfect in every other respect.

However, there are certain behaviours and values that they should surely be held accountable for. While it's not part of their skill as a professional athlete, it is a part of being at the elite level in sport that comes with the the job description. When a young hopeful is training to be the best that they can be, they know that if they fulfil their

hopes and dreams they will find themselves centre stage. If that's not something they want then maybe they should be counselled to choose a different career path. In the same article citing Packer's drink-driving, Scottish footballer Erin Cuthbert recognises the obligations that come with her position saying: 'All 23 of us are now role models. I realise the responsibility that we've got for little kids growing up now. They look up to us. We need to continue our success on the pitch.'[9] This may feel like a big burden to shoulder but must be true given the platform they have. It's also critically important when talking about any of those mentioned: a black woman from an underprivileged background, a female rugby player and a female football player, to remember the powerful example any of them play in breaking down barriers and stereotypes for a new generation of women. However, they, like the rest of us, are still human and no one is perfect.

In reality, even looking to the extreme of the heroes and heroines in movies and fiction, perfect role models do not really exist. Take, for example, comic book superheroes: the Incredible Hulk, Superman and Spiderman had their powers thrown upon them and all arguably have neurotic tendencies. The X-Men are mutants, different from everyone on Earth, making them outsiders who struggle to fit in. Even the heroes without superpowers have flaws – James Bond drinks heavily, gambles and drives recklessly, seduces women and then leaves them for another. Hermione Granger from Harry Potter is argumentative, can be condescending, stubborn and when she's stressed takes her frustrations out on others. Without flaws these characters simply aren't relatable even as our heroes and heroines. We cannot connect with, trust or have empathy for them – factors we have seen as essential for us to model our behaviour on others and our mirror neurons to imitate

their good points. Flawed characters give us something we can understand and see in ourselves; they give us hope despite being fictional and even if it's not conscious we feel that if they can do that, then so can we. The same is true of good real-life role models.

All of us are role models in one way or another. We have explored the fundamental factors concerned with this through the book: connection, trust, empathy and exposure. These are the key factors to being a role model. This, however, is true of the Unibomber, ISIS leaders, Kim Kardashian, on the one hand, and Mahatma Gandhi, Mother Theresa and Jameela Jamila on the other. We discussed how the Jokela shooter Pekka Auvinen connected with the Unibomber, built trust with his online friends and felt empathy towards their intentions; and how young radicals connect with ISIS, trust them and avidly watch footage creating high levels of exposure. The less extreme example of Kim Kardashian illustrates someone who connects with young girls sharing things that engage with the teenage and emerging adult brain: looking good, being part of the in-crowd and having social standing. There has to be more to it then surely. While these factors facilitate mirroring, that doesn't make the imitation good. So what does?

One person can make a huge difference

As a society there are generalised ideals over what's good and what's not, which will differ depending on culture and the groups to which we align ourselves. In general terms 'good' relates to things like being considerate towards and helping others, especially those who are less fortunate than ourselves, learning and growing as a person in order to fulfil our potential and contribute to society, and making the world a better place for the next generation. These factors

are not isolated to one religion or philosophy. But we have seen how more and more evidence is emerging from a biological and neurological standpoint that points to the same thing – humans are a prosocial race. It stands to reason that these are the factors we'd expect to be the motivation of a 'good' role model. Added to this we'd expect a 'good' role model to know and accept the responsibility, be open-minded and maintain a level of self-awareness in order to best serve themselves and others.

We discussed both our reacting brain and observing brain earlier in the book. In summary, the reacting brain is fast-thinking and intuitive. It is not conscious and responds quickly to environmental cues. This, as we have seen in the research on generosity, shows us to respond charitably towards other people – unless under threat, at which point survival drivers such as 'fighting' come to the fore. The observing brain relates to our neocortex, the slower-thinking part of our brain where decision-making and planning is carried out. It is the conscious deliberate part of our brain relating to rational thought. It is less driven by impulses and basic drivers such a need to eat, reproduce and protect territory and more by thinking which relates to a higher-level purpose. Research indicates that we are at our peak level of well-being and feel most fulfilled when using our observing brain to contribute to the broader social agenda and to a society where we can all live agreeably.

One may furtively conclude from this that bad role models either have intentions that are clouded by other drivers – for example, Kim Kardashian's drivers to achieve via sex, attraction and money (which relates to status) – or that they themselves have been strongly convinced to make decisions via their observing rational brain that do not align with what nature intended. When we are at rest and

feeling safe our more advanced observing brain allows us to contemplate the world and make sense of it, to search for deeper meaning. However, we can infer that modern-day life and the constant stresses and strains that puts on our brains can override this way of operating, as seen with bad role models.

Indeed, Nelson Mandela, whom I consider a role model and whose intentions were always overridingly positive, namely to end apartheid and oppression, did so initially in a way that was not prosocial. My mother-in-law grew up in apartheid South Africa as a Chinese immigrant speaking English and Afrikaans. She saw Mandela in his early years using violence towards others in pursuit of his aims. As leader of the ANC, he planted homemade bombs in official buildings and in power stations as a way of making the government 'sit up and listen'. Understandably she still views him as a terrorist, in large part because she saw youngsters modelling that behaviour around her. His strong character together with the status he held will have increased not only his prominence but the tendency for people to mirror his behaviour, attitude and beliefs. And youngsters, as we have discussed, are particularly susceptible to imitating violence.

I, however, grew up knowing the Mandela who was unfairly incarcerated and left prison after 27 years to do a great deal of good in the world. I understand where my mother-in-law sits on this despite seeing him as a someone I personally admire. Mandela underwent a profound process of self-reflection in prison: rather than becoming bitter, he became wiser and used his time to grow his knowledge. He was treated harshly but leveraged this as an opportunity to examine his own negative emotions and even resisted feeling anger towards his captors, trying to understand their point of view (cognitive empathy). He

read numerous biographies, studied for his law degree and gained further insights about the world by corresponding with prominent people. He learnt the value of self-control and discipline. Crucially, he also had a curious and inquiring mind, which drove him to seek the observations and lessons that could be wrought from every situation. From Marcus Aurelius to the Egyptian pharaohs, he was fascinated by leadership itself. He absorbed centuries of wisdom, stretching from the ancient world to the modern, that taught him about the pitfalls of power. He fed his own mirror neurons with a mass of information on how to behave effectively as a leader and how to engage mirror thinking in others, not just through his actions but through the stories that he used to communicate.

Once freed, Mandela immediately sought to unite a divided country in which people of different races had been separated by apartheid for generations, but his mode of operating had shifted. Where before his reacting brain driver of violence was dominant, he had begun to use mirror thinking to put himself in the shoes of others and empathise, to see both sides of the narrative and use this knowledge in a helpful and prosocial way. In doing so he had come to understand how those unconscious impulses that once drove him were driving others. By fostering a sense of shared ownership and belonging in relation to territory, Mandela created a sense of collective responsibility.

He was loved by millions around the world and adored by children. But he was self-aware enough to know and point out many times that he was 'no angel'[10] – taking responsibility for his position as a role model and being open about his faults. That essence of being human and fallible is what also allowed him to connect with so many people.

A present-day example of someone who could be considered a good role model is Angelina Jolie. On one hand she fulfils many of the primitive brain drivers women aspire to and men are attracted to, having been listed on numerous 'most beautiful women in the world' lists including those of *Vogue* and *Vanity Fair*. However, she put those factors in second place to being a talented actress, articulate and determined to make a positive impact on society. Playing Lara Croft in *Tomb Raider*, an iconic role with great sex appeal, some feminists may question what she represents. But Jolie rejected the original outfits designed for her, saying that they showed too much of her body and sent a negative message to young girls. This is an example of purposefully drawing away from the primitive sex driver, aiming to focus more on her personality as an athletic, intelligent archaeologist. Lara Croft and *Tomb Raider* were originally developed as a video game with the character intended to counter stereotypical female portrayals. We've seen how the mirror neuron synchronises with stories being told, which creates a very strong and direct connection with people when it comes to role-modelling, especially through the medium of screens.

It was when filming in war-torn Cambodia in 2001 that Jolie saw people suffering and she is quoted as saying 'my eyes started to open'.[11] This led her to explore more about refugee crises across the world, after which she carried out an 18-day tour of Sierra Leone and Tanzania visiting refugee camps. Jolie refers to this as an experience that gave her a greater understanding of the world and a deep desire to give back. That drive came from the empathy for the people she met enabled via the mirror system. Over the following decade Jolie has travelled to 30 countries to carry out field missions and visit refugee camps[12] as goodwill ambassador for the UN High

Commission for Refugees (UNHCR). She has also worked tirelessly on the issues of child immigration, support of vulnerable children and education, human rights and women's rights. Although initially driven from a reaction to seeing people in distress, a prosocial reacting brain driver, she then moved forward to use her observing brain as a way of fulfilling a need to give back in a considered and decisive way. Taking action with meaningful thinking, not just the broader social agenda but the broader *societal* agenda, and most certainly centred on contributing to a society where we can all live agreeably.

However, Jolie is human, fallible and flawed like the rest of us. There has been speculation over whether she has had facial plastic surgery, she once talked openly about how much she liked sadomasochism, and she has been married and divorced three times. Perhaps this illustrates where a line should be drawn between private and public lives. Jolie, like anyone else, has the right to live her life as she chooses. How do we encourage good role models who are prominent to share aspects of themselves that make them human while providing them with the respectful boundaries to live their own lives? And how do we communicate to those following the lives of Jolie or anyone who is a good role model, not to take everything on board? The mirror neuron cannot discern good from bad; that takes judgement, and for younger people that can be hard. From childhood, through adolescence into emerging adulthood in the mid-20s, judgements are predominantly driven by a need to fit in with a certain naivety over what's best. Therefore guidance of what is good and bad, what to mirror and counter-mirror, may be helpful to this population.

Mandela and Jolie are two different examples of role models most of us would consider 'good'. Although Jolie is only in her 40s, Mandela was 72 years old when he came

out of prison. It does take time to know ourselves, to be able to manage our reacting brain and to really get a sense of our purpose, but some manage it despite not having years to gain wisdom. Greta Thunberg rose to prominence at the age of just 15 when she started skipping school and sitting outside the Swedish parliament building with a sign saying 'School strike for climate'. Malala Yousafzai became the youngest Nobel Peace Prize winner as a Pakistani activist for female education. Malala was also 15 when she became known at a global level. Both of these amazing young individuals have suffered abuse in their roles. Malala was unforgettably shot in the head by the Taliban for insisting that girls have the right to an education. Thunberg has been at the receiving end of nasty commentary, most notably from the Presidents of Russia, the US and France.

Starting out on her own, Thunberg was inspired by Rosa Parks, saying: 'I learnt she was an introvert, and I'm also an introvert', and discovering this made her realise that 'one person can make such a huge difference'. She mirrored what had been done before in pursuit of her own aim, but also showed a discerning judgement. Her sit-out every Friday from August 2018 began to inspire other school-age students to do the same in their own communities. A wide body of research shows that people are more likely to model the behaviour of those who are similar to them.[13] Thunberg's protests have created consequences cross-generationally, but modelling of the protests have largely been in populations of children a similar age to her. In addition, as her prominence has risen, so has the prestige associated with her attitudes and behaviour, making it increasingly attractive for other teenagers worldwide to mirror her behaviour, attitude and approach. During 2019 school climate strikes were participated in by tens of thousands of children across various locations throughout

the world. On Friday, 15 March 2019, more than 1.4 million students took part in over 300 cities around the world.[14] Thunberg addressed the UN in September 2019: 'You have stolen my dreams and my childhood with your empty words ... we are in the beginning of a mass extinction and all you can talk about is money and fairytales of economic growth. How dare you?'[15]

Here we see the emotion that she conveys and the imagery in her language, which will evoke the imagination of listeners. Whether intentionally or not, she is using storytelling to allow others to connect with the message she is conveying. As we have seen in previous chapters, this storytelling, particularly its emotive language, will synchronise the brains of listeners to her own via the mirror neuron system.

The British rapper and singer Stormzy was named as one of *Time* magazine's 2019 next-generation leaders. In 2017 Stormzy was awarded Person of the Year by the University of Oxford's African and Caribbean Society. In an interview with the BBC, Renee Kapuku, president of Oxford's ACS, spoke about why Stormzy was chosen. 'He's a great example of how young black people can progress while holding on to their roots ... He's never been afraid to speak out against injustices and has promoted the positivity within our community.'[16]

Stormzy rose to fame at 21; now at 26, he feels the weight that's on his shoulders doesn't necessarily reflect the stage of growth he has reached as a person, and from a psychological perspective that would be true – he is still in emerging adulthood. He wrote on Instagram:

I am deeply flawed and still learning how to be a man and still figuring out how to grow into the person I need to be but within all of that confusion and all the juggling of being a human and

trying to be a superhuman – I have purpose. And my purpose has led me here.[17]

This in itself serves as a constructive message to young people as just one example of where he's gone wrong and openly accepted accountability for it. As a result he is modelling that it's OK to make mistakes when you're young, as long as you aim to be a better person as a result.

All of these examples, young and old, show how good role models emerge and influence through positive prosocial intent. Initially that comes from the reacting brain and our natural tendency to help others. But the planned and continued action together with the search for meaning and desire to contribute positively to society comes from the slower and more advanced observing brain. All of these role models have proactively chosen to remain accepting of their faults and to be answerable for the position of influence that they have. But what happens when this self-awareness and desire for responsibility is not there or is there and then lost. Do they remain good role models then?

Leading by example

Good leaders are an example of role models. The work I do with leaders is predominantly about helping them to understand themselves better, and to appreciate and modify the impact that they are having on other people and the world. While this is to optimise their leadership, it is also optimising role-modelling, and they need to think about how mirroring impacts the culture and values of the organisation. The risks of not remaining self-aware or taking full responsibility for your impact on other people in leadership, celebrity and life more broadly range from limiting your capability to shaping people in a negative way. In day-to-day life we tend to get pulled up if we're being

annoying, not conforming to social norms or upsetting other people, but leaders and celebrities enter a world where these helpful natural boundaries no longer exist. For example, when a leader becomes so out of touch with reality they believe the rules are different for them. Good leaders can turn bad in even the most democratic nations. After all, the leader, the celebrity and the follower are only human.

Why might a leader specifically start off good but turn bad? It often stems from something known as 'hubris syndrome', which describes an exaggerated pride and an overwhelming self-confidence that results directly from power or fame. A former doctor, Lord David Owen was a British politician who became Foreign Secretary in the 1970s. He witnessed the psychological impact of power on leaders first hand. In 2009, Owen partnered with Jonathan Davidson, professor of psychiatry at Duke University in North Carolina, to write a paper outlining the factors involved in hubris syndrome.[18] Davidson argued that hubris syndrome is an acquired personality disorder in contrast to most other personality disorders, which are present throughout adulthood regardless of circumstance. The hubristic leader is 'intoxicated' by power, believing that they are almost omnipotent while becoming increasingly oblivious to subtleties within the circumstances they face. One of the key aspects of good leadership and holding any position of responsibility is being in tune with the more intangible dynamics within the environment. In the case of hubris syndrome this is almost entirely lost. A few of the symptoms that Owen and Davidson outline include the following:

- a disproportionate concern with image and presentation;
- excessive confidence in the their own judgement and contempt for the advice or criticism of others;

- exaggerated self-belief, bordering on a sense of omnipotence, in what they personally can achieve.

The mirror system needs to operate within the context of social norms. In our ancient ancestors' time no one would ever become disconnected enough from a population to be able to escape from the expectations of a group. The natural order of a tribe would mean that a leader displaying hubris would rapidly be removed. However, today where the population size of a city can be several million and technology enables us to be attached to but not in check with 'normality', it's far easier for a leader to get out of touch. Then, because of those same factors, it becomes almost impossible to remove a leader who in ancient times would have been considered 'bad' for the population.

In the paper written by Owen and Davidson they looked for clinical symptoms of a developed hubris syndrome in heads of government in the US and UK over the past 100 years. They found that seven out of 18 US Presidents could be described as having hubristic traits, with one, George W. Bush, actually having full-blown hubris syndrome. Among the 26 UK Prime Ministers, seven had hubristic traits and four developed the actual syndrome, including David Lloyd George, Neville Chamberlain, Margaret Thatcher and Tony Blair. Tony Blair provides perhaps the most intriguing and compelling example in recent British history; Owen and Davidson describe what they believe to be Blair's tipping point into hubris:

Tony Blair's hubris syndrome started to develop over NATO's bombing of Kosovo in 1999, two years after coming into office. At one stage, President Clinton angrily told Blair to 'pull himself together' and halt 'domestic grandstanding'. He was starting to display excessive pride in his own judgements. One of Clinton's aides mocked Blair's 'Churchillian tone' and one of his officials,

who frequently saw Blair said of him, 'Tony is doing too much, he's overdoing it and he's overplaying his hand'. Another of Clinton's staff accused Blair of 'sprinkling too much adrenalin on his cornflakes'.[19]

Although we can assume well-intentioned, many insiders believe that Blair's decision-making around the invasion of Iraq failed to take into account professional advice or even counsel from his own inner circle. Having gone through the Chilcot Report in depth, I co-authored a paper to the UK government with Peter Kinderman, then president of the British Psychological Society and professor of clinical psychology at the University of Liverpool. In this we outlined where he had become disconnected and how to prevent the same mistakes again. A large part of this hinges on being self-aware. Blair had, at this point in time, made an extraordinary transformation from the politician who, in his earlier career, had so often been held up as an example of tact, emotional intelligence and interpersonal flexibility.

The problem, for most ordinary citizens, is that we only find out the full truth of a leader's behaviour much later, preventing our democratic cycles from effecting the change we would in hindsight like to have seen. Rival politicians and media commentators may report worrying traits at the time they begin to manifest – Trump springs to mind as a current example with ample commentary – but even their own agendas tend to compromise the message and the leader's public relations team is often able to spin disclosures. We would indeed hope that their inner circle would raise their concerns, but with their own careers linked so closely to the leader's success this is unlikely to happen.

By contrast, Mandela seemed aware of hubris syndrome and how to avoid it at least in later life. So rather than bringing about his own downfall through narcissism, he

sought to pursue the principles he believed were right for the majority of ordinary people in his country. This was, however, the result of many years of reflection while incarcerated – not something most leaders, prominent people or any of us have experienced. As detailed in his book *Conversations with Myself*, he clearly knew those people:

> *In real life we deal, not with gods, but with ordinary humans like ourselves: men and women who are full of contradictions, who are stable and fickle, strong and weak, famous and infamous, people in whose bloodstream the muckworm battles daily with potent pesticides.*[20]

Mandela sought to maintain self-awareness. The impetus towards such insights came from himself, not anyone else. While he was in prison, there was nobody helping him towards this level of understanding and there was no clearly defined route of learning or education laid out ahead of him. We can all take wisdom from this.

What makes a good role model?

From a psychological perspective one of the key points of commonality that enables the positive role models we've discussed is their unwavering belief in the cause they are representing. There is a clear sense of meaning and purpose behind what they are standing for. Viktor Frankl, a psychiatrist, neurologist and Holocaust survivor, gives a powerful example of how critical purpose is in his book *Man's Search for Meaning*.[21] He relates his encounters at Auschwitz and other concentration camps and how finding a sense of meaning, in even the most cruel of experiences, kept him going and gave him a reason to live. Frankl interviewed hundreds of fellow prisoners, and found that those who survived the mistreatment and were able to fight

back from illness had a deeper sense of purpose. This was what kept them going. Frankl famously argued that within the context of normal life, people who lack meaning fill what he called the 'resultant void' with hedonistic pleasures: power, materialism, obsessions and compulsions – in other words, those things that the reacting brain chases after but gains no lasting satisfaction from.[22] One could argue that these are the things that the Kardashians of the world chase and encourage others to pursue. They are the exact opposite to what we're looking to be modelled by good role models. Having a sense of purpose and striving to go after factors that have an impact beyond ourselves, the things that tick the box of advanced brain thinking, is so powerful that it's been found to have a vast range of positive outcomes. In terms of mental health people are more able to curb their anxiety,[23] symptoms of depression can be reduced[24] and our ability to handle pain can be improved.[25] Physical benefits include protecting against heart disease,[26] diminishing the impacts of Alzheimer's[27] and even lengthening our lives.[28] In addition to all of this, meaning is a major component of well-being and life satisfaction.[29] So, it's not hard to see how this serves as a compass and shield to some of the pressures faced by high-profile figures. It is certainly something that we explore when working as psychologists with senior leaders. But it can be helpful to any role model and indeed any of us to have a sense of purpose in order to help guide us through life, protect our mental well-being and enable us to stand as a more positive citizen in humanity.

The second commonality of the good role models explored is that they take responsibility not only for the impact they have, but also for remaining self-aware. Every person has a unique set of strengths and fallibilities. Everyone has flaws, people who love them and those who will dislike them, and we all do right and wrong. What is

important is realising the responsibility that comes with holding a prominent role in society, whether that's through media fame, politics, business, or being a parent. What does matters is accepting that obligation. This is something that good role models do; for example, Jamil openly recognises that she is not perfect and calls herself a 'feminist in progress'[30]. She acknowledges that some may doubt her intentions given her looks. However, she bravely asserts her position and how she wishes to use that privilege to help others get their voices heard. It's important for all of us not to mix up the perfection portrayed in fictional or retold stories of heroes and heroines with what a good role model really is. No role model is perfect in any domain of life, whether teachers, healthcare providers, parents, relatives, athletes, leaders or movie stars. It's what we do with those flaws and how we live with and portray them that matters, which comes down to self-awareness. That attitude, together with our actions, is what will be mirrored by those who look up to us or simply spend time in our company.

Changing the World

On 5 October 2019, in the Thai National Park of Khao Yai, 13 elephants attempted to cross a river at the top of a 150m waterfall known as Haew Narok or Hell's Falls. It was monsoon season and the current of the swollen river was strong, making it particularly treacherous. As they made their way across a 3-year-old calf slipped and fell over the edge. Later the bodies of 10 more elephants were found downstream. The BBC reported local official Badin Chansrikam as saying, 'Probably, one of the smaller elephants might have slid and the adult ones were trying to rescue them but instead, were swept away by the water.'[1]

The BBC also spoke to Dr Joshua Plotnik, an assistant professor of psychology at Hunter College City University of New York who specialises in elephant behaviour. Plotnik said it's 'certainly reasonable to suspect that when an elephant in a family group is in danger the other elephants might do everything they can to go help.'[2]

A mother and her calf were found struggling on a rock nearby and rescued by the Park. They were the only survivors of the herd. Scientists are concerned for the emotional well-being of the remaining elephants, as they are known to grieve the death of one let alone a whole herd of relatives. Plotnik went on to say 'This is a large-brained, intelligent, social, empathetic animal... I would argue they would suffer the same kind of trauma we would suffer.'[3] The scientists are also deeply concerned about the loss of knowledge; if the herd's matriarchial leader died in the fall it means that they will have lost generations of knowledge

about the jungle they live in. They believe that over the longer term this could impact their behaviour.

What's this got to do with us? Elephants don't impart this knowledge by writing it down or instructing each other on how to behave, but through observational learning, in the same way we pass on social and emotional learning. As humans we have the capability to build on knowledge, particularly scientific and technical knowledge through capturing and sharing it, allowing huge advancements. However, our social and emotional learning is still largely dependent on the people we grow up with, the cultures we live in and the way in which each generation develops their mirror neuron system. In a *New York Times* article, Patricia Greenfield, professor of developmental psychology at UCLA writes 'Mirror neurons provide a powerful biological foundation for the evolution of culture; [we now] see that mirror neurons absorb culture directly, with each generation teaching the next by social sharing, imitation and observation.'[4]

It's believed that elephants also depend on a mirror system, to learn this information in the same way as humans. Are we too at risk of losing our capabilities, not to navigate the jungle but to understand the social world in which we all exist? Is our increasing reliance on technology and science creating the same potential issue for us as a society as falling over the edge of a waterfall? Are we undermining our capability to be human?

Will tech shatter the mirror?

Our incredible ability to pass on our knowledge of technology and science, building on it not just between generations but within, is also destabilising society. That same technology, the increasing reliance on and addiction to screens, is

dramatically undermining the opportunity to develop our mirror systems. This gets in the way of us sharing and evolving our social and emotional understanding of the world both as individuals and as communities. It's preventing our ability to flourish as human beings, which as we've seen throughout this book requires constantly adapting to the myriad of social nuances that rule our lives. Without this natural way of being we are also getting sick – poor mental health being just one illustration of the outcomes.

Today, mental health is one of the main causes of the overall disease burden worldwide[5] and it is on the increase. The cost to the global economy is estimated to be $16 trillion by 2030.[6] NHS Digital released figures in 2017 showing this to be a particular problem in young people. In 2004, 1 in 10 children aged 5–15 had a mental health disorder and by 2017 this had risen to one in nine.[7] In England a staggering one in six people aged 16–64 have a mental health problem. One of the core underlying reasons for this is a diminished opportunity for social and emotional learning, connecting with others and using our mirror system. At the level of inoculation, protecting children through upskilling them with social and emotional skills, it's critical to provide constant exposure to situations and interactions that will help develop their mirror thinking. This will not only build resilience, but also enable them to live optimally as humans in the way nature intended. At the other end of the spectrum role models can be used to help raise awareness of the problems that already exist.

Prominent role models have begun to communicate publicly about their own mental health across a number of campaigns backed by health professionals and experts. In the UK, campaigns such as #EveryMindMatters launched by Public Health England involves a range of role models such as Glenn Close, Gillian Anderson, Jordan Stephens, Davina

McCall and Nadiya Hussain. The next generation of royals, Prince William, Prince Harry, the Duchess of Cambridge and Duchess of Sussex, introduced a campaign called Heads Together, which aims to 'tackle stigma and change the conversation on mental health'.[8] All of these and many other role models globally are being more overt about their own struggles. Harry, for example, explained in an interview with the *Telegraph* that losing his mother had a 'quite serious effect' on his personal and professional life, that he shut down his emotions for 20 years and that left him feeling 'very close to a complete breakdown on numerous occasions'. This, he says, triggered him to seek help through counselling, which has put him in a far better place.[9]

Such a public proclamation from someone in a family that has traditionally modelled the British 'stiff upper lip' makes it feel more acceptable to experience difficulties. It also provides a direct route towards what to do, the actions to mirror in order to seek help. Unfortunately, however, mental health is complex. These movements are undoubtably beginning to shift the way society views issues – a collective mirroring of understanding a different approach – but this alone will not create resolution.

We are at a point in history where we can more effectively treat mental illness than ever before. The concern is that despite people becoming more willing to seek help, we're also seeing the use of prescriptions for mental illness increase at an unprecedented rate. The speed at which this is happening suggests this is not just caused by more people speaking out. Technology, social media, a faster pace of life, more dispersed families, less social support and a range of other factors all contribute to us living in a way that is mismatched with how our brain has evolved to work optimally. As society in the West is becoming ever more individualistic in outlook, the neuroscientific knowledge we are accumulating emphasises how highly dependent we are on other people. As Iacoboni

says, 'Mirror neurons … show that we are not alone, but are biologically wired and evolutionarily designed to be deeply interconnected with one another.'[10]

Knowing this, we can see that removing opportunities for us to connect is like amputating a limb or starving a child of the nutrients they need to remain healthy and grow. We are in effect being robbed of the chance to be human.

The communication trap

Our complex digital world also exacerbates another problem relating to the mental health epidemic by giving well-meaning novices a voice. In the time of our ancient ancestors a tribe's members all had different experts who accumulated knowledge and then shared it beneficially. For example, the medicine man or woman helped when people were sick; the best hunter tracked down the most prized meat; the canoe carver built the most effective boat. This in one way or another remained true until very recently, when technology opened our world up to literally millions of people we don't know. Now we are bombarded with information and, beyond traditional fields like medicine, we no longer know who to go to for advice. Our natural mechanisms fail. Looking to see where most tribe members go to for help with a particular problem can translate to who has the most followers on social media. The logic does not, however, confer expertise. Who knows what they are talking about and who doesn't? There are, for example, more than 13 million posts about mental health on Instagram, many with comments like the following:

- 'Taking a nap in place of eating a meal or snack is avoidance.' (User with 17,600 followers)
- 'You will continue to suffer if you have an emotional reaction to everything that is said to

you. True power is sitting back and observing everything with logic; true power is restraint.' (User with 36,000 followers)

Both of these statements are incredibly unhelpful, however well-meaning. They are not grounded in any psychology and could lead thousands of followers down a mental health rabbit hole. Psychology is particularly problematic because everyone 'thinks' they know how it works and until recently people would not have sought advice from a psychologist because of the stigma attached. However, our minds and behaviour are complex and made even more so as a result of the mismatch between our brain and the world we live in.

A fine line exists for mental health and it is one I feel strongly about. While it's incredibly helpful for publicly prominent role models to share their experiences and to say what has helped them, it takes an expert to be able to offer advice. Used in the right way, like the Heads Together and #EveryMindMatters campaigns, role models for mental health can have a massively positive impact. They serve to shake up societies' long-held views, such as a stance that 'boys shouldn't cry'. We are, however, arguably at a point where there also needs to be more action. This is something that can only be responsibly role-modelled with advice from professionals both in terms of treatment and also inoculating against the root cause.

How do we inoculate and limit the incidences that arise in the first place? To do this we need to use mirroring more effectively throughout life and realise that learning how to be human is not a given. Think back to the case of the feral children who, without the opportunity to mirror talking, walking and eating as a human, simply couldn't do it. However much feral children are then taught fundamental life skills, they will always be a step behind and most probably

always left wanting in comparison with the children who have been able to mirror these things from birth. In the same way, without sufficient exposure to learning social and emotional skills, we limit our capacity to function at our best – to flourish and thrive. Academics call this ability to pass on this type of learning 'cumulative cultural evolution'. This has enabled us to create a world that no one could generate on their own in one lifetime. Knowledge is ratcheted up one generation after another, which is evident in the incredible advances all around us. But what happens if we limit the learning where the softer sides of culture are concerned, elements relating to our behaviour and our minds? The way in which we grow, behave, think, understand the intentions of others and connect with those around us all comes through mirroring people's actions and beliefs on to our own brain. If we're dependent on screens, too busy to really listen, desperate to achieve the next target, pushing our kids in academic pursuits and focused primarily on ourselves, can that happen optimally?

An analogy of how cumulative cultural evolution operates was given by Alex Mesoudi, a lecturer in psychology at Queen Mary University of London in 2018. He uses the example of learning to read and write, a capability which in itself enables us to increase our intelligence. Once we can read and write we can learn more and communicate that learning, which enables further evolution of our individual and collective capabilities.[11] The same is true of how we learn to use and develop the mirror system. For example, when starting to talk we learn a few words and are then are able to ask questions in order to learn more. In interpreting someone else's opinion, we are then able to ask if that is what they are thinking and get feedback, which adapts our knowledge. We can imagine, tell stories, empathise, understand our own emotions and decipher how to navigate our social world. But if we're not getting enough input, we

simply cannot optimally or even sufficiently develop these capabilities, thus limiting our spiritual, moral, social and cultural capability.

Unfortunately, even teaching emotional well-being to children can be somewhat counter-productive. Tony Eaude, who works as an independent research consultant with a particular interest in young children's spiritual, moral, social and cultural development, suggests that when happiness and emotional well-being are considered explicit ends in themselves, they tend to promote individualisation, introspection and a sense of vulnerability. As a result, well-meaning interventions do not have the intended outcome. The basic concepts of well-being can result in children being discouraged from engaging with the complexity and ambiguity of everyday emotional responses, limiting learning. The skills required to enable a child or adult to become resilient originate in real-life interactions. They need to be learnt in the way nature intended. When it comes to children, Eaude stresses the importance of adults being emotionally attuned to them in order to help build up the attributes associated with good mental health or simply positive functioning as a human. For example, understanding how another person experiences emotion and responding accordingly, which of course is dependent on the mirror system. A confident child may be more able to experiment and take risks whereas a more anxious child may need more support and reassurance. To be able to do this requires us recognising and embracing both our independence and interdependence.[12] It also reflects the continual need to rebalance and readjust to our world, but most importantly to other people. It's what allows our mirror system to thrive. We need each other, and we need to continually interact at a meaningful and nuanced level both to flourish as individuals and to progress culture.

Seeking to do good within an unnatural system (the world we live in) without guidance from research on how and why it works can backfire in other ways too. Angelina Jolie is someone with prosocial intentions and uses her prominence as a force for good. In May 2013 Jolie made a very brave and honest move to speak publicly about her decision to have a preventative mastectomy, writing an op-ed piece for the *New York Times*. In the article Jolie explained that her mother had died of cancer and that her own children were afraid of losing her in the same way. She was tested for the BRCA1 gene, revealing that she had an 87 per cent risk of developing breast cancer and a 50 per cent risk of developing ovarian cancer. Her response was to have a double mastectomy and to go public about it in order for other women to benefit from her experience.[13] One would imagine this role-modelled incredibly helpful behaviour and intention.

Indeed, a study carried out by the *British Medical Journal* published in December of the same year, revealed that tests for the breast cancer BRCA gene increased by a dramatic 64 per cent following the piece. The cost to the US healthcare system was estimated to be at least $13.5 million in the two weeks after Jolie's op-ed was published. The concern was that there was no related uptick in mastectomy rates, which suggests the tests did not lead to increased breast cancer diagnoses.[14] Anupam Jena, professor of healthcare policy at Harvard Medical School, said: 'From a physician's perspective, a celebrity announcement is great when we are worried about underutilisation of a preventive test or screening, because it gets more patients into the office ... But when it comes to tests that may be overutilised, a celebrity testimonial could exacerbate that problem.'[15]

This is not Jolie's fault: she was trying to help but one can only assume that she wasn't being given the right guidance in her quest. She needed guidance from experts in a range of

areas, for example epidemiologists, healthcare professionals, psychologists and the media. Jolie took note of the results and published a follow-up piece in 2015, explaining that testing and treatment should be carried out on a case-by-case basis. Celebrities are an example of role models who can have a huge societal impact, but one that needs to be carefully planned in order to have the intended impact.

Beyond individuals, governments have occasionally latched on to the potential impact of role models and used them to approach the resolution of issues. Unfortunately, when this isn't done with proper consideration of the evidence and the complexity of factors involved, it can also go wrong. The UK government has implemented a number of mentoring schemes as a solution to social issues in underprivileged settings. Predominantly these interventions have targeted 'at-risk' youths with the aim of curbing behavioural problems that can become more serious issues later in life. Helen Roberts, professor of child health research at University College London, looked at what happens when these schemes are implemented without a proper understanding of the research and evidence. Roberts and her team followed one programme for three years and found that youths who had previously been arrested for minor offences before being mentored were even more likely to be arrested following the scheme than those who had not been mentored.[16] The issue is that many of these schemes are introduced because they have good face validity – on the surface they look like a great option, but they are implemented without a clear understanding of the mechanisms involved in making them work. The most commonly cited reason for failure is that the relationship between mentor and mentee breaks down. As discussed throughout this book, trust is essential to mentoring relationships and even more so for at-risk children. A break in trust can result in young people feeling even more

hopeless, lonely and rejected than they did to start with. This illustrates how mirroring is part of a far more complex system, especially in our advanced world. If role-modelling is forced without consideration of the evidence or naturalistic processes it can go badly wrong.

The power of community

In spite of examples where the intended results have not been produced, there are also instances where role-modelling has had a measurably positive impact on society despite not being the main objective. For example, in India in April 1993 the government passed a constitutional amendment that required all village councils, traditionally populated by higher-caste men, to hold regular elections open to all. The other hugely contentious mandate was that one-third of the seats had to be reserved for women. The project was dubbed by the *New York Times* an 'epic social experiment'[17] and hailed by the UN as 'one of the best innovations in grassroots democracy in the world'.[18] This directive would impact a population of more than 800 million people.[19] Before the legislation was passed, only 5 per cent of local leadership roles were carried out by women, but by the year 2000 this had increased to more than 40 per cent.[20]

The direct intention of this project was to increase female representation in political forums where women had been excluded from village politics for centuries. However, in 2012, development economist Lori Beaman set about exploring the unintended by-product of this intervention. Beaman was interested in whether the changes in gender balance had positively shaped parents' and children's beliefs about what women could achieve regarding their education and careers. This, they proposed, could have happened through a direct role-model effect. But could this mandate shift the age-old belief expressed

by one villager? 'Women should be confined to the household and men should be village heads ... The work of a woman is to cook the food and clean the clothes.'[21]

Beaman and her colleagues collected data from a rural district located about 200km from Kolkata, which included 8,453 girls aged 11–15 from 495 villages. Astonishingly, they found that the gender gap in educational attainment was completely erased. Controlling for other factors, Beaman was able to show that women in leadership positions and 'their presence as positive role models for the younger generation' influenced the ambitions of girls themselves and their parents' aspirations for them.[22]

Sudha Pillai, joint secretary in India's Ministry of Rural Development, said: 'It has given something to people who were absolute nobodies and had no way of making it on their own.'[23]

The presence of positive role models has provided opportunities for modelling not only of behaviour, but also attitudes. Before these quotas existed, neither parents nor children had seen women playing a role in leadership. How could they imagine what that looked like? How could a girl imagine themselves reaching that position or parents believe it was a possibility? Once that mirror was made available it had an enormously positive impact on the communities involved. But why did this instance of role-modelling work in such a positive way, when others previously mentioned didn't always have the desired effect?

The simplest reason is that this took place within an existing community that enabled processes of learning to take place effortlessly. Relationships are already in place, connection and trust are a given, groups already exist and there is a regular level of exposure. It works with the way our brain evolved to mirror.

That's not to say that deliberate role-modelling can't or won't work, but it reminds us of the importance of using

research as soon as something steps outside the confines of the naturally formed community. Clearly, mentoring schemes can work, but if they are interventions that come from outside the community they need to be guided by experts. The story of an immensely successful mentoring programme started way back at the turn of the last century.

Ernest Kent Coulter was born in Columbus, Ohio in 1871, the son of a physician. He graduated from Ohio State University and in 1893 became a journalist for a local paper,[24] going on to become assistant city editor for the *New York Evening Sun*. As a reporter in New York, Coulter became increasingly concerned by the poverty, crime, absent parents and inadequate schooling he saw children experiencing. He wanted to do something that would allow him to help the poor and began to pursue a career in law. But this wasn't enough to settle his discomfort, and in 1904 he spoke at a local church meeting with the aim of creating action:

> *There is only one possible way to serve that youngster and that is to have some earnest, true man volunteer to be his big brother, to look after him, help him do right; make the little chap feel that there is at least one human being in this great city who takes a personal interest in him, who cares whether he lives or dies. I call for a volunteer.*[25]

Coulter had intuitively understood the mirror system, the need for these children to connect with and learn from people living a better life. Forty members of the club volunteered to become mentors. Coulter's scheme, which he named 'Big Brothers', not only gained momentum, but due to his utter commitment as a lifelong advocate continues to this day.[26]

Now called Big Brothers Big Sisters of America (BBBS), it is the longest running and largest of its type in the world. Unlike many worthy schemes, it has evidence in support of what it does, how it operates and the outcomes of its efforts.

Today BBBS matches young people from low-income backgrounds with adult volunteers who are typically between 20 and 34 years of age and have a college degree. The scheme begins through volunteer reachouts from the young person's parent or guardian. The potential role models are then screened by a caseworker, which includes interviewing to ensure that they are likely to form a positive relationship with their mentee, home visits and criminal background and reference checks to ensure that they are not a safety risk.

Once matched, the mentor and youth typically meet two to four times per month for at least a year and engage in different activities depending on the mentee's preferences (for example, studying, cooking, playing sports). The typical meeting lasts 3–4 hours. For the first year, caseworkers maintain monthly contact with the mentor as well as the youth and his or her parent, to offer support and help resolve any problems in the relationship. Mentors are encouraged to form a supportive friendship with the youths, as opposed to modifying the youth's behaviour or character.[27] There are numerous moving stories of the outcomes.

For example, 11-year-old Terrell was, according to his aunt, in a 'really dark place' and 'missing something' from his life.[28] He was signed up to the scheme and matched with Terence, who had himself been mentored when he was younger. Terrell lived with his aunt because both of his parents were in prison. His little brother had died aged three and he was separated from his older brother and younger sister. Unsurprisingly, he had deep issues with trust and anger, responding quickly and aggressively to situations he found difficult. Terrell's aunt and uncle wanted to help, but also had reservations about the scheme. Given what Terrell had been through, the last thing they wanted, in his aunt's words, was 'to introduce him to someone new who could potentially not hang around'. Terrell was also reticent, talking about how he

felt at the time: 'With my background, with what I've been through in my life, I didn't trust people a lot.'

But Terence was committed and developed the connection needed to help Terrell. He never pushed him to talk about things he didn't want to, but remained consistent, showing him that he wasn't going anywhere. A year into their relationship Terence recalls how Terrell first began to open up. They drove past a cemetery and Terrell said 'my brother's over there, he's buried over there'.

His aunt recalls: 'Terence stepped right in and before I knew it, I could see the light start to glow in Terrell again.' Terrell says that being able to open up to Terence and having him as a role model has changed his life. Terrell doesn't skip class when his friends do. He knows what he wants out of life and is focused on getting there. 'My future plans are to go to college, join the National Guard, be a dentist,' Terrell says. He also wants to be 'a Big Brother like Terence and pass it on'.[29] Having someone to model provided Terrell with a guide to how he could be and how things could turn out learning from someone very similar to himself. This was someone who could provide the opportunity for direct social and emotional learning, typically less available in a busy household.

It's also very likely that the empathy Terence offered served to buffer the negative effects of Terrell's environment. We've seen the research showing the mitigating impact that empathy can have on similar situations. A mentor who is able to use their own mirror system for empathic understanding will not only mitigate issues, but help to develop that capability in children. While Terrell may not be privy to the neurological mechanisms, he's clear about the pragmatic outcomes, saying: 'I promise you, without this programme, getting matched with Terence and my uncle getting involved, I'd be somewhere following the wrong people in the wrong crowd.'

In-depth analysis of the impacts of the BBBS scheme has
been carried out using a randomised controlled trial. The
1,138 young people chosen for the research was made up of
56 per cent minorities, with 43 per cent living in
underprivileged households. The effects of the scheme were
measured 18 months after youths were matched with a mentor.
The findings were unequivocally positive, indicating:[30]

- youths were 46 per cent less likely to start using
  illegal drugs, 27 per cent less likely to begin
  drinking alcohol and displayed 32 per cent lower
  incidence of hitting someone;
- they were significantly less likely to skip school;
- a marginally significant, positive impact on grade
  point average and more confidence of performance
  in schoolwork;
- an improved level of trust and better relationships
  with parents, families and peers.

Additional protective factors resulting from the
relationships included:

- exposure to cultural norms that oppose antisocial
  behaviour and substance use;
- promotion of healthy beliefs;
- goal-setting and a positive orientation towards the
  future;
- more positive attitude to school and increased
  confidence in ability;
- improved relationships with prosocial peers;
- improved communication, interpersonal, decision-
  making, critical thinking, coping and self-
  management skills.

This scheme shows the immensely positive impacts that
role-modelling can have in society if done 'right'.

Unfortunately, most schemes, because they are not based on evidence and don't take account of 'best practices', often fail to work.[31] Role models need to be given support in doing this, especially when it takes the form of an 'intervention', rather than a naturally occurring relationship. However, when it works, the outcome is profound, not just helping to minimise negative social outcomes, but also providing a route by which individuals are able to fulfil their potential. The long-term benefits of this to both the youngster and society are of immeasurable value.

Role models have the potential to create a positive impact across a range of minorities, especially during adolescence. Not being able to see or relate to anyone who feels similar can leave teenagers feeling exceptionally vulnerable, underconfident and uncertain of life in general. Take, for example, the LGBTQ youth population, for whom a lack of role models has been linked to an increase in health and behavioural risks[32] such as drinking, self-harm and even suicide. By contrast, having a role model helps positive adolescent development, providing a means by which to build emotional resilience, a sense of self-worth and confidence in the future.[33]

Jason Bird, assistant professor in the department of social work at Rutgers University in New Jersey, explored the impact of role models on health outcomes for LGBTQ youth. Bird found that a majority of the participants reported having inaccessible role models. In the US, LGBTQ individuals make up approximately 3.5 per cent to 8.2 per cent of the population, meaning that from a pragmatic perspective it's difficult to find a role model 'like me' to engage with. In the cases where a youngster finds an aspirational role-model, this inaccessibility has been shown to actually increase psychological distress. This is because, as an LGBTQ youth, there is a high need for advice, comfort and a safe space to share thoughts and feelings, for

which they need an interactive relationship. Being able to see but not connect with someone can make them feel even more isolated and lonely.

A proposed resolution to this is making use of the very technology that is hindering us elsewhere. In 2014 a study carried out at the University of Toronto looked specifically at the impacts of identity formation in the LGBTQ community. The research showed that when web-based technology provided direct contact with role models who were not otherwise accessible, the impact was significant and hugely positive. It enabled the youths to explore and become comfortable with their identity, provided them with the support and advice they needed and offered a place for them to share their feelings before coming out offline.[34] This is a fantastic example of technology helping rather than hindering empathic connection and opportunities for role-modelling and possibly something that could be replicated in other communities.

Sport is an incredibly powerful way to engage populations and create positive societal change. It wasn't that long ago when I was growing up, but I don't remember any female athletes from my childhood years. The representation of women in sport is thankfully changing. Kelly Holmes, Erin Cuthbert and Marlie Packer are all testament to that. During the recent Women's (football) World Cup, which was covered extensively on British television, the BBC reported a 'record-breaking' 6.9 million viewers. But this still pales in comparison to the 26.5 million watching the 2018 England knockout in the men's football.[35] And this is only one example, as one scholar says: 'The under-representation and marginalisation of females across a range of sports media has been well documented.'[36]

The proportion of girls who participate in physical activity is considerably smaller than boys.[37] This may be for a number of complex reasons, but one definite impact is the

lack of female role models in sport, in spite of the women we've cited. Studies carried out in Australia, the US, Canada and Britain have all found that a lack of positive role models acts as a critical barrier to female participation in sport.[38] On the flip side, research in Australia has also shown that exposure to female role models encourages adolescent participation in physical activity and sports programmes.[39]

A groundbreaking study specifically looking into this phenomenon was led by Dr Janet Young, an exercise and sport psychologist at the College of Sport and Exercise Science at Victoria University in Australia. Young and her colleagues looked at 730 girls in school years 7 (age 11–12) and 11 (age 15–16), asking them whether they had a role model. This was not limited to sport and so could include anyone. They were also asked what that role model's gender, age, type and sporting background was. The physical activity of the participants themselves was also recorded. These girls were part of the study for three years. Their results showed that the majority of the girls in the study said they had a role model who was female, played sport and was under 50 years of age. The most frequently mentioned were family members, friends or sports celebrities. Young suggests that this also reflects Australian culture where sports personalities are all highly prominent. Sport is arguably a lot more prevalent there than in other countries, and with a higher representation of women in sport it makes it easier for these girls to find a role model to emulate.

Crucially, the girls with role models who played sport were more physically active themselves than the girls who had a role model who did not play sport. Young's study not only highlights the relationship between female sports celebrities and physical activity, but also the role that family members and peers can play in levels of physical activity. This point is really significant and repeated across all sorts of studies – if parents are physically active their children are

more likely to be so. If you are a role model of any sort your levels of physical activity will influence those of the people around you, especially youngsters.

Other populations, notably indigenous women in Australia, show 'startlingly low' participation in physical activity compared with the rest of the population. Only 23.3 per cent of indigenous women participate in sport or physical activity, compared with 66.7 per cent for non-indigenous Australian women. Young women in this population described the lack of indigenous women athletes in the media to serve as role models as one major missing factor.[40] The same issue has been found in African countries. One study looking specifically at the potential of 'sporting role models' to promote empowerment emphasising gender issues carried out analysis of research from Malawi, Zambia and South Africa. The findings were that the lack of women in sport came down to one common denominator – a lack of female sporting role models.[41]

While things are becoming marginally better within mainstream sport, minorities are clearly lacking representation; whether that's across gender, race or sexuality, it's critical to have sports professionals who are visible. The reality, in spite of what basketball player Charles Barkley said, is that sports players are role models. Children will look up to and emulate sports stars whatever their behaviour. When that is good, and when the athlete represents a minority group, it provides a window to another world of possibility that may not otherwise exist. Role models enhance dreams and aspirations, enable confidence and provide a route by which others can follow in the footsteps of those who have gone before them. But those who would willingly follow them need to be able to see those who are like them and to really believe in their path.

Aspirational role models in sport are important for both boys and girls of any background. Children look up to and

mirror their sporting role models, emulating their behaviours, values and approach to life. Athletes are rewarded for hard work, determination and the resilience they show in facing obstacles – and children see this. To get to the top they have to have a growth mindset in all they do, facing failure, disappointment, and injury and picking themselves up to try again. They are not simply there because of their looks or because they have made endless videos on YouTube. Athletes represent so many positives that we can only be pleased about children emulating. Although this mirroring is from a far greater distance than any we've spoken about so far, it has been shown to have a massive influence on development, gender identity and finding a place within the world. This is becoming increasingly important in a world where we have less and less interaction with traditionally significant role models (grandparents, aunts, uncles) due to the way society is evolving. Those role models that children see in the media are not only proving ever more prominent in a child's development, but also increasingly significant. Gertrud Pfister, professor of sport sociology at the University of Copenhagen, says:

> [sporting] role models and idols stimulate individuals to identify and to imitate patterns of interpretation and behaviour. Therefore, they play a vital role particularly in childhood and adolescence: they provide children with ways of finding their way in their environment and in society. There is a consensus that role models and idols have great significance in youth culture in that they contribute to the image, strengthen identification with the 'group' and make possible a demarcation between the 'in-group' and those outside it.[42]

The business of changing minds

Moving away from macro-level impacts towards what still involves huge swathes of minority populations, are the

organisations that act as employers. Both big and small, these environments are far more regulated when it comes to quotas and expectations than society more broadly. Yet the same issues still exist. Minorities in business, girls in STEM (science, technology, engineering and mathematics subjects), women in leadership, people with disabilities – they all lack representation despite an acknowledgement of the economic and decision-making impacts. There is public recognition of the need to balance the numbers in all of these areas, nonetheless the same issues still exist. To break the cycle minorities need to be overtly modelled, making their presence and inclusion feel 'normal' both to the majority and those who are under-represented. To mirror, people need to be able to see what it looks like and feel able to emulate the behaviours. If you are a black woman with talent and aspirations, but you see no other black women who are or have been leaders in your industry, it's far harder to mirror that behaviour. You not only have to be able to imagine it yourself, but also convince others that it's possible and break down doors along the way – not an easy task.

Trailblazers who have done this tend to have extremely strong personalities, making sacrifices that others aren't willing to make. The first woman who has succeeded in a particular male-dominated culture may have put so much time and energy towards getting to where she has that she's never had children. A younger woman might think: 'I don't want to mirror her; I don't want to make that sacrifice.' We do, after all, tend to see things in holistic terms, rather than dissecting the parts that are relevant to us. So how do we ensure that the first trailblazer leads to real change rather than simply being an anomaly? To tip the balance, a certain volume of people breaking through is needed who can collectively mirror and offer different role models for women with a range of personalities and preferences. As

more women have become successful business leaders – including women of varied ethnicity and from diverse backgrounds – we have started to see it become a little easier for other women to realise the route through for themselves. Over time this should create more of a virtuous circle. The same is true for any minority: a single role model often isn't enough. More role models are needed to make it feel more normal to everyone, and makes mirroring far more accessible and possible. The phrase 'if she can't see it, she can't be it' is being used in a range of campaigns seeking to create diversity and equality (although obviously it's not always 'she'). Those behind the campaigns may not know about the mirror neuron, but they are clearly aware that without someone to learn from the cycle will never get broken.

However, creating this volume is not easy, nor is it something that happens overnight – it takes considerable effort. One person who has taken on that challenge and in doing so has acted as a role model herself is Brenda Trenowden CBE. From 2016 to January 2020 Brenda chaired the 30% Club, which was set up with the aim of achieving a minimum of 30% female representation on FTSE100 boards. In this role she has encouraged, persuaded, convinced and corralled CEOs globally to understand and support the need for diversity. The campaign hit a milestone in September 2019, when the number of female directors on the boards of the UK's 100 largest listed companies hit 30.42 per cent.[43] This shift creates a perpetually positive cycle – the more that women and minorities are seen, the more they can be imitated. Brenda herself is one of these role models to me and many others. She is also a friend and someone who I'm very lucky to be able to call my mentor.

The impact of diverse role models reaches far beyond the executive board room. Research from Microsoft, for example, shows that the number of girls interested in STEM

decreases as they move through education. Despite entering school with similar levels of ability in maths to boys, there is a trend for them to lose interest. The overall result is that women are under-represented in STEM fields, especially in areas such as engineering and computer science,[44] which are in huge demand globally. The World Economic Forum explains how rapid advances in artificial intelligence, along with robotics and other emerging technologies, means that the nature of jobs is changing rapidly. The future job market is likely to become more clearly split between non computer-based skills and technical.[45] The prediction is that at least 133 million new roles will be generated globally as a result of the new division of labour between humans, machines and algorithms, requiring women to make up a significant proportion of the workforce. However, research has shown that as societies become more wealthy and the gender gap closes, women will be even less likely to gain degrees in STEM subjects.[46] This is being called the 'gender-equality paradox'.[47] So how do we combat this issue?

Microsoft's research, spanning 12 European countries and including nearly 12,000 females aged 11–30, showed that the number of girls and young women interested in STEM across Europe, on average, almost doubles when they have a role model to inspire them.[48] The results also revealed that having a role model for a particular subject area, such as chemistry, shows positive uplift in all STEM subjects. Role models give girls and women greater confidence in their ability to achieve within STEM, more passion for the subjects and more interest in pursuing careers in technical fields. They are able to more easily see themselves via their mirror system in those roles if they can see women who are already there.

Role-modelling can be leveraged in society to combat other social issues, such as bullying. In the context of schools

this conjures up an image of a thug towering over a helpless younger boy with a posse of his friends in tow. Unfortunately, bullying is also prevalent in the workplace, where cultural norms – themselves perpetuated by the mirror neuron – often serve to replicate and support it more than in the playground. It is also becoming a worryingly common phenomena online, not only for youngsters but adults, too. Social psychologist, Harvard lecturer and author Amy Cuddy has experienced this herself, having been accused of hyping her research findings. The claims are unfounded, yet the obsessiveness with which they have been made have been disproportionate and unnerving. At its worst she has even received death threats. To say this is scary is an understatement, especially given that these are supposedly rational, world leading experts in the area of psychology. If anyone should know better when it comes to behaviour then surely it should be them. Cuddy has bravely stood up to those bullies and to bullying more broadly. In fact, it's the subject of her second book *Bullies, Bystanders and Bravehearts*. Amy agrees that role models are critical to disrupting the power of the bullies. By stepping in rather than playing what is known as the 'bystander' role, a role model displays an alternative behavioural norm to other onlookers, whether online or off. By being explicit about what they are doing, a role model's actions become immensely powerful, creating a template for others to replicate. This is yet another example of where role models can have a positive impact at a micro level through to a macro level, especially where the internet is concerned.[49]

Society needs its own inoculation programme

Paying attention to the astounding capabilities of the mirror system is critical in so many ways. If we allow ourselves to

be swept along by our fast-paced technical world, neglecting our social and emotional learning of the world, we risk, like the elephants, falling over the metaphorical waterfall and losing our capability to be human. While technology and science can be easily shared between and within generations through written material and instruction, the same is not true for most aspects of culture: the nuances of human behaviour, emotional wisdom, language, storytelling, or creativity, for example. We also risk living more and more in isolation from others, mirroring only piecemeal rather than living the shared experiences of life that the mirror system enables. The predicted cost of a lack of social-emotional learning enabled by the mirror system is thought to be £17bn in the UK alone.

We can already see how this is impacting society, with issues such as mental health becoming ever more prevalent. The work of role models to raise awareness of mental health is fantastic, but it doesn't prevent the problem. We need inoculation, not just cure. The complexity of our world – access to millions of people rather than 150, which is believed to be the maximum number of people our brain evolved to cope with – our dependence on technology and the 'always on' lifestyle all serve to interfere with natural role-modelling and social and emotional learning. More screen time is time away from cultivating our mirror system, more fragmented communities are depriving us of the opportunity to connect and develop our emotional wisdom, which protects our mental health. People are struggling for a sense of belonging, which drives us towards technology, exacerbating the issue and tipping extreme, unsocial thoughts towards online groups that encourage aggression. By recognising this and looking for opportunities to use evidence to help bypass the issues of complexity and technology we can reignite learning how to be human, to

connect, to be prosocial in a way that will enhance our lives as individuals and build our capability as a human race. We need to rebuild communities, and encourage and enable prosocial behaviours to create a positive cycle of mirroring. This will only become more critical as the use of AI within workplaces and society more broadly increases. As this occurs we will need our ability to be human more than ever, our innate potential to outshine, not be outshone, by the advancements in science and technology.

Beyond retaining it as a natural way of learning how to be human we've seen that deliberately leveraging role-modelling, with consideration of evidence when done at scale, can have dramatically positive effects. To make better use of this mechanism we need to implement thoughtful, considered and specific interventions as well as enhancing naturalistic opportunities for mirroring. Where this has been done we can see that it works. At a local level, in systems and communities that already exist, there are ways in which governments can help to make the societal outcomes far more impactful. For example, trainee teachers need to be provided with role models and be taught the mechanisms underlying social and emotional learning. They also need to have the freedom to teach in a way that enables them to share how to be human, not just the content of the syllabus. If they are not allowed to fulfil their own potential, how can they pass on the opportunity to their pupils?

It would be immensely powerful for healthcare providers to be given training in different types of empathy, with strong and positive role models provided to them who themselves are supported in their behaviour. People across different professions, sports coaches, managers, leaders, would benefit hugely from understanding the fundamental power of mirroring so that it can be used to have a positive impact. Within the community this knowledge would

help parents, relatives and friends to optimise the role they play in influencing others and positively shaping their brains. We have the mirror system for a reason – we evolved as highly social beings. Yet we are taking our opportunities to be human away. We will never be perfect, but with knowledge we can at least understand how our beliefs, behaviours and attitudes are mirrored in the brain of others, especially those closest to us.

Sports stars, movie stars, musicians, celebrities, politicians and all those in prominent public positions would all benefit from learning about mirroring and the responsibility they have. In a utopian world they would all have executive coaches to support them, honing their good points, mitigating their faults and presenting their values in a way that positively influences thousands of followers. While we intuitively 'feel' that these people should be good role models, which is massively evident in press coverage of public figures, they too are human. They need help, as anyone would, to become more self-aware and to understand their impact.

The outcome for anyone who recognises their position as a role model is hugely positive. It's actually about being human and sharing that capability with others, which is incredibly rewarding. It also provides people with the opportunity to grow and fulfil their own potential, to understand themselves better and ultimately to be happy, more successful and more mentally and physically healthy, while also influencing others positively. This creates a positive cycle. If you have it and you share it, it empowers others to have it and share it themselves.

PART FOUR

YOUR GUIDE TO HARNESSING THE POWER OF MIRROR THINKING

The Mirror You Hold

In July 2011 Amani Simpson was handing out flyers for an upcoming music event outside a nightclub in Enfield, London, where he'd grown up. One of Amani's friends began disagreeing with a group of youths about stolen goods, and as the argument escalated Amani stepped in to protect his friend. The 20-strong gang set upon Amani, slashing his puffa jacket with knives, slicing into shreds of material through his coat and doing the same to his flesh. He was stabbed deeply seven times. Lying in the ambulance, he wondered whether he would ever see his family again. It was at that point he made a promise to both God and himself that if he survived, he would help other young people to stop them from getting mixed up in violence and crime.[1]

Amani made a short film highlighting what was going through his head during the attack. It showed how he desperately searched for meaning and questioned his faith in God. It is now his life's mission to share the experience with schoolchildren. In an interview with the *Guardian* newspaper he said:

> I believe in positive role models, the need for more BAME [black and minority ethnic] leaders. In the school I went to I wasn't represented or understood. You need someone who is relatable to. That's why I like going into schools and colleges, empowering kids on the ground, because I can tell them I've been in your shoes, I know what it feels like to be you.[2]

Role-modelling isn't just reserved for those who have suffered, who stand up to stereotypes, or who are leaders in the traditional sense of the word. We are all role models and we can all learn to be better. This may feel daunting, odd, or something that's not for you. Even the senior leaders I work with often struggle to see themselves as role models, despite knowing it's expected of them. The same is true whatever we do in life. We are all role models, yet can all struggle to see ourselves as such. One of the role models on the Big Brothers Big Sisters scheme, Cynric, explains how he was initially reticent to sign up because he thought it was for people who had it all figured out. 'I always felt like being a mentor was a thing I should do as a man and as someone who cared about their community,' he says. 'But for a long time I didn't think I was the right guy.' Eventually he realised that it was the mistakes he'd made in life and the experiences he'd had that would make him a better role model. He has now been mentoring the same boy for seven years, who says 'He [Cynric] helped me get through those tough times, and now I'm confident in myself.'[3] This is a message that we'd surely all love to hear.

Why be a role model?

Being a role model infers a great deal of benefit. One role-modelling study, aimed at facilitating empowerment and tackling gender issues within Malawi, Zambia and South Africa, showed how it isn't just the modelee who benefits but that the 'reciprocity of empowerment'[4] improved the well-being of role models themselves. Giving and sharing with others is part of what makes us human and has huge psychological and physiological benefits.

Prosocial behaviour, which includes role-modelling, is becoming more widely recognised as a vehicle for improved mental health and well-being across society. Significant

evidence shows that focusing on other people[5] rather than ourselves consistently makes us happier. Katherine Nelson, an American developmental psychologist, published research in the journal *Emotion* that contrasted the mood and well-being boosting effects of prosocial behaviour with self-orientated behaviour over a six-week period. The 2015 study, which included 472 people, found that prosocial behaviour in the test group led to significantly bigger increases in 'psychological flourishing' than the self-focused group. Flourishing in this context means positive emotional well-being, high life satisfaction, good relationships with others, being socially accepted and having a sense of purpose in life.[6]

A 2017 study carried out by Jennifer Crocker, professor of social psychology at the University of Ohio, points to similar findings. Crocker explained that as humans we are 'hardwired' to promote both self-interest and concern for others depending on our survival situation. From an evolutionary perspective self-interest came into play when fleeing a predator, but survival at a species level meant depending on each other to live in cooperative groups, helping one another to remain safe. She explained that we are constructed in a way that means 'giving to others can be rewarding despite its obvious material costs, and selfishness can be costly despite its immediate material benefits. In other words, humans should be psychologically disposed to find benefits in giving that counterbalance the costs.'[7]

Crocker's review shows that in the majority of everyday situations giving benefits our psychological well-being, physical health and the quality of our relationships. She proposes that the mechanisms that enable this include positive affect (*i.e.* a more optimistic outlook), increased confidence, a greater sense of connection to others and a clearer sense of purpose.[8]

Susan Whitbourne, professor emerita of psychological and brain sciences at the University of Massachusetts

Amherst, showed that making a difference to the lives of others is one of the key aspects to fulfilment. She explored happiness levels in midlife adults and found that no matter what their job, those who reached out to younger people and helped them overcome life obstacles were most fulfilled.[9] In other words those people who were involved with some sort of role-modelling experienced the greatest levels of happiness.[10] Even the act of volunteering to be a role model improves well-being, leading to better self-health ratings, increased life satisfaction, decreased mortality, higher levels of contentment and lower levels of depressive symptoms.[11]

Added to all of this research, being a role model in the work environment has been shown to benefit through:

- providing a chance to reflect on your own behaviour and approach, which can enhance performance and improve levels of self-awareness;
- enhancing job satisfaction;[12]
- improving emotional intelligence and relationship skills;
- enhancing recognition from peers, followers and superiors;
- enabling you to pass on your own learning and experience;
- increasing your understanding of what's going on around you at a social or political level and learning to see things from different perspectives;
- developing your capability to develop others (a fundamental skill of career progression and job satisfaction);
- growing your leadership skills with a greater understanding of how to motivate and engage people.[13]

The mere process of seeking to improve self-awareness, connections with others, build trust and clarify your own values in the service of being a good role model provides further positive benefits. In short, it's well worth doing.

The three levels of role model

There are three different types of role-modelling you can fulfil: personal, situational or aspirational. They fall into the areas below.

Role model			
	Personal role model	Situational role model	Aspirational role model
People included	Parents Siblings Relatives Friends	Relatives Teachers Sports coaches Friends Colleagues Bosses Healthcare professionals Youth workers Members of the clergy	Celebrities Television personalities Social media influencers Film stars Campaigners Leaders Athletes Prominent figures
May also include	Teachers Sports coaches Colleagues Bosses Youth workers Members of the clergy		Fictional characters
Intensity of interaction	High	Medium	Low
Length of relationship	Long-term	Variable	Variable
Reciprocity	Bilateral	Limited bilateral	Unilateral

(Adapted from MacCallum & Beltmann 2002[14] and Meier 2013[15])

How to role-model

Research shows that to be a really good role model, whether personal, situational or aspirational, requires some assistance. If training is not available, these pointers will guide you along the right lines. One of the best ways to learn any of these skills is to find a personal or aspirational role model who's good at whichever aspect you are looking to develop in your own role-modelling.

Remember, role-modelling is as much about not doing as it is doing: for example, not swearing in front of children if you don't want them to swear, or not doing drugs if you don't believe it's something others should imitate. If you can't refrain from these behaviours altogether then do them in private. I swear a lot when my kids aren't with me, but try and refrain when they are. This is particularly important if you're an aspirational role model. Think about what you are role-modelling to other people, especially children – like it or not, it is part of taking on the position in society that you have. Your private life is yours to do with what you want, but when you're in the public eye you need to be conscious of the messages you're sending.

Personal role model

Personal role-modelling depends a great deal on establishing strong, high-quality relationships through connection, trust, empathy and exposure to the person. You may want to be explicit about the relationship, actually offering to be a personal role model; or it may be a relationship that doesn't need a label, for example if you're an uncle or aunt. There are elements of executive coaching that can be extremely helpful for this type of relationship, the details of which we'll explore below.

Beyond the fundamentals, being a good role-model comes down to the factors discussed in Chapter Ten.

Firstly, it's good to take a look at what your motivations are. You need to be careful that it's not about feeling in control over someone else's life. It shouldn't be about enjoying the power or superiority the position gives you, or even trying to look like a decent person. The motivation has to come from really wanting to make a difference. Good role-modelling is undertaken in pursuit of meaning, driving for outcomes such as helping someone to learn, grow, feel good about themselves and fulfil their potential.

Secondly, are you prepared to take responsibility? Role-modelling, although naturally occurring all the time, is a responsibility, especially when it becomes conscious and intentional. Doing it to the best of your ability means remaining self-aware and asking for feedback. You should be open-minded about what's working and what's not and be prepared to share your own mistakes, setbacks and life experiences in order to help your modelee learn.

Trust and connection

Trust and connection are absolutely critical as a foundation to any personal role-modelling relationship. In some circumstances being a role model is not a choice, as with a parent for example – which tends to infer a natural trust and connection with your child. But taking the time to think about that consciously can still make a big difference to the quality of your relationship.

At the other end of the scale, if you are becoming a personal role model to someone you've never met, especially someone from a different background or dissimilar personal circumstances to you, trust and connection have to be built. That may take time and patience, but it's an essential

component of having a positive impact. You will have to be present and live up to any commitments you make; trust is quickly eroded by letting someone down, especially when they are vulnerable.

Motivation

As alluded to above it's important to consciously and proactively focus on your modelee's goals rather than your own. I have to check myself on this when I'm coaching – what I want or think is best is not necessarily right for the coachee. I may, for example, think that someone should apply for a more senior role, but when I explore the situation with them in more depth I learn that they have concerns about work–life balance and the impact it would have on their family. Putting my goal or beliefs about the situation first would push the wrong agenda. I could even inadvertently convince them to do something that doesn't suit their needs. It's really important to explore your modelee's aspirations with an open mind. The goals you explore should be in their best interests, not in the interests that you think would be best for them.

Connection, trust, exposure and responsibility – emotional intelligence as a vehicle for good role-modelling

Emotional intelligence, or as I call it emotional wisdom, is a useful skill to have regardless of what you are doing in life and especially helpful for role-modelling. With more advanced levels of emotional wisdom come the abilities to manage your own emotions more effectively, communicate more successfully, connect with people more meaningfully, navigate emotionally fraught situations and mitigate conflict.

A good level of emotional wisdom helps you to manage stress and anxiety better, freeing you up to make clearer judgments, which in turn means you are better able to help your modelee to work productively toward their goals.[16]

When it comes to role-modelling, emotional wisdom forms a critical foundation to connection and trust, and also forms the basis on which cognitive empathy is developed both in you and the other person.

All relationships are shaped by our emotions,[17] so it makes sense that in order to positively influence a relationship, connect with someone and build trust we must have a good sense of our own emotions. It's important to be consciously aware of how they are impacting us and to read the other person's emotional response so that we are able to adapt appropriately. For example, if we say something that makes someone look anxious and upset, do we stay on that subject, address the topic directly or steer the conversation on to something else? What would provide the most helpful outcome?

Daniel Goleman, the psychologist who popularised the term 'emotional intelligence', breaks it down into four component parts, which are modified to meet the needs of role-modelling as follows:

- **Self-awareness** – the ability to recognise your emotions and understand how they affect your thoughts and behaviour.
- **Conscious role-modelling and self-management** – being conscious of your behaviour as a role model and the impact that has, and being able to manage impulsive feelings and behaviours in a way that's helpful to you and the other person.
- **Empathy** – being able to notice and appropriately respond to emotional cues. This, as we've discussed, can be broken down further into

emotional and cognitive empathy. Ideally enough
mastery of both exists to enable you to connect to
and feel, but not become overwhelmed by, your
modelee's emotions.

- **Building trust** – the ability to communicate and
interact with people effectively; to use your social
skills adeptly to create relationships that you're
able to maintain over time.

These may sound like skills that you don't have. That is
why I refer to this as 'emotional wisdom', because research
shows that all of these factors can be developed, we can all
become better at them, it's not a fixed capability to which
the term 'intelligence' implies. If you would like to explore
these more for yourself then my previous book *Defining You*
takes you through a process of evolving these skills. For
now, however, a more detailed description of each of the
four factors is as follows:

Self-awareness

This is the critical foundation on which the other three
skills are built. Being self-aware requires understanding
yourself, your personality and how that impacts others,
strengths, passions, blindspots and values. It's knowing
where and when you need help, learning from your mistakes
and identifying what you need to improve. Self-awareness
takes a constant effort of consciousness and fine tuning.
This is because our relationships, the world around us and
who we are within it are constantly evolving and changing.

Conscious role-modelling and self-management

From a neurological perspective this is about the strength of
the connections between your more advanced observing
brain and your more primitive reacting brain. The connections
between the pre-frontal lobe (observing brain) and the

emotional centres of the brain are still developing through emerging adulthood, the years between the ages of 18 and 29. The pre-frontal lobe is the 'executive' region that manages emotion. The more developed the connections, the better able you are to control your impulses and manage your emotions.[18] Learning to step back and observe your emotions rather than connecting with them takes time. It isn't an easy thing to do, but is something you can learn more about in *Defining You* and in Russ Harris's brilliant book *The Happiness Trap*, which provides some very useful tips and techniques to work through. You can also improve by being consciously aware of your emotions and through meditation.

When it comes to role-modelling and forming a connection with your modelee, you need to try to quieten down your reacting brain and the emotions that it elicits, allowing yourself to be in the moment with the person you are talking to. During any conversation our reacting brain provides us with all sorts of thoughts and emotions, such as deciding what we're going to say next, needing to interrupt so we don't forget what we've just thought of, jumping to conclusions about what the other person's leading up to, forming opinions over what type of person they are, deciding what you're going to have for dinner, wondering where they got their shirt from. While it is hard, it's important to only observe those thoughts without responding to or engaging with them, to stop your reacting brain from racing ahead with its own agenda and give your modelee time to express themselves properly. Doing this will in itself begin to develop your capability, which you can then apply in other areas of life.

Empathy

Being able to self-manage also facilitates the next level of emotional wisdom, the way in which we use cognitive and emotional empathy. It's our more natural empathic

response, emotional empathy, that allows us to immediately feel what others are feeling. Cognitive empathy is believed to be more advanced, both in terms of the brain mechanisms and with regard to our own development. It is the type of empathy that allows us to step back from an initial reaction and look at it from a more rational standpoint, rather than engaging with it at a level that can feel overwhelming. If you want to remind yourself more about this then look back to the chapter on empathy.

As a personal role model you need to use both emotional and cognitive empathy. It's essential to have emotional empathy in order to really understand and put yourself in the shoes of your modelee. However, you also need to be able to remove yourself from their emotion to prevent it from having a negative impact on your mental health and well-being. Using empathy, connecting, listening and being conscious and self-aware will all help to build trust.

Trust
This involves all of the other elements discussed, the ability to really manage your own emotions and agenda in order to understand theirs, but also a follow-through on commitments and promises made. This is especially important if your modelee is someone vulnerable. Stepping away or not following through can leave someone in a worse place than when you started.

While role-modelling effectively is more challenging with lower levels of emotional wisdom, it should not put anyone off trying, as the relationship itself will help you to develop your skills in this area. Paying attention, feeling your responses, and being conscious of reactions in someone else all provide the space for your own mirror system to develop. Each iterative interaction improves your social and emotional skills. You can also develop both your emotional wisdom and your capability as a role model by

exploring altruistic goals, showing genuine interest, wanting to know someone without judging them. Above all else, being patient and letting a modelee open up at their own pace will build trust, which is the essential underpinning to creating a successful outcome.

Responsibility

You have the responsibility to continue to do all of this, not just make a one-off effort, but remain conscious of what you are role-modelling, to maintain the level of exposure. You also need to ensure that you can 'walk the talk'. This doesn't mean being perfect. Part of 'walking the talk' is sharing your own vulnerabilities, weaknesses and failures. This not only allows you to connect more authentically, but also to help your modelee to see that it's OK to make mistakes. It also helps them to understand how to deal with mistakes and how to avoid making the same ones themselves. Recall the mentor Cynric who was part of the BBBS scheme: he showed his modelee what and where he'd gone wrong and how it could be avoided. He said, 'I can tell – by what he says – that Kam thinks about the mistakes I made when I was in his shoes and how I dealt with it (or didn't), when he figures out how to handle problems in his own life.'[19]

In effect, you are consciously giving your modelee an opportunity to counter role-model your own behaviour and decision-making. You are drawing their attention and therefore their mirror thinking into focus on a particular event, providing opportunities for both mirroring and counter-mirroring.

Developmental focus

If you are familiar with coaching you will probably also know that there is a continuum of how to engage someone

in helpful conversations. At one end of the scale is a prescriptive and directive style and at the other a more facilitative, non-directive style. The same is true when it comes to how a personal role model interacts with a modelee. The non-directive approach relates to the connection and trust-building elements discussed earlier as opposed to the directive approach, which is often referred to as 'tell'.

Take, for example, a parent who is rushing to help their child to finish their geography homework on the water cycle the morning it is due to be handed in. They are late for school and really need to get it completed as quickly as possible. In this situation the parent is more likely to use a directive than a non-directive approach because of the time pressure. It is easiest to tell them the answers – 'evaporation needs to go in this box here', 'precipitation in this one'. However, if they have more time, say they are helping with the homework at the weekend, they may take a more non-directive open approach, asking their child what they have learnt about the water cycle, whether they can remember the names of any of the parts of the cycle, how the cycle works and why, *etc.*

Business managers and leaders who are stressed or under extreme time pressure typically use a directive style of coaching, telling people what they should do, whereas managers and leaders who have more time or are more practised in coaching will ask questions and guide people to find the answers themselves. An experienced leader will use a combination of both, as will a skilled role model, with a tendency to always be more on the facilitative end than the tell end. The tell side of the continuum does not build the same level of trust or connection, doesn't create the same level of buy-in and is far less inspirational. Imagine you are on the receiving end of someone barking orders or telling you what to do. It's not fun, nor is it what you want unless you are specifically looking for advice or instruction.

Role-Modelling Continuum

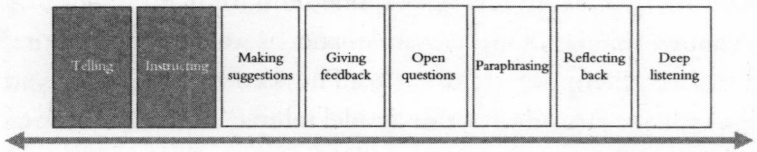

| Telling | Instructing | Making suggestions | Giving feedback | Open questions | Paraphrasing | Reflecting back | Deep listening |

Directive Style / 'Tell'   Non-Directive Style /
                                                            Without judgement

Adapted from *The Coaching Continuum* by Myles Downey

Research carried out on the BBBS scheme shows that the most effective and enduring role model relationships are formed at the non-directive end of the spectrum. By contrast, those at the tell end are most likely to fail. The study revealed that when someone used the directive approach, they tended to believe that they were there to 'fix' their modelees, to make right certain deficiencies or to steer them towards the values, attitudes and behaviours that they personally thought were positive. The role model set out the goals without including the modelee in decision-making and they decided on the pace of the relationship.[20] At this prescriptive end of the spectrum, role models were reluctant to adjust their expectations of the modelee or their beliefs of how quickly their behaviour could change,[21] which ultimately resulted in the relationship failing.

Analogous to teachers in schools, managers in work environments, parents with children or anyone trying to help, we tend to go into a problem looking for a solution. But our brain and behaviour do not work like that. We cannot 'solve' people, neither ourselves nor others, like they are a problem. For example, telling someone who doesn't exercise enough simply to start exercising doesn't work. It's most helpful to them to try to understand the root cause: why they don't exercise, when they have in the past, what they like and don't like about it, and how they feel when they do exercise. Exploring this allows someone to find the

solutions for themselves; it's not only illuminating, but also empowering. Giving open-minded emotional support provides the opportunity for someone to safely explore and also mirror attitudes, outlooks, behaviours and values from a different source.

However, in certain circumstances someone may need more critical feedback and help with goal-setting. For example, this could be in a sporting context where instructional guidance on a technique or approach to training is essential. The same will be true in some work situations. For example, when I'm coaching people in business I will often listen and question, but I will also sometimes offer my advice from the perspective of either a psychologist or from the experience I have had with other leaders. I may say: 'It sounds to me like you are being influenced by the expectations of your peers rather than doing what you think is right. Why not try positioning your idea in a different way at the next board meeting?' Then I might move back to the developmental end of the spectrum, asking them: 'What could that look like?'

As a personal role model there may be times where your modelee is looking for advice or suggestions and getting frustrated if you won't tell them the answers. This is where you need to make a judgement on whether switching to the more directive end of the continuum will be helpful. But the default, unless in the context of sport or goal-setting, should be to return to the non-directive end of the spectrum. It's far more effective trying to help them to find their own solutions.

Exposure

When it comes to personal role-modelling, beyond relationships where there is natural exposure, such as for a parent and child, there is a need to ensure contact

through being accessible and committed. Research has shown that this makes a dramatic difference to how effective a role-modelling relationship is. If you go into it half-hearted it won't work and will let down the modelee. You have to follow through over the long term, be accessible (with obvious boundaries), and be patient in order to allow the relationship to evolve and grow at its own rate. Things may not appear to be happening and you may not feel like you're making a positive impact straight away, but building trust takes time and behavioural learning requires repeated exposure to different attitudes and approaches. Research shows that the most effective role-modelling relationships evolve naturally over time. This is especially important if you're working with someone young or who has emotional issues. You may remember that one of the role models on the BBBS scheme said it took nearly a year before his modelee opened up to him. Commitment to someone builds not only trust, but also their self-esteem and confidence. It makes them feel worth something and able to explore what their purpose is. Withdrawing that commitment causes more harm than good, often putting a modelee in a worse place than they started.

Situational role model

It's more difficult for a situational role model to build trust and a connection, typically because of a lower level of exposure. In the case of a doctor or nurse that means engaging quickly. In this situation role-modelling is about rapidly building a relationship and showing empathy. For example, the healthcare professional mirroring the behaviour of the patient to make them feel at ease and to take on board what they are saying into their own mental world. It's also arguably about the healthcare professional

role-modelling to the patient and their relatives the respect, care and hope that they should be taking on board once they've left their care. In these relationships trust is to some extent innate and comes as a result of professional standing. It can, however, be quickly eroded with a poorly calculated remark. The most critical thing for situational role models to do is understand how to create connection and build trust quickly with low exposure. This requires high levels of cognitive empathy. Other factors replicate those outlined in the section on personal role-modelling.

Aspirational role model

Aspirational role models, such as sports stars, musicians, actors or leaders like Martin Luther King Jr, influence thousands or millions of people who they cannot possibly know individually. But they do connect more effectively by having an understanding and empathy with their audience. In the days of King, his audience were exposed to him almost exclusively via television and radio, but today we have multiple digital platforms where aspirational role models can convey their message – whether that's social media, podcasts or the internet, the routes are plentiful. What is communicated and how will differ greatly between ISIS, the Kardashians, Angelina Jolie or Jameela Jamil, but they all do the same thing: they tap into our emotions, build trust and use clever communication to connect.

If you are an aspirational role model, storytelling is your best option for building the foundation of a positive relationship with your audience. Think about how even today, King's words conjure up images and emotions by simply reading them off the page. Or how Maya Angelou's poetry engages and transports us to another world. Stories don't have to be complex – the best TED Talks are stories given in 15 minutes or less.

As we've discussed, stories engage us via the mirror system. It can feel intimidating thinking of a way to deliver your message like this – but it shouldn't. It is, after all, the most natural way to communicate and something you do on a daily basis without even realising. For example, recounting your weekend to someone, or your experience on holiday is storytelling.

We can all learn to communicate better. Research shows that we tend to think we are much better communicators than we really are. I often say to the leaders I work with that it's an easy development area to identify as it applies to everyone – however good you are you can be better. It's a skill that can help you to role-model through connecting at a more profound level. It's also something that can help us in myriad other ways – to argue our point more clearly at work or in a personal dispute, to help us work more effectively as part of a team, to improve our ability to connect with our teenage kids, to communicate better with our partner reducing arguments and improving connection, or to explain our latest idea so that other people understand and get excited about it. For a number of reasons it's worth investing the time in working out how to be a better communicator and of course how to tell a good story. Here are some pointers on how to approach shaping your communication, looking specifically at storytelling as a vehicle.

Craft your open

J. D. Schramm is a lecturer in organisational behaviour at Stanford Business School and specialises in communication. When it comes to storytelling, Schramm recommends parachuting in, with no preamble.[22] He points out that the best storytellers engage the audience in the action right away in order to capture attention. In effect, this is switching

on the mirror neurons. This doesn't have to be complex or elaborate: in fact, children's books give a good example of how this can be done simply. For example, Julia Donaldson's award-winning book *The Gruffalo* starts with 'A mouse took a stroll through the deep dark wood. A fox saw the mouse and the mouse looked good.'

In these two sentences Donaldson has captured attention. The lone mouse is minding his own business in a scary dark place and then, a predator sees him and immediately we feel a sense of risk. Carefully chosen words throw us straight into the story in a clear and simple way.

Craft your close

Our brains operate well within frameworks. Things that are simple and clear are far easier for us to remember and understand. That doesn't mean we shouldn't add colour, intensity and passion to what comes between, but that at the start and end, simplicity and carefully chosen words make the difference between the whole story making sense or not. Being remembered or forgotten, acted on or brushed aside. Returning to *The Gruffalo*, the final two sentences show how this can be done: 'All was quiet in the deep dark wood. The mouse found a nut and the nut was good.' We don't have to read the whole story to know that in the end the mouse was fine. It was peaceful in the wood even though it was still 'deep and dark', giving a sense of calm. Donaldson takes us away from the danger and back to daily life – the mouse finding a nut, which provides a sense of ease. The mouse is no longer on the menu, but has instead found himself something good to eat. The two sentences she uses as an opening and these two sentences as a close can be filled in by our own brain without even knowing the rest of the story.

Light up the mirror neurons – what comes in between

Analogies, metaphors, imagery – these are what make the difference between running through a story as if you are recounting what you did last weekend and orating like the greatest speakers of all time. We discussed how analogies, metaphor and imagery all activate the mirror neurons in various areas of the brain triggering our core senses: vision, hearing, smell, taste and touch. As a result of engaging different senses in storytelling, more areas of the brain of the listener are also engaged. It helps them to put their own meaning on to the message, which is far more engaging, motivating and interesting for the listener than simply being told something.

Poetry is a way of making this tangible. Schramm explains that poems use fewer words to carry more meaning. The added benefit is that poetry provides the opportunity for dramatic pause in order to emphasise a particular point. In the same way that a piece of music is as much about the quiet between notes as it is the music, so is a well-told story about the rhythm, emphasis and silences. It is a way of conveying far greater meaning to the brain without the need to use lengthy explanation. Take, for example, the following:

> I am trying to remember you,
> and
> let you go
> at
> the same time.

This poem, 'The Mourn' by Nayyirah Waheed, conjures up so much in so few words. It makes me think about losing my dad, wanting desperately to hang on to his

memory and not let those images of him fade away, while also frantically trying to move on and shrug off the grief. It's incredibly emotive, immediately reconnecting me with my own experiences. This may mean something entirely different to you. Someone else may read it and think of a lover they have separated from or even someone who has annoyed them. It can be easily accessed and translated into our own meaning, carrying a great deal of power with it.

Within a talk the use of analogy, metaphor and imagery may take on a different form. For example, in the speech that J. K. Rowling gave to students at Harvard University she said, 'There is an expiry date on blaming your parents for steering you in the wrong direction; the moment you are old enough to take the wheel, responsibility lies with you.'

Martin Luther King's use of metaphor is another example: 'Let us not seek to satisfy our thirst for freedom by drinking from the cup of bitterness and hatred.'[23]

Or Maya Angelou's use of imagery: ' ... but it didn't hide my skinny legs, which had been greased with Blue Seal Vaseline and powdered with the Arkansas red clay. The age-faded color made my skin look dirty like mud, and everyone in church was looking at my skinny legs.' In this extract from I *Know Why the Caged Bird Sings*, about Angelou's life growing up facing racism and abuse in America's Deep South, she describes her humiliation. Without knowing the entire story, we can easily conjure up the setting, imagine how she looked, what she felt, even how she got to church. I could go on. The point is that these short sentences carry far more weight and significance than a typical description. Using any of these tools – analogy, metaphor, imagery or poetry – makes a massive difference to the impact of the story you tell.

Less is more – looking at Donaldson's very simple example displays this clearly. It's difficult to convey more

with fewer words, but so powerful. When you're crafting your communication it's worth going through and weeding out the unimportant points, or the 'bits' that draw away from the story. A message is far more potent if the listener is able to join the dots between points. It gives the listener's brain the chance to be in the story and work things out for themselves. They become more engaged.

Emotional connection – social psychologist Brené Brown is an adept storyteller. She also studies connection, empathy and belonging. In TEDxHouston, June 2010, Brown gave an often quoted presentation, the recording of which has been watched by millions. She walked the talk in her transcript, explaining that she had to see a therapist because in researching vulnerability she had uncovered things about herself. Brené is also funny, which helps soften the emotional message and makes it feel more palatable. She continues the talk, explaining how accepting rather than numbing her vulnerability allows her to connect more effectively with others.

Sharing personal feelings and showing a level of vulnerability taps into our empathy and is therefore dependent on the mirror neuron. It provides a route by which to connect with the audience and build trust despite – as an aspirational role model – never actually meeting them. Brené has shared her own vulnerability with 44 million people as a result of her TEDx recording, a number that will no doubt continue to rise over the next few years.

Context and audience

The entire story needs to be framed with both the audience and message you are trying to convey in mind. What are you trying to say and to whom? What are they interested in, what motivates them, scares them, excites them? For

example, when Churchill delivered his speech on 4 June 1940 it was directed at the nation of Britain, which he referred to as 'our island': 'We shall defend our island, whatever the cost may be; we shall fight on the beaches, we shall fight on the landing grounds, we shall fight in the fields and in the streets, we shall fight in the hills; we shall never surrender.'

Churchill frames his message in terms of the critical importance of continuing with the war whatever the cost, rallying people to unite against the enemy or out-group, hooking the more emotive primitive drivers of listeners.

There are a number of ways to develop your skills in communicating and storytelling more effectively:

- **Watch footage of people giving speeches** – this activates your own mirror neurons, assisting your learning, especially if you are conscious of what you are taking on and what you want to counter-mirror.
- **Read through the transcripts of great historical speeches** – this will also activate your mirror neurons.
- **Go through books and pull out passages that resonate** – why do they resonate? What is it that's said and how?
- **Visualise and walk through the story in your own mind** – and engage your mirror neurons in shaping what you say.
- **Practise in front of the mirror or film yourself** – and play it back in order to refine your message, emphasising the bits you like and working on the bits that you don't.

All of the elements of being an aspirational role model are the same as for the personal role model, except of course

the one-to-one interactions. As an aspirational role model you need to be clear on your motivations for role-modelling, your values and purpose, ensuring that you remain self-aware. Once in such a position, you start to wield a great deal of influence and it is something you must take responsibility for. This role often comes about accidentally, as Charles Barkley said: 'I'm not a role model. Just because I dunk a basketball doesn't mean I should raise your kids'; perhaps not raise them, but success brings with it responsibilities. Remember that whether you mean to or not, your behaviour and every action is impacting someone else. If you make that conscious and purposeful it can have a far more positive effect.

There is evidence that prosocial behaviour increases well-being even without having direct contact with the person on the receiving end, so that responsibility has many benefits for you as a role model as well as bestowing benefits on others.[24] Think about how you can use role-modelling to continue to grow and learn as a person, and in a way that truly adds value to the people you are influencing.

This chapter has explored how to be a role-model whether that's personal, situational or aspriational. But even as the role model you need people to look to and model, which is what we'll talk about in the final chapter.

CHAPTER TWELVE

CHAPTER TWELVE

Choosing Your Mirrors

In this chapter we will look at why you would want a role model, who to choose, what to look for in them and how to approach being a role modelee to get the most out of it. Finding a role model not only includes personal aspects, but also situational and aspirational.

Why role-model anyone?

We mirror the people around us all the time. The person sat in the seat opposite us on the train yawns and we yawn, someone on the street smiles and we smile back without thinking, the person on the table next to us in the coffee shop crosses their legs and so do we. We also mirror more lasting behaviours: the way we talk may be influenced by a co-worker, the opinions we have by our partner or someone we've heard on the radio, our values by our parents. All the time, every day we are mirroring other people. We are role-modelling whether we intend to or not.

It makes sense to bring mirroring into consciousness, to choose what and who we mirror *and* what and who not to; taking us in the direction we want in life, rather than being unintentionally diverted off track. We can choose role models and behaviours that help us to grow and improve, to fulfil our potential and to take us where we want to go in life. However successful you already are, there's always room to grow. We all always need role models and, even if it's not in search of success, they can provide personal fulfilment, an example of how to live a more healthy life,

how to have more fun, how to enable more rewarding relationships, be a better parent, be more mentally well and a whole host of other positives.

What are you looking for?

First and foremost, whoever you are and whatever your goals, you are looking for someone who will support you in fulfilling your potential – someone who helps you work towards your life purpose. You may be unsure about what your potential might be or without a clear idea of your purpose. If this is the case there are two approaches you could take – either a bit of personal exploration[1] on your own, or finding a personal role model who can help you to explore and define what it is you're aiming for. Either way this is something that will take a little patience and persistence. The fundamental areas you're looking to define are your values, strengths, passions, areas for development and blind spots. You're then looking to use this information to help you explore what gives you meaning and purpose in life *and* how to harness that to fulfil your potential.

Approach to being a role modelee

Having identified these points, it's really important to keep reminding yourself of them. Don't worry if you're not completely clear on all of them, you can use your role models to help you to explore them further; whether that's a personal role model or watching other people from more of a distance, it doesn't matter. One thing is certain: whoever you role-model you don't want to copy anyone outright. Ultimately, you're learning behaviours and approaches, but the core values and personality you have

should remain stable. You may in some instances find that a role model's values move you so deeply that you readjust your own, but even then you need to remain true to who you are. It's also important to remember that a role model is not a point of comparison. We can never and should never try to be someone else. We can mirror aspects of what they do and how they do it, but only if they resonate with our own personality and values.

It is key to approach any relationship, whether personal, situational or aspirational, with a curious open-minded attitude. Imagine you are a detective, observing which points of your role model can help you to develop your own behaviour. It may be that you fundamentally just need the support of a role model in a relationship, or it could be that you are looking to emulate certain elements of who they are and how they reached the point in life that they have. For example, I hate networking and although I come across as outgoing, I'm actually quite introverted. So, I need to find a role model who is introverted, but able to network and work out how they do it. That may mean watching or exploring it with them and then applying it in a way that would work for me.

Who to role-model

Who should you role-model? Remember that you've been role-modelling the people around you from the day you were born. This is not new, it's simply that you're making a conscious decision over who to mirror and why. That really does come down to your needs. You may simply want to refine part of your behaviour: you may want to become an entrepreneur and therefore look to people like Richard Branson, and read his biography and media articles on him. That may be accompanied by finding a personal

role model who is an entrepreneur or watching someone in your community who is successful.

It could be that your needs are more personal and emotional. For example, we looked at people within the LBGT community; when teenagers are trying to work out who they are, understand their identity and decide when and how to come out to relatives, it is critical for them to have someone who understands, and can offer support and advice. That's not going to come from an aspirational role model, and even with personal role models it would help if they have an understanding and experience of what you are going through. In this situation, if there's no one in your community you can identify with, it may be easiest to find that support through online support networks.

It's useful to start with a broad understanding of what your needs are and then work out who is going to best meet those needs. This should be someone who can support you, who you can identify with and who exhibits behaviours you aspire to. This doesn't all have to come down to one person. When I'm working with leaders they often struggle to identify role models. Earlier in their career they may have looked to people with more experience, but now they are one of those people themselves. However, they still want to learn and they still can: it may just mean pulling together aspects of lots of different people to emulate and mirror. Perhaps Martin Luther King for his communication skills, Gandhi for his ability to rally people together in a peaceful way, Alan Mulally from Ford for pulling a company through crisis, Alex Ferguson for his discipline and focus. They may look outside of leadership to sport – for example, Bethany Hamilton's surfing comeback after losing an arm in a shark attack – and beyond to someone like Maya Angelou for her wisdom, courage and determination; or the pilot Captain

Chesley 'Sully' Sullenberger who landed a plane on the Hudson River in New York after losing the power in both engines, for how to stay calm and work as a team. There are so many people who have done incredible things in the world; we just need to explore and remain open-minded in order to see them. They may not even be that far away. Often we can look to one of our parents, who have more in common with us than anyone else, to think about how they do or did something exceptionally well and how we can mirror that more consciously and effectively.

You may also want to identify people who you are going to consciously counter-mirror – the 'bits' of someone you don't want to be like. For example, in medicine junior doctors often say they learn how not to treat a patient from seeing someone more senior behaving unethically or making a flippant remark. The only thing to be careful of here is to make sure that you don't surround yourself with too many people who you want to counter-mirror. We can't always be conscious of everything we are mirroring or absorbing from others and this is why the choice of role models that you want to mirror is so critical. While some junior doctors may successfully counter-mirror, others may mirror the unethical behaviour.

Even a 'good' role model is not good if they're not helping you to become the best person you can be, however much they fulfil any other criteria. What makes a good role model is not universal because we all have individual differences. For example, I admire Greta Thunberg, but my eldest daughter and husband don't think much of her at all. And that's OK. We all have unique preferences, needs and ideas about the world.

You can choose to role-model one person, or 10, 20, 50, 100. It's up to you. Although too many and you could end up getting a little lost. The key thing is looking at your needs and finding people who will fulfil them.

There are three different types of role model you can mirror: personal, situational or aspirational. They fall into the areas below.

Role model			
	Personal role model	Situational role model	Aspirational role model
People included	Parents Siblings Relatives Friend	Healthcare professional Relatives Teacher Sports coach Friend Colleague Boss Youth worker Member of the clergy	Celebrity Television personality Social media influencer Film star Campaigner Leader Athlete Prominent figure
May also include	Teacher Sports coach Colleague Boss Youth worker Member of the clergy		Fictional character
Intensity of interaction	High	Medium	Low
Length of relationship	Long term	Variable	Variable
Setting	Informal	Formal	Virtual
Reciprocity	Bilateral	Limited bilateral	Unilateral
Mirror thinking			

Personal

One of the most important things to look for in a personal role model is someone who makes you feel good. Think to the points we've discussed throughout the book; you are looking for someone who you connect with, trust, who you see a lot of, or who can commit time to you if you ask. Ideally

the person will also have a solid level of empathy – for several reasons. Empathy will enable them to make you feel better about yourself than someone with low levels of empathy; model social and emotional skills in a way that you can learn from and help you to build relationships more effectively.

You may want to explicitly identify your needs with your personal role model, explaining to them what you're trying to achieve by doing that. Or you may find that simply having them as a sounding board – as someone who is able to share their own experiences with you, what's worked, what hasn't and why – is enough. It may be that you choose one personal role model who is more like a mentor and others who are people you are simply being around in order to observe and mirror their behaviour.

Try to be open, curious, and consider what fits with your needs and why and what is less helpful. Watch and learn.

Situational

A situational role model may be someone observed from a slight distance. Perhaps it's the man running an exercise class you attend and the way that he motivates or engages with people in the class. Or it might be your family doctor, who puts you at ease with her manner and approach. Maybe a co-worker whose work ethic you admire. These are the people who you may come into contact with quite frequently, but who you don't have a personal relationship with.

Aspirational

Aspirational role models can include anyone, but they tend to be people who you are unlikely to ever meet in person. It may be because they are a historical figure, someone very famous, someone fictional, an athlete or a prominent

person in the public eye. One example is Elon Musk, who is famous (among many other things) as the co-founder of Tesla and founder of X.com, which later merged with PayPal. Musk comes up with fantastical ideas about linking computers to our brains, or creating a system of underground tunnels under Los Angeles that will allow cars to travel at 130 miles per hour, or space tourism, or colonising Mars and many other ideas. These may seem crazy now, but so would PayPal and Tesla have a few decades ago. Musk said of himself as a child that 'I read all the comics I could buy.'[2] He was wrapped up in comics and totally immersed himself in the content. Musk's particular favourites were Batman, Superman, Green Lantern, Doctor Strange and Iron Man. It's believed that the science-led storylines in comic books of the 1980s may well have sparked his interest in space travel, technology and energy. David Lewis, comic book author and comics scholar, said, 'I have to imagine Musk absorbed this idea that there's this heroism to being smart and innovative,'[3] mirroring aspects of Batman and Ironman. Lewis also says that 'if he was reading comics, he was enjoying and ingesting morality' and that possibly 'inspired him to envision himself as a potential superhero, to write his own superhero story'.[4] Musk's role models became part of his own belief system, values and the vision he has of doing something useful for society via technology.

Mandela represents a leader who combined 'personal', situational and aspirational role models. In terms of his aspirational role models, he read biographies, listened to historians, visited historical sites associated with leaders he admired or thought he could learn from. From Marcus Aurelius to the Egyptian pharaohs, he read and learnt everything he could. He absorbed centuries of wisdom, stretching from the ancient world to the modern, to help him learn about the pitfalls of leadership.

Then there are the current prominent figures – the politicians, business leaders and thought leaders. Whoever they are you will inevitably be able to watch them on television, see them on social media, read about them in the news and they will most likely have talks online, possibly biographies or autobiographies.

Aspirational role models also include sports stars, musicians and movie stars. People who have got to where they have through talent and hard work. They are not perfect; it's important to remember that. You don't want to mirror their entire behaviour, nor do you want to feel let down when they misbehave. Love and admire them for their 'good' bits as well as the aspects that you can helpfully mirror, but don't expect them to be the perfect package. They are human, too. Remember that while you can aspire to be them, you are a different person with different circumstances. Work on being the best version of yourself. Also look beneath the surface. Jonny Wilkinson, the former England rugby player renowned for his ability to kick, didn't just get there by luck or talent. He put in hours and hours of hard work and has more recently said that he was so obsessive about perfecting the kick that it became a problem for him in terms of his mental health. Things are not always what they seem.

It's also important with any on-screen role model to not globally accept who they are. As we spoke about in Chapter Ten, we have a natural tendency to see the success of someone to mean everything they do, all that they are, is worth emulating. Some of it will be constructed by PRs and agents, some will be spun by advertisers wanting to sell a product; not all of it is real, nor is all of it part of what makes them successful. Even more so, you will not see what they may have sacrificed to be who they appear to be. Look at the real-life pragmatic aspects of their success – their commitment to a goal, determination, consideration of others in order to find the things that are really worth emulating.

This is particularly important to remember if you choose a celebrity who has reached fame through no particular talent or achievement. They would not have been successful in our evolutionary society and while our society has moved on, our brain and ways of being human have not. Some or many Instagram, YouTube or reality TV stars may be great people and worth mirroring. They may be good communicators – perhaps that's got them where they are – and that may well be worth mirroring if it fits with your own personality type, preferences and objectives. However, if you are looking to be successful by being like them, that's another thing completely. Even if you want to be a reality TV star or an influencer, simply mirroring them may not work for you. The landscape is changing so quickly that the factors involved and windows of opportunity are continually moving. Compare a sports star, a leader, a prominent person of any sort today with how they would be 50 or 100 years or more in the past and you will see the same fundamental principles for achieving success; that substance is often lacking when it comes to being famous for the sake of it. If you really want to mirror a celebrity, then work out if what they're doing has a purpose that aligns with your values. Think through whether behaving like them will really help you to achieve whatever it is you want to, and dissect the aspects that you consider helpful and differentiate those from those which are not.

Mapping your role models

The following exercise will help you to map your role models against specific areas you'd like to focus on in your life. What these areas are is up to you, and depends on your core drivers and needs. Each of the sections below have a few examples by them, but these are more of a rough guideline than a strict model for you to follow.

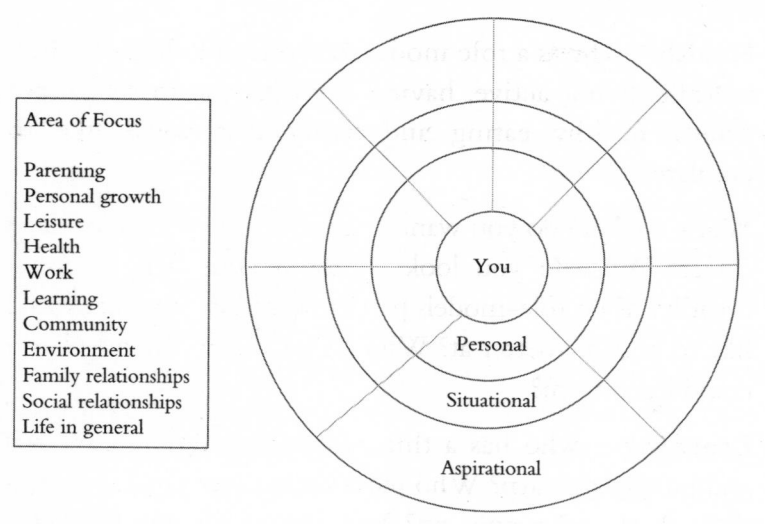

Area of Focus

Parenting
Personal growth
Leisure
Health
Work
Learning
Community
Environment
Family relationships
Social relationships
Life in general

Figure 1

Area of focus

How would you like to be and what personal strengths or qualities do you want to develop within different areas of your life? Those areas could be any of the following or others that you choose to define for yourself:

Parenting – how do you want to parent your children? Who do you want to look to in order to guide your parenting or help you to be better at certain aspects of parenting?

Personal growth – who do you look to in order to grow as a person in terms of your values, attitude, personal development, spirituality?

Leisure – who do you want to emulate or mirror when it comes to your spare time, activities, hobbies, attitude to leisure? How would you like to use your creativity, to relax and have fun? What activities would you like to undertake? What type of holiday would you like to go on?

Health – who is a role model in terms of living a healthy lifestyle, being active, having a positive attitude toward fitness, healthy eating and living that you'd like to emulate?

Work – where do you want to go in terms of your work or career? Who do you look up to in your field or more broadly? Who role-models particular behaviours that you'd like to become better at? Who do you respect and feel you could learn from?

Learning – who has a thirst for knowledge, a curiosity and hunger to learn? Who picks themselves up after facing difficulties and carries on? Who has a lifelong thirst for education?

Community – who do you know or see that is community-minded in a way that you respect or look up to? Is there anything you can mirror from them? What do people stand for at the level of local community or society more broadly that you admire?

Environment – is there someone who looks after the environment, climate and natural world in a way that resonates with you? Do you want to mirror or role-model any aspects of their behavior, attitudes and approach?

Family relationships – who treats their partner, parents, children and relatives in a way that you would like to mirror? What can you work on when it comes to your family relationships and who in your family displays the kind of behaviour you would like to emulate?

Social relationships – who do you know who builds positive and constructive social relationships? Who links people together? Who surrounds themselves with people that make them feel good about themselves? Who is a good friend to others?

Life in general – whose values, approach to life and attitude do you respect or admire and would like to emulate?

Choose which areas you would like to focus on. It may just be one, for example, family relationships, or it could be one broken down further as shown in the example in Figure 2.

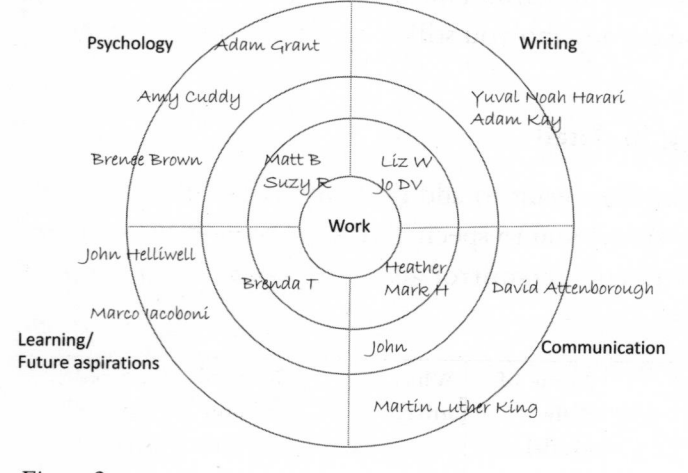

Figure 2

Or it could be several areas, as shown in Figure 3.

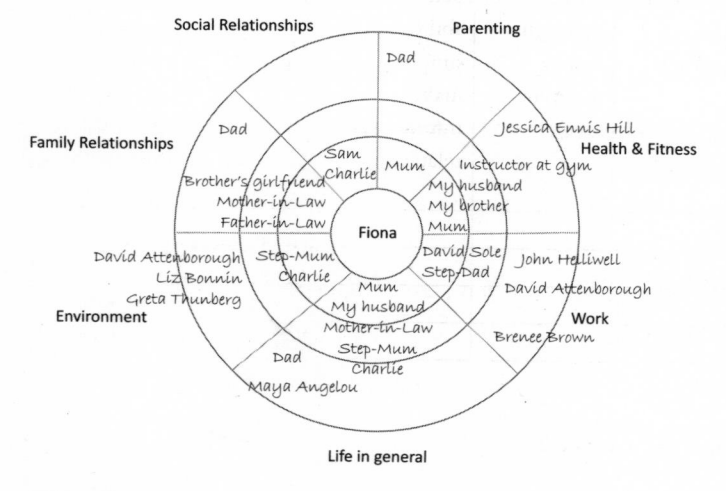

Figure 3

Write the names of people who you would like to mirror into each of the circles, putting personal role models in the first layer, situational in the second and aspirational in the third. In Figure 3, my dad is in aspirational rather than personal role model because he died a number of years ago, making it impossible to have a personal relationship with him moving forward. This may be the same for a relative or close friend who you still think of or wish to emulate.

Adding in detail

You may then want to add more detail by filling in Table 1. This allows you to specify what it is you want to mirror or even to counter-mirror and how you will measure your progress.

Area of Focus	Name of Role Model (type)	What to mirror	What to counter mirror	How will I measure progress
e.g. Work (specifically communication in presenting)	Harry (situational – work colleague from a different area)	Understanding of technical details and ability to simplify and make information relatable	Clipped speaking style	Ask someone I trust for feedback on my own communication style before and after trying new approach

CONCLUSION
How the Mirror Makes Us Human

The mirror neuron makes us human. It enables us to talk, learn, pass on knowledge, connect with others, to love, to have meaningful relationships. It allows us to experience the joy and sadness of those around us. Without it we would not be creative; we would be unable to daydream, imagine and tell stories, or to produce great works of art, music, film and literature. We simply wouldn't have evolved from the cave dwellers of prehistory to the human race we are today. It literally makes us who we are.

That also means it is responsible for the things we wish we weren't. Role models and mirroring enable many of the issues we live with, including a rise in terrorism, increases in youth violence, a growing number of eating disorders and the mental health crisis that has escalated via social media.

Prominent Anglo-American historian David Christian is renowned for generating an interdisciplinary approach known as 'Big History'. He believes that what makes humans different from other creatures is our ability to learn collectively. He defines this as 'the ability to share, store and build upon information'.[1] As humans we collectively started learning with our foraging ancestors around the same time as our brains stopped evolving 50,000 years ago. Our ancestors communicated information that enabled them to adapt to life in different climates, to share knowledge about food sources and to advance tool

development. Knowledge was passed on from generation to generation. And at each stage, with each generation, that knowledge about how to thrive in their environment was adapted, refined and gradually advanced. Almost 44,000 years ago we started leaving our stories in the form of cave paintings, informing generations upon generations of our past lives and creating that platform for inter-generational mirroring.

After all, the transference of learning, taught to the next generation through watching, doing and storytelling, was and still is reliant upon the mirror system. The development of ideas took several generations a step further forward. It wasn't until around 3300 BC that people developed the ability to write. Suddenly this allowed a dramatic leap ahead in collective learning; it was possible for ideas to be recorded, exchanged more rapidly and quickly expanded upon. Our ancestors were no longer purely dependent on the mirror system. However, much of the progression still relied upon mirror *thinking* – the creation of social structures, justice, shared religious beliefs, established human rights and commonly held human values.

In just a few decades, technology such as the internet has allowed an astonishing increase in the speed and quantity of information transfer. The extent of learning that took place in a single village across one generation hundreds of years ago is now possible across a global population in a matter of seconds – expanding the scale and speed of collective learning exponentially.

The possibilities for such learning are mind-boggling. Take, for example, NASA's Open Innovation project, which leverages knowledge from citizens across the globe to solve specific problems. NASA's Space Apps Challenge is described as 'a two-day hackathon where teams of technologists, scientists, designers, artists, educators,

entrepreneurs, developers and students across the globe
collaborate and engage with publicly available data to
design innovative solutions for global challenges'.[2] The
project brought together more than 8,000 people in 91
different locations to solve 40 global challenges in just 48
hours, with the momentous aim of 'helping to improve life
on Earth'. Solutions included technologies such as an app
called CROPP that gathers information to provide real-
time crop risk assessment for farmers, helping them to
improve their harvests. Locusts, diseases and other bugs
destroy up to 30 per cent of crops, which directly affects
the livelihood of a farmer. This innovation makes use of
simple plastic bottles with sensors in them. The sensors
gather data from the fields, which is sent to servers in the
cloud and then combined with data from satellite images in
order to provide warning signals to farmers so they can be
prepared for potential threats. This can dramatically lessen
the risk of crops being decimated. Such amazing technology,
which could revolutionise farming, was designed across
continents in a mere two days. More and more organisations
are teaming up in the same way as NASA to enable the
transfer of knowledge and innovation across global
boundaries, speeding up the time in which answers can be
found. Solutions for food security, energy production and
medical science are actively being sought.

The question is why, despite such amazing advances in
the way we share scientific learning, are things still going
wrong in the world? Why, among other things, are there
poverty, crime, abuse, terrorism and obesity? Are we
focusing on the wrong things? Are we essentially looking
in the wrong mirrors?

We are at a pivotal moment as a species: in spite of
radically improving our capability to solve issues we are
also smothering our mirror system by undermining

opportunities for natural social sharing, imitation and observation. We are creating solutions at an unprecedented rate, but we are creating problems at an arguably greater rate. The pace at which we are living is dampening the opportunities for each of us to develop fully over the course of our lifetimes, suffocating our potential as humans. For example, a study carried out in 2010 by Sara Konrath, an associate professor of philanthropic studies at the University of Michigan, looked at nearly 14,000 people and showed that levels of empathy declined by 48 per cent between 1979 and 2009, with the sharpest decline being between 2000 and 2009.[3] This is primarily because, with science and technology, we are taking people further away from our natural way of operating. We're wandering around like social and emotional zombies, too busy and distracted to engage with the nuances that develop our capability to be empathic, socially competent or emotionally literate. Our heads are lost scrolling through Twitter and Instagram, rather than looking up and out at how we could better fulfil our potential. If you or I don't fulfil our potential, the chances are that neither will the next person. And, worryingly, without developing empathy we can't form effective relationships with each other. Where does that leave society as a whole?

Unfortunately, it does not stop there. Not only is our mirror system being smothered by a faster pace of life, but the balance of our scientific and technical advances tend to favour commercial organisations rather than societal or human concerns. While there are amazing solutions being produced, such as CROPP, these advances are more frequently leveraged in creating algorithms to promote products on commercial platforms, not in making the world a better place. Even the knowledge we are gaining in behavioural science tends to be more heavily used to take

advantage of us rather than work to our advantage as humans. The tech giants, for example, employ some of the best scholars from the most prestigious schools to use behavioural insights for commercial gain. Some of the most creative minds in the world expend huge amounts of brain power on how to hook us into their apps or making that recommendation of what to buy next magically appear on our social media feed. Some people have even claimed that social media can predict a relationship break-up before those in the relationship can and start using that knowledge to 'sell' us a new lifestyle accordingly. Meanwhile, governments are slow and even reluctant to take on board those very same insights to enable more effective policy and to address other societal concerns. This mismatch and imbalance mean that civilisation is actually at risk of going backwards where humanity is concerned and research backs this up.

As we sit and watch the news and see what feels like ever more mass shootings, increasing rates of depression and suicide, and heightened levels of hatred and extremism, we all want to do something – but we don't know how. We try to shout louder, but use technology to do it, posting tens of millions of messages online every day, which only serves to overwhelm and undermine our ability to be human. We use scientific and technological advances to create solutions. For example, debilitating illnesses such as depression can now be treated with a drug, something that was not possible a century ago. But we also use advances in science and technology to achieve a faster pace of life, often for commercial gain, that results in an ever-increasing mismatch between the brain and our environment. This in turn means that while we can now treat depression, overall levels of poor mental health are rising dramatically. The suicide rate in the US has increased by 31 per cent since

2001.[4] In other words, the drugs are clearly not solving the problem.

We need inoculation not cure.

Neuroscience has already yielded some incredible insights and there will be more to come. The next step is harnessing that knowledge and integrating it with other advances – such as those in artificial intelligence – in a way that aligns with and makes optimal use of who we are as humans. All of the evidence shows that when we use our brain in its most natural way, harnessing role models and collective mirror thinking as the basis from which to share social and emotional learning, we have the potential to do amazing things. Coupled with using technological advances to the advantage of humans, we will make the world a better place.

If we work with our brains rather than against them and use this knowledge, we could break numerous negative cycles in our own lives and enhance the lives of the next generation. Paying attention to these factors and not letting the technological advances in our world smother our capability to be human would help ensure that everyone is more able to realise their full potential.

Significantly, evidence shows that prioritising behavioural skills for our children is critical. Ensuring children are exposed to social and emotional learning in school delivers positive outcomes including better mental health, improved physical health, and a higher likelihood of getting a good job and having a rewarding lifestyle. To do this, teachers need to be empowered to pass on these skills, not disabled by the barrage of testing required. And, perhaps most importantly, our children need to be freed from the brutal, addictive hold of social media. If we can improve mirror thinking in young people, research shows that it will help

to dismantle the momentum of abuse, violence and crime being passed from one generation to another.

At a collective level, paying closer attention to our social and emotional worlds, and building a better understanding of who we are would help alleviate countless global issues, including the election of poor leaders, economic crises, the obesity epidemic, the risk we face from terrorism, international conflicts, global warming and even ease poverty.

So how can we work to ensure that this happens? How do we impose more regulation on how technology is used when we see negative impacts in society? Drinking, gambling, drug use and even sugar are all regulated because they can damage individual lives and communities. Very few people would criticise these regulations. Solutions don't have to be groundbreaking to return us to our natural way of being – the age that children are allowed on social media platforms could be higher or time spent per day limited by age. This would ensure that kids spend more time learning face to face about the social and emotional nuances of the worlds they live in. Leveraging behavioural insights for good rather than gain needs to be seen as a priority not an afterthought for our governments and the corporations that make super profits from their activities.

You now have a little more insight into how hugely interconnected we are as humans. The question is – how will you respond? Will you be a social, emotional zombie or wake up to the world and people around you? You are unique as an individual, but your uniqueness only counts when we interact with others, stimulating the lives of those around us within your own mind. We have a shared experience of the world, a shared understanding along with dependence on each other and an ability to thrive. In the same way we need to eat and drink water to survive – we need to interact with other people. In the same way that

the water quality and nutritional content of our food impacts our body, the interactions that we have impact our brain and our soul. Without that connection, our very morals and values are all at risk of being lost.

If you choose to make the effort to 'observe' what's going on around you, which behaviours you take on board and how you respond, you can take some degree of control in how your brain is being shaped. You can choose to reflect the world you wish to see in your own behaviour and, while you or I may not be able to change the whole of society, we can certainly start a virtuous cycle of our own. We each meet roughly 80,000 people in our life, and if they take away something good from us and pass it on to the next 80,000 people, we theoretically could impact 6.4 billion people. If they then pass it on, the maths speaks for itself.

Imagine if you stop staring at your phone the next time you buy a coffee and actually look up and smile at the barista before you order – that simple interaction could create a ripple effect. Imagine that if you watch your child play with all your attention and don't answer a text message, you will teach them the importance of affection and praise through mirroring. The quality of each and every interaction improves every single relationship and increases that chance of us passing on knowledge, and, powerfully, an understanding of what human relationships could and should be. The invisible domino effect of one positive interaction will be huge – in fact it will impact the whole of humanity.

References

Introduction

1. Hofman, M. A. 2014. Evolution of the human brain: when bigger is better. *Frontiers in neuroanatomy* 8, 15.
2. Maclean, P. 1985. Evolutionary psychiatry and the triune brain. *Psychological Medicine* 15(2): 219–221.
3. www.lexico.com/en/definition/role_model
4. Ramachandran, V. S. (2000). Mirror neurons and imitation learning as the driving force behind 'the great leap forward' in human evolution. www.edge.org/3rd_culture/ramachandran/ramachandran_index.html
5. Cannon, E. N. & Woodward, A. L. 2008. Action anticipation and interference: a test of prospective gaze. CogSci Annual Conference of the Cognitive Science Society Vol. 2008, p. 981.
6. Rhodes, J. E. & DuBois, D. L. 2008. Mentoring relationships and programs for youth. *Current Directions in Psychological Science* 17(4): 254–258.

Chapter One

1. www.developingchild.harvard.edu/science/key-concepts/brain-architecture
2. www.developingchild.harvard.edu/science/key-concepts/brain-architecture
3. There is currently disagreement over whether we are born with or develop the aspects of the mirror system, but I personally ascribe to the latter.
4. Užgiris, I. Č., Benson, J. B., Kruper, J. C. & Vasek, M. E. 1989. Contextual influences on imitative interactions between mothers and infants. *Action in social context*. Springer, Boston, 103–127.
5. Fogel, A., Toda, S., & Kawai, M. 1988. Mother-infant face-to-face interaction in Japan and the United States: a laboratory comparison using three-month-old infants. *Developmental Psychology* 24(3): 398.
6. www.developingchild.harvard.edu/resources/inbrief-science-of-ecd
7. McNeil, M. C., Polloway, E. A. & Smith, J. D. 1984. Feral and isolated children: Historical review and analysis. *Education and training of the mentally retarded* 70–79.
8. Meltzoff, A. N. & Moore, M. K. 1977. Imitation of facial and manual gestures by human neonates. *Science* 198(4312): 75–78.
9. Heyes, C. 2018. *Cognitive Gadgets: The cultural evolution of thinking*. Harvard University Press, Cambridge, MA.
10. Ramachandran, V. S. (2000). Mirror neurons and imitation learning as the driving force behind 'the great leap forward' in human evolution. www.edge.org/3rd_culture/ramachandran/ramachandran_index.html

11 Epigenetics refers to the environmental influences that lead to a gene being switched on or off, which results in each person's mirror system developing and adapting through exposure to different experiences, relying heavily on these interactions with the social environment.

12 Pawlby, S. J. 1977. *Imitative Interaction: Studies in mother-infant interaction.* New York Academic Press, 203–224.

13 Haviland, J. M. & Lilac, M. 1987. The induced after affect response: 10-week-old infants responses to three emotion expressions. *Developmental Psychology* 24: 223–229.

14 Lenzi, D., Trentini, C., Pantano, P., Macaluso, E., Iacoboni, M., Lenzi, G. L. & Ammaniti, M. 2009. Neural basis of maternal communication and emotional expression processing during infant preverbal stage. *Cerebral Cortex* 19(5): 1124–1133.

15 Ebisch, S. J., Aureli, T., Bafunno, D., Cardone, D., Romani, G. L., & Merla, A. 2012. Mother and child in synchrony: thermal facial imprints of autonomic contagion. *Biological psychology* 89(1): 123–129.

16 Yang, C. 2006. *The Infinite Gift: How children learn and unlearn the languages of the world.* Scribner, New York.

17 Hoff, E., Core, C., Place, S., Rumiche, R., Señor, M. & Parra, M. 2012. Dual language exposure and early bilingual development. *Journal of Child Language* 39(1): 1–27.

18 Plante-Hébert, J. & Boucher, V. J. 2015. Effects of nasality and utterance length on the recognition of familiar speakers. International Congress of Phonetic Science, Glasgow, United Kingdom.

19 Von Kriegstein, K. & Giraud, A. L. 2006. Implicit multisensory associations influence voice recognition. *PLoS biology* 4(10).

20 Tettamanti, M., Buccino, G., Saccuman M. C., Gallese, V., Danna, M., Scifo, P., Fazio, F., Rizzolatti, G., Cappa, S. F. & Parani, D. 2005. Listening to action-related sentences activates fronto-parietal motor circuits. *Journal of Cognitive Neuroscience* 17: 273–281.

21 Fazio, P., Cantagallo, A., Craighero, L., D'ausilio, A., Roy, A. C., Pozzo, T., Calzolari, F., Granieri, E. & Fadiga, L. 2009. Encoding of human action in Broca's area. *Brain* 132(7): 1980–88.

22 www.developingchild.harvard.edu/resources/inbrief-science-of-ecd

23 www.hunewsservice.com/newsteens-look-up-to-parents-not-celebrities-and-athletes-as-role-models

24 Madhavan, S. & Crowell, J. 2014. Who would you like to be like? Family, village and national role models among black youth in rural South Africa. *Journal of Adolescent Research* 29(6): 716–737.

25 www.scmp.com/magazines/post-magazine/long-reads/article/2169346/one-year-adopted-girl-reunited-birth-parents

26 Widom, C. S., Czaja, S. J. & DuMont, K. A. 2015. Intergenerational transmission of child abuse and neglect: real or detection bias? *Science* 347(6229): 1480–1485.

27 Kandel, D. B., Griesler, P. C. & Hu, M. C. 2015. Intergenerational patterns of smoking and nicotine dependence among US adolescents. *American Journal of Public Health* 105(11):e63–e72.

28 Murden, F. 2018. *Defining You: How to profile yourself and unlock your full potential.* Nicholas Brealey, London.

29 https://www.goodreads.com/quotes/492199-my-parents-raised-me-to-never-feel-like-i-was

30 Murden, F. 2018. *Defining You: How to profile yourself and unlock your full potential.* Nicholas Brealey, London.

31   Lindquist, M. J., Sol, J. & Van Praag, M. 2015. Why do entrepreneurial parents have entrepreneurial children?. *Journal of Labor Economics* 33(2): 269–296.

32   www.telegraph.co.uk/culture/film/starsandstories/11395314/Fifty-Shades-Dakota-Johnson-on-sex-scenes-and-her-famous-parents.html

33   Beede, D. N., Julian, T. A., Langdon, D., McKittrick, G., Khan, B. & Doms, M. E. 2011. Women in STEM: a gender gap to innovation. *Economics and Statistics Administration Issue Brief* 4–11.

34   Olsson, M. I. T. & Martiny, S. E. 2018. Does exposure to counterstereotypical role models influence girls' and women's gender stereotypes and career choices? A review of social psychological research. *Frontiers in Psychology* 9: 2264.

35   Olsson, M. I. T. & Martiny, S. E. 2018. Does exposure to counterstereotypical role models influence girls' and women's gender stereotypes and career choices? A review of social psychological research. *Frontiers in Psychology* 9, 2264.

36   www.time.com/4821462/melinda-gates-advice-from-father

37   www.evoke.org/articles/june-2019/Data-Driven/Fresh_Takes/the-difference-a-dad-can-make

38   Geher, G. 2000. Perceived and actual characteristics of parents and partners: a test of a Freudian model of mate selection. *Current Psychology* 19(3): 194–214.

39   www.npr.org/2016/07/26/487431756/michelle-obamas-prepared-remarks-for-democratic-national-convention?t=1579631389701

40   Vaughn, A. E., Martin, C. L. & Ward, D. S. 2018. What matters most – what parents model or what parents eat?. *Appetite* 126: 102–107.

41   Reicks, M., Banna, J., Cluskey, M., Gunther, C., Hongu, N., Richards, R., Topham, G. & Wong, S. S. 2015. Influence of parenting practices on eating behaviors of early adolescents during independent eating occasions: implications for obesity prevention. *Nutrients* 7(10): 8783–8801.

Chapter Two

1   www.telegraph.co.uk/health-fitness/body/alistair-brownlee-mum-wouldnt-have-been-happy-if-id-left-jonny-b

2   www.telegraph.co.uk/health-fitness/body/alistair-brownlee-mum-wouldnt-have-been-happy-if-id-left-jonny-b

3   www.joshuas.io/brownlee-brothers-brotherhood-beyond

4   Alba, R. D. & Kadushin, C. 1976. The intersection of social circles: a new measure of social proximity in networks. *Sociological Methods & Research* 5(1): 77–102.

5   Tukahirwa, J. T., Mol, A. P. J. & Oosterveer, P. 2011. Access of urban poor to NGO/CBO-supplied sanitation and solid waste services in Uganda: the role of social proximity. *Habitat International* 35(4): 582–591.

6   McHale, S. M. & Crouter, A. C. 1996. *The family contexts of children's sibling relationships*. Ablex Publishing, New York.

7   Nicoletti, C. & Rabe, B. 2019. Sibling spillover effects in school achievement. *Journal of Applied Econometrics* 34(4): 482–501.

8   Tucker, C. J., Updegraff, K. A., McHale, S. M. & Crouter, A. C. 1999. Older siblings as socializers of younger siblings' empathy. *The Journal of Early Adolescence* 19(2): 176–198.

9   Jambon, M., Madigan, S., Plamondon, A., Daniel, E. & Jenkins, J. 2018. The development of empathic concern in siblings: a reciprocal influence model. *Child Development*.

10   Pollack, W. S. 2006. The 'war' for boys: hearing 'real boys' voices, healing their pain. *Professional Psychology: Research and Practice* 37(2): 190.

11   Iacoboni, M. 2009. Imitation, empathy and mirror neurons. *Annual Review of Psychology* 60: 653–670.

12   Pfeifer, J. H. & Dapretto, M. 2011. Mirror, mirror, in my mind: empathy, interpersonal competence and the mirror neuron system. *The Social Neuroscience of Empathy* 183.

13   Rizzolatti, G. 2005. The mirror neuron system and its function in humans. *Anatomy and Embryology* 210(5–6): 419–421.

14   Slomkowski, C., Rende, R., Novak, S., Lloyd-Richardson, E. & Niaura, R. 2005. Sibling effects on smoking in adolescence: evidence for social influence from a genetically informative design. *Addiction* 100(4): 430–438.

15   Wall-Wieler, E., Roos, L. L. & Nickel, N. C. 2018. Adolescent pregnancy outcomes among sisters and mothers: a population-based retrospective cohort study using linkable administrative data. *Public Health Reports* 133(1): 100–108.

16   Lyngstad, T. H. & Prskawetz, A. 2010. Do siblings' fertility decisions influence each other? *Demography* 47(4): 923–934.

17   www.fortune.com/2013/03/22/the-hatred-and-bitterness-behind-two-of-the-worlds-most-popular-brands

18   www.adidassler.org/en/life-and-work/chronicle

19   Smit, B. 2008. *Sneaker Wars: The enemy brothers who founded Adidas and Puma and the family feud that forever changed the business of sport.* CCCO/HarperCollins, New York.

20   www.bundesligafanatic.com/20160817/adidas-vs-puma-part-2-key-battles

21   www.thesun.co.uk/sport/1642200/ed-brownlee-tells-the-sun-what-its-like-to-be-the-big-burly-one-following-olympic-triathlon-brothers-jonny-and-alistairs-win

22   Bank D. P. & Kahn M. D. 1997. *Adult Sibling Relationship. The Sibling Bond.* Basic Books, New York.

23   Yang, J., Hou, X., Wei, D., Wang, K., Li, Y. and Qiu, J. 2017. Only-child and non-only-child exhibit differences in creativity and agreeableness: evidence from behavioral and anatomical structural studies. *Brain Imaging and Behaviour* 11(2): 493–502.

24   McHale, S. M., Updegraff, K. A. & Whiteman, S. D. 2012. Sibling relationships and influences in childhood and adolescence. *Journal of Marriage and Family* 74(5): 913–930.

25   Society for Research in Child Development. Younger and older siblings contribute positively to each other's developing empathy. *ScienceDaily* 20 February 2018.

26   Chambers, S. A., Rowa-Dewar, N., Radley, A. & Dobbie, F. 2017. A systematic review of grandparents' influence on grandchildren's cancer risk factors. *PloS One* 12(11).

27   www.ox.ac.uk/research/research-impact/grandparents-contribute-childrens-wellbeing

28   Profe, W. & Wild, L. G. 2017. Mother, father and grandparent involvement: associations with adolescent mental health and substance use. *Journal of Family Issues* 38(6): 776–797.

29   Zeng, Z. & Xie, Y. 2014. The effects of grandparents on children's schooling: evidence from rural China. *Demography* 51(2): 599–617.

30   www.gla.ac.uk/news/archiveofnews/2017/november/headline_559766_en.html

31   Elias, N., Nimrod, G. & Lemish, D. 2019. The ultimate treat? Young Israeli children's media use under their grandparents' care. *Journal of Children and Media* 13(4): 472–483.

32   Nimrod, G., Elias, N. & Lemish, D. 2019. Measuring mediation of children's media use. *International Journal of Communication* 13: 17.

33   The opening sentences from Mandela's statement from the dock at the Rivonia Trial, April 1964.

34   Johnson, S. K., Buckingham, M. H., Morris, S. L., Suzuki, S., Weiner, M. B., Hershberg, R. M., Fremont, E. R., Batanova, M., Aymong, C. C., Hunter, C. J. & Bowers, E. P. 2016. Adolescents' character role models: exploring who young people look up to as examples of how to be a good person. *Research in Human Development* 13(2): 126–141.

35   Beam, M. R., Chen, C. & Greenberger, E. 2002. The nature of adolescents' relationships with their 'very important' non-parental adults. *American Journal of Community Psychology* 30(2): 305–325.

36   Hurd, N. M., Zimmerman, M. A. & Reischl, T. M. 2011. Role model behavior and youth violence: a study of positive and negative effects. *The Journal of Early Adolescence* 31(2): 323–354.

37   www.nytimes.com/1984/04/09/style/relationships-the-roles-of-uncles-and-aunts.html

Chapter Three

1   Guinn, J., 2010. *Go Down Together: The true, untold story of Bonnie and Clyde.* Simon and Schuster, New York. 59.

2   www.theatlantic.com/magazine/archive/2003/09/people-like-us/302774

3   Telzer, E. H., Fuligni, A. J., Lieberman, M. D. & Galván, A. 2013. Ventral striatum activation to prosocial rewards predicts longitudinal declines in adolescent risk-taking. *Developmental Cognitive Neuroscience* 3: 45–52.

4   Klucharev, V., Munneke, M. A., Smidts, A. & Fernández, G. 2011. Downregulation of the posterior medial frontal cortex prevents social conformity. *Journal of Neuroscience* 31(33): 11934–11940.

5   Campbell-Meiklejohn, D. K., Bach, D. R., Roepstorff, A., Dolan, R. J. & Frith, C. D. 2010. How the opinion of others affects our valuation of objects. *Current Biology* 20(13): 1165–1170.

6   Christakis, N. A. & Fowler, J. H. 2007. The spread of obesity in a large social network over 32 years. *New England Journal of Medicine* 357(4): 370–379.

7   Christakis, N. A. & Fowler, J. H. 2007. The spread of obesity in a large social network over 32 years. *New England Journal of Medicine* 357(4): 370–379.

8   Katzenbach J. R. & Khan, Z. 2010. Positive peer pressure: a powerful ally to change. *Harvard Business Review* 6 April 2010.

9   Paluck, E. L., Shepherd, H. & Aronow, P. M. 2016. Changing climates of
     conflict: a social network experiment in 56 schools. Proceedings of the
     National Academy of Sciences 113(3): 566–571.

Chapter Four

1   www.independent.co.uk/voices/aylan-kurdi-death-three-year-
     anniversary-child-refugee-home-office-a8518276.html
2   www.theguardian.com/world/2015/dec/22/abdullah-kurdi-
     father-boy-on-beach-alan-refugee-tragedy
3   www.theguardian.com/world/2015/sep/02/
     shocking-image-of-drowned-syrian-boy-shows-tragic-plight-of-
     refugees
4   www.independent.co.uk/voices/aylan-kurdi-death-three-year-
     anniversary-child-refugee-home-office-a8518276.html
5   Hein, G., Engelmann, J. B., Vollberg, M. C. & Tobler, P. N. 2016. How
     learning shapes the empathic brain. Proceedings of the National Academy of
     Sciences 113(1): 80–85.
6   www.theguardian.com/society/2018/oct/04/increasing-number-
     of-britons-think-empathy-is-on-the-wane
7   Konrath, S. H., O'Brien, E. H. & Hsing, C. 2011. Changes in dispositional
     empathy in American college students over time: a meta-analysis.
     Personality and Social Psychology Review 15(2): 180–198.
8   Ferrari, P. F., Gallese, V., Rizzolatti, G. & Fogassi, L. 2003. Mirror
     neurons responding to the observation of ingestive and communicative
     mouth actions in the monkey ventral premotor cortex. European Journal of
     Neuroscience 17(8): 1703–1714.
9   Hutchison, W. D., Davis, K. D., Lozano, A. M., Tasker, R. R. & Dostrovsky,
     J. O. 1999. Pain-related neurons in the human cingulate cortex. Nature
     Neuroscience 2(5): 403.
10   Hutchison, W. D., Davis, K. D., Lozano, A. M., Tasker, R. R. &
     Dostrovsky, J. O. 1999. Pain-related neurons in the human cingulate
     cortex. Nature Neuroscience 2(5): 403–405.
11   Mukamel, R., Ekstrom, A. D., Kaplan, J., Iacoboni, M. & Fried, I. 2010.
     Single-neuron responses in humans during execution and observation of
     actions. Current Biology 20(8): 750–756.
12   Christov-Moore, L., Simpson, E. A., Coudé, G., Grigaityte, K., Iacoboni,
     M. & Ferrari, P. F. 2014. Empathy: gender effects in brain and behavior.
     Neuroscience & Biobehavioral Reviews 46: 604–627.
13   Krevans, J. R. & Benson, J. A. 1983. Evaluation of humanistic qualities in
     the internist. Annals of Internal Medicine 99(5): 720–724.
14   Osgood, V. New Medical Education and Training Standards. General Medical
     Council meeting, 2 June 2015.
15   Newton, B. W., Barber, L., Clardy, J., Cleveland, E. & O'Sullivan, P. 2008.
     Is there hardening of the heart during medical school? Academic Medicine 83(3):
     244–249.
16   Neumann, M., Edelhäuser, F., Tauschel, D., Fischer, M. R., Wirtz, M.,
     Woopen, C., Haramati, A. & Scheffer, C. 2011. Empathy decline and its
     reasons: a systematic review of studies with medical students and residents.
     Academic Medicine 86(8): 996–1009.

17   Neumann, M., Edelhäuser, F., Tauschel, D., Fischer, M. R., Wirtz, M., Woopen, C., Haramati, A. & Scheffer, C. 2011. Empathy decline and its reasons: a systematic review of studies with medical students and residents. *Academic Medicine* 86(8): 996–1009.

18   Hojat, M., Vergare, M. J., Maxwell, K., Brainard, G., Herrine, S. K., Isenberg, G. A., Veloski, J. & Gonnella, J. S. 2009. The devil is in the third year: a longitudinal study of erosion of empathy in medical school. *Academic Medicine* 84(9): 1182–1191.

19   Mirani, S. H., Shaikh, N. A. & Tahir, A. 2019. Assessment of clinical empathy among medical students using the Jefferson Scale of Empathy – student version. *Cureus* 11(2).

20   Mostafa, A., Hoque, R., Mostafa, M., Rana, M. M. & Mostafa, F. 2014. Empathy in undergraduate medical students of Bangladesh: psychometric analysis and differences by gender, academic year and specialty preferences. *ISRN Psychiatry* 375439.

21   Triffaux, J. M., Tisseron, S. & Nasello, J. A. 2019. Decline of empathy among medical students: dehumanization or useful coping process?. *L'Encéphale* 45(1): 3–8.

22   Pagano, A., Robinson, K., Ricketts, C., Cundy Jones, J., Henderson, L., Cartwright, W. & Batt, A. M. 2019. *Empathy levels in Canadian paramedic students: a longitudinal study.*

23   Ameh, P. O., Uti, O. G. & Daramola, O. O. 2019. Empathy among dental students in a Nigerian institution. *European Journal of Dental Education* 23(2): 135–142.

24   Devi, N. A., Eapen, A. A. & Manickam, L. S. S. 2018. A comparative cross-sectional study on the level of empathy between the freshmen to senior undergraduate student nurses. *International Journal for Advance Research and Development* 3(9): 10–14.

25   Nunes, P., Williams, S., Sa, B. & Stevenson, K., 2011. A study of empathy decline in students from five health disciplines during their first year of training. *International Journal of Medical Education* 2: 12–17.

26   Singh, S. 2005. Empathy: lost or found in medical education?. *Medscape General Medicine* 7(3): 74.

27   Namely the anterior cingulate cortex, anterior insular cortex, periaqueductal gray.

28   Newton, B. W., Barber, L., Clardy, J., Cleveland, E. & O'Sullivan, P. 2008. Is there hardening of the heart during medical school?. *Academic Medicine* 83(3): 244–249.

29   Bauer J. 2005. *Why I Feel What You Feel. Communication and the Mystery of Mirror Neurons* [in German]. Hoffmann und Campe; Hamburg, Germany.

30   Nielsen, H. G. & Tulinius, C. 2009. Preventing burnout among general practitioners: is there a possible route?. *Education for Primary Care* 20(5): 353–359.

31   Thirioux, B., Birault, F. & Jaafari, N. 2016. Empathy is a protective factor of burnout in physicians: new neuro-phenomenological hypotheses regarding empathy and sympathy in care relationship. *Frontiers in Psychology* 7: 763.

32   Goldman, A. I. 2011. Two routes to empathy: insights from cognitive neuroscience *Empathy: Philosophical and Psychological Perspectives*, eds A. Coplan and P. Goldie. Oxford University Press, 31–44.

33   Heyes, C. 2018. Empathy is not in our genes. *Neuroscience & Biobehavioral Reviews* 95: 499–507.

34   As neuroscientists are understanding more about these functions in the brain they are realising that they may not be clearly separable, *e.g.*

Christov-Moore, L., Reggente, N., Douglas, P. K., Feusner, J. & Iacoboni, M. 2019. Predicting empathy from resting brain connectivity: a multivariate approach *bioRxiv*: 539551. However, there is agreement that this is a useful way of explaining the functions.

35   Greimel, E., Schulte-Rüther, M., Fink, G. R., Piefke, M., Herpertz-Dahlmann, B. & Konrad, K. 2010. Development of neural correlates of empathy from childhood to early adulthood: an fMRI study in boys and adult men. *Journal of Neural Transmission* 117(6): 781–791.

36   Christov-Moore, L. & Iacoboni, M. 2016. Self-other resonance, its control and prosocial inclinations: brain–behavior relationships. *Human Brain Mapping* 37(4):1544–1558.

37   Benbassat, J. 2014. Role-modeling in medical education: the importance of a reflective imitation. *Academic Medicine* 89(4): 550.

38   Passi, V., Doug, M., Peile, J. T. & Johnson, N. 2010. Developing medical professionalism in future doctors: a systematic review. *International Journal of Medical Education* 1: 19–29.

39   Passi, V. & Johnson, N. 2016. The hidden process of positive doctor role modelling. *Medical Teacher* 38(7):700–707.

40   www.bma.org.uk/advice/career/progress-your-career/teaching

41   Smith, L. S. 2005. Joys of teaching nursing. *Nursing 2019* 35: 134–135.

42   Maudsley, R. F. 2001. Role models and the learning environment: essential elements in effective medical education. *Academic Medicine* 76(5): 432–434.

Chapter Five

1   www.apbspeakers.com/speaker/louanne-johnson

2   www.people.com/archive/boot-camp-candy-vol-44-no-10

3   Olson, K. 2014. *The Invisible Classroom. Relationships, neuroscience and mindfulness in school.* Norton & Co, New York.

4   Johnson, S. K., Buckingham, M. H., Morris, S. L., Suzuki, S., Weiner, M. B., Hershberg, R. M. & Bowers, E. P. 2016. Adolescents' character role models: exploring who young people look up to as examples of how to be a good person. *Research in Human Development* 13(2): 126–141.

5   Jackson, C. K. 2018. What do test scores miss? The importance of teacher effects on non-test score outcomes. *Journal of Political Economy* 126(5): 2072–2107.

6   Jackson, C. K. 2018. What do test scores miss? The importance of teacher effects on non-test score outcomes. *Journal of Political Economy* 126(5): 2072–2107.

7   www.people.com/archive/boot-camp-candy-vol-44-no-10

8   Sakiz, G., Pape, S. J. & Hoy, A. W. 2012. Does perceived teacher affective support matter for middle school students in mathematics classrooms? *Journal of School Psychology* 50(2): 235–255.

9   DuBois, D. L. & Silverthorn, N. 2005. Natural mentoring relationships and adolescent health: evidence from a national study. *American Journal of Public Health* 95(3): 518–524.

10   Allee-Smith, P. J., Im, M. H., Hughes, J. N. & Clemens, N. H. 2018. Mentor Support Provisions Scale: measure dimensionality, measurement invariance and associations with adolescent school functioning. *Journal of School Psychology* 67: 69–87.

11   Rhodes, J. E. & DuBois, D. L. 2008. Mentoring relationships and programs for youth. *Current Directions in Psychological Science* 17(4): 254–258.

12   Oberle, E. & Schonert-Reichl, K. A. 2016. Stress contagion in the classroom? The link between classroom teacher burnout and morning cortisol in elementary school students. *Social Science & Medicine* 159: 30–37.

13   Murden, F. 2018. *Defining You: How to profile yourself and unlock your full potential*. Nicholas Brealey, London.

14   Tomova, L., Majdandžić, J., Hummer, A., Windischberger, C., Heinrichs, M. & Lamm, C. 2017. Increased neural responses to empathy for pain might explain how acute stress increases prosociality. *Social Cognitive and Affective Neuroscience* 12(3): 401–408.

15   Murden, F. 2018. *Defining You: How to profile yourself and unlock your full potential*. Nicholas Brealey, London.

16   Tomova, L., Majdandžić, J., Hummer, A., Windischberger, C., Heinrichs, M. & Lamm, C. 2017. Increased neural responses to empathy for pain might explain how acute stress increases prosociality. *Social Cognitive and Affective Neuroscience* 12(3): 401–408.

17   Oberle, E. & Schonert-Reichl, K. A. 2016. Stress contagion in the classroom? The link between classroom teacher burnout and morning cortisol in elementary school students. *Social Science & Medicine* 159: 30–37.

18   DuBois, D. L. & Silverthorn, N. 2005. Natural mentoring relationships and adolescent health: evidence from a national study. *American Journal of Public Health* 95: 518.

19   Rhodes, J. E. & DuBois, D. L. 2008. Mentoring relationships and programs for youth. *Current Directions in Psychological Science* 17(4): 254–258.

20   Feinstein, L. 2015. *Social and Emotional Learning: Skills for life and work*. Early Intervention Foundation, UK.

21   I prefer to call emotional intelligence emotional wisdom. Intelligence gives the impression of a fixed capability, whereas whatever our age we can improve our social and emotional skills.

22   Cherniss, C., Extein, M., Goleman, D. & Weissberg, R. P. 2006. Emotional intelligence: what does the research really indicate?. *Educational Psychologist* 41(4): 239–245.

23   Feinstein, L. 2015. *Social and Emotional Learning: Skills for life and work*. Early Intervention Foundation, UK.

24   Feinstein, L. 2015. *Social and Emotional Learning: Skills for life and work*. Early Intervention Foundation, UK.

25   www.bbc.co.uk/scotland/sportscotland/asportingnation/article/0062/page02.shtml

26   www.telegraph.co.uk/sport/rugbyunion/11099705/Scotland-rugby-legend-reveals-abuse-over-Scottish-independence-No-statement.html

27   www.bbc.co.uk/sport/live/rugby-union/31807582

28   www.telegraph.co.uk/sport/rugbyunion/11099705/Scotland-rugby-legend-reveals-abuse-over-Scottish-independence-No-statement.html

29   Bath, R. 2003. *Rugby Union: The Complete Guide*. Carlton Books, UK.

30   www.smithsonianmag.com/innovation/why-are-finlands-schools-successful-49859555

31   www.siliconrepublic.com/careers/finland-education-schools-slush

32   Lohman, M. C. 2006. Factors influencing teachers' engagement in informal learning activities. *Journal of Workplace Learning* 18: 141–156.
33   Lunenberg, M., Korthagen, F. & Swennen, A. 2007. The teacher educator as a role model. *Teaching and Teacher Education* 23(5): 586–601.
34   Eurich, T. 2017. *Insight: Why we're not as self-aware as we think, and how seeing ourselves clearly helps us succeed at work and in life.* Crown Books, US.
35   www.fionamurden.com/2018/02/12/knowing-you-knowing-me
36   Geeraerts, K., Tynjälä, P., Heikkinen, H. L., Markkanen, I., Pennanen, M. & Gijbels, D. 2015. Peer-group mentoring as a tool for teacher development. *European Journal of Teacher Education* 38(3): 358–377.
37   Geeraerts, K., Tynjälä, P., Heikkinen, H. L., Markkanen, I., Pennanen, M. & Gijbels, D. 2015. Peer-group mentoring as a tool for teacher development. *European Journal of Teacher Education* 38(3): 358–377.

Chapter Six

1   www.christianheadlines.com/news/these-are-the-12-pastors-who-are-most-effective-preachers.html
2   http://content.time.com/time/specials/packages/article/0,28804,199323 5_1993243_1993257,00.html
3   King Jr, M. L. 1950. *An Autobiography of Religious Development: The papers of Martin Luther King Jr* 1: 360–361.
4   http://en.wikipedia.org/wiki/Benjamin_Mays
5   Hansen, D. D. 2003. *The Dream: Martin Luther King Jr and the Speech that Inspired a Nation.* HarperCollins, New York.
6   www.nationalarchives.gov.uk/education/heroesvillains/transcript/g6cs3s4t.htm
7   *A 'Dream' Remembered.* NewsHour. August 28, 2003. Retrieved July 19, 2006
8   Decety, J. & Grèzes, J. 2006. The power of simulation: imagining one's own and others' behavior. *Brain Research* 1079(1): 4–14.
9   González, J., Barros-Loscertales, A., Pulvermüller, F., Meseguer, V., Sanjuán, A., Belloch, V. & Ávila, C. 2006. Reading cinnamon activates olfactory brain regions. *Neuroimage* 32(2): 906–912.
10   Lacey, S., Stilla, R. & Sathian, K. 2012. Metaphorically feeling: comprehending textural metaphors activates somatosensory cortex. *Brain and Language* 120(3): 416–421.
11   Katuscáková, M. 2015. Sharing scientific knowledge through telling stories and digital storytelling. European Conference on Knowledge Management 408.
12   Stephens, G. J., Silbert, L. J. & Hasson, U. 2010. Speaker–listener neural coupling underlies successful communication. *Proceedings of the National Academy of Sciences* 107(32): 14425–14430.
13   Stephens, G. J., Silbert, L. J. & Hasson, U. 2010. Speaker–listener neural coupling underlies successful communication. *Proceedings of the National Academy of Sciences* 107(32): 14425–14430.
14   Hasson, U., Ghazanfar, A. A., Galantucci, B., Garrod, S. & Keysers, C. 2012. Brain-to-brain coupling: a mechanism for creating and sharing a social world. *Trends in Cognitive Sciences* 16(2): 114–121.

15   Yuan, Y., Major-Girardin, J. & Brown, S. 2018. Storytelling is intrinsically mentalistic: a functional magnetic resonance imaging study of narrative production across modalities. *Journal of Cognitive Neuroscience* 30(9): 1298–1314.

16   www.greatergood.berkeley.edu/article/item/how_stories_change_brain

17   www.greatergood.berkeley.edu/article/item/how_stories_change_brain

18   http://news.berkeley.edu/berkeley_blog/the-science-of-the-story

19   www.campaignlive.co.uk/article/case-study-always-likeagirl/1366870

20   www.adidas-group.com/en/media/news-archive/press-releases/2004/impossible-nothing-adidas-launches-new-global-brand-advertising-

21   Tyng, C. M., Amin, H. U., Saad, M. N. & Malik, A. S. 2017. The influences of emotion on learning and memory. *Frontiers in Psychology* 8: 1454.

22   McMillan, R., Kaufman, S. B. & Singer, J. L. 2013. Ode to positive constructive daydreaming. *Frontiers in Psychology* 4: 626.

23   McMillan, R., Kaufman, S. B. & Singer, J. L. 2013. Ode to positive constructive daydreaming. *Frontiers in Psychology* 4: 626.

24   www.psycom.net/schizophrenia-hallucinations-delusions

25   Allen, K. 2015. Hallucination and imagination. *Australasian Journal of Philosophy* 93(2): 287–302.

26   McCormick, L. M., Brumm, M. C., Beadle, J. N., Paradiso, S., Yamada, T., Andreasen, N. 2012. Mirror neuron function, psychosis and empathy in schizophrenia. *Psychiatry Research* 201(3): 233–239.

27   Mehta, U. M., Thirthalli, J., Aneelraj, D., Jadhav, P., Gangadhar, B. N. & Keshavan, M. S. 2014. Mirror neuron dysfunction in schizophrenia and its functional implications: a systematic review. *Schizophrenia Research* 160(1-3): 9–19.

28   McMillan, R., Kaufman, S. B. & Singer, J. L. 2013. Ode to positive constructive daydreaming. *Frontiers in Psychology* 4: 626.

29   Hansen, D. D. 2003. *The Dream: Martin Luther King Jr and the speech that inspired a nation.* HarperCollins, New York.

30   Beaty, R. E., Benedek, M., Silvia, P. J. & Schacter, D. L. 2016. Creative cognition and brain network dynamics. *Trends in Cognitive Sciences* 20(2): 87–95.

31   Mula, M., Hermann, B. & Trimble, M. R. 2016. Neuropsychiatry of creativity. *Epilepsy & Behavior* 57: 225–229.

32   www.web.archive.org/web/20110919034257/http://www.independent.co.uk/news/obituaries/john-nelson-729400.html

33   www.bbc.co.uk/newsbeat/article/36107807/12-incredible-and-slightly-crazy-things-about-prince

34   www.bbc.co.uk/newsbeat/article/36107807/12-incredible-and-slightly-crazy-things-about-prince

35   www.startribune.com/dancers-recall-prince-as-a-hard-working-darling-in-tights-and-ballet-slippers/378179261

36   Beaty, R. E., Benedek, M., Wilkins, R. W., Jauk, E., Fink, A., Silvia, P. J., Hodges, D. A., Koschutnig, K. & Neubauer, A. C. 2014. Creativity and the default network: a functional connectivity analysis of the creative brain at rest. *Neuropsychologia* 64: 92–98.

37   King, E. & Waddington, C. (Eds.). 2017. *Music and Empathy.* Taylor & Francis, London.

38 Molnar-Szakacs, I. & Overy, K. 2006. Music and mirror neurons: from motion to 'e'motion. *Social Cognitive and Affective Neuroscience* 1(3): 235–241.

39 Molnar-Szakacs, I. & Overy, K. 2006. Music and mirror neurons: from motion to 'e'motion. *Social Cognitive and Affective Neuroscience* 1(3): 235–241.

40 Preiss, D. D., Ibaceta, M., Ortiz, D., Carvacho, H. & Grau, V. 2019. An exploratory study on mind wandering, metacognition and verbal creativity in Chilean high school students. *Frontiers in Psychology* 10: 1118.

41 Immordino-Yang, M. H., Christodoulou, J. A. & Singh, V. 2012. Rest is not idleness: implications of the brain's default mode for human development and education. *Perspectives on Psychological Science* 7: 352–364.

42 Dewey, J. 1933. *How We Think: A restatement of reflective thinking to the educative process.* D. C. Heath, Boston. (Original work published in 1910.)

43 www.fionamurden.com/2019/03/22/the-power-of-reflection

44 Di Stefano, G., Gino, F., Pisano, G. P. & Staats, B. R. 2016. Making experience count: the role of reflection in individual learning. *Harvard Business School NOM Unit Working Paper* 14–93.

45 Immordino-Yang, M. H., Christodoulou, J. A. & Singh, V. 2012. Rest is not idleness: implications of the brain's default mode for human development and education. *Perspectives on Psychological Science* 7: 352–364.

46 Immordino-Yang, M. H., Christodoulou, J. A. & Singh, V. 2012. Rest is not idleness: implications of the brain's default mode for human development and education. *Perspectives on Psychological Science* 7: 352–364.

47 McMillan, R., Kaufman, S. B. & Singer, J. L. 2013. Ode to positive constructive daydreaming. *Frontiers in Psychology* 4: 626.

48 Trapnell, P. & Sinclair, L. 2012, January. *Texting frequency and the moral shallowing hypothesis.* Poster presented at the Annual Meeting of the Society for Personality and Social Psychology, San Diego, CA.

Chapter Seven

1   www.independent.co.uk/sport/general/boxing-ali-v-frazier-it-was-like-death-closest-thing-to-dyin-that-i-know-of-316051.html

2   Dower, John. *Thrilla in Manila.* 2008. HBO Documentary Films.

3   Dower, John. *Thrilla in Manila.* 2008. HBO Documentary Films.

4   www.independent.co.uk/sport/general/boxing-ali-v-frazier-it-was-like-death-closest-thing-to-dyin-that-i-know-of-316051.html

5   www.independent.co.uk/sport/general/boxing-ali-v-frazier-it-was-like-death-closest-thing-to-dyin-that-i-know-of-316051.html

6   54 Facts you probably don't know about Don King. 14 January 2008. *Boxing News 24.*

7   www.worldatlas.com/articles/what-are-the-most-popular-sports-in-the-world.html

8   Iacoboni, M. 2009. *Mirroring People: The new science of how we connect with others.* Farrar, Straus and Giroux, New York.

9   www.washingtonpost.com/sports/ali-frazier-fights-were-colossal-events-on-theradio/2011/11/08/gIQAO1c62M_story.html

10 Gazzola, V., Aziz-Zadeh, L. & Keysers, C. 2006. Empathy and the somatotopic auditory mirror system in humans. *Current Biology* 16: 1824–1829.

11   Cannon, E. N. & Woodward, A. L. 2008. Action anticipation and interference: a test of prospective gaze. CogSci Annual Conference of the Cognitive Science Society. Vol. 2008: 981.

12   Kumar, A., Killingsworth, M. A. & Gilovich, T. 2014. Waiting for merlot: anticipatory consumption of experiential and material purchases. *Psychological Science* 25(10): 1924–1931.

13   Mukamel, R., Ekstrom, A. D., Kaplan, J., Iacoboni, M. & Fried, I. 2010. Single-neuron responses in humans during execution and observation of actions. *Current Biology* 20(8): 750–756.

14   www.tenniscompanion.org/serve-toss

15   Zetou, E., Tzetzis, G., Vernadakis, N. & Kioumourtzoglou, E. 2002. Modeling in learning two volleyball skills. *Perceptual and Motor Skills* 94(3): 1131–1142.

16   Hendriks, M., & Treur, J. (November 2010). Modeling super-mirroring functionality in action execution, imagination, mirroring and imitation. *International Conference on Computational Collective Intelligence* 330–342.

17   Fryling, M. J., Johnston, C. & Hayes, L. J. 2011. Understanding observational learning: an interbehavioral approach. *The Analysis of Verbal Behavior* 27(1): 191–203.

18   Raiola, G., Tafuri, D. & Gomez Paloma, F. 2014. Physical activity and sport skills and its relation to mind theory on motor control. *Sport Science* 7(1): 52–56.

19   Raiola, G., Tafuri, D. & Gomez Paloma, F. 2014. Physical activity and sport skills and its relation to mind theory on motor control. *Sport Science* 7(1): 52–56.

20   Zhang, L., Pi, Y., Zhu, H., Shen, C., Zhang, J. & Wu, Y. 2018. Motor experience with a sport-specific implement affects motor imagery. *PeerJ* 6:e4687.

21   www.telegraph.co.uk/men/active/10568898/Sports-visualisation-how-to-imagine-your-way-to-success.html

22   www.telegraph.co.uk/men/active/10568898/Sports-visualisation-how-to-imagine-your-way-to-success.html

23   www.smithsonianmag.com/history/phineas-gage-neurosciences-most-famous-patient-11390067

24   Harlow, J. M. 1993. Recovery from the passage of an iron bar through the head. *History of Psychiatry* 4(14): 274–281.

25   Harlow, J. M. 1993. Recovery from the passage of an iron bar through the head. *History of Psychiatry* 4(14): 274–281.

26   Lamm, C., Bukowski, H. & Silani, G. 2016. From shared to distinct self-other representations in empathy: evidence from neurotypical function and socio-cognitive disorders. *Philosophical Transactions of the Royal Society B: Biological Sciences* 371(1686): 20150083.

27   Decety, J., Chen, C., Harenski, C. & Kiehl, K. A. 2013. An fMRI study of affective perspective taking in individuals with psychopathy: imagining another in pain does not evoke empathy. *Frontiers in Human Neuroscience* (7): 489.

28   Knight, M. 2014. Psychopaths' broken empathy circuit. *SA Mind* 25,1,19.

29   Iacoboni, M. 2009. *Mirroring People: The new science of how we connect with others.* Farrar, Straus and Giroux, New York.

30   Kahl, S., & Kopp, S. 2018. A predictive processing model of perception and action for self-other distinction. *Frontiers in Psychology* 9: 2421.

31   Christov-Moore, L., Sugiyama, T., Grigaityte, K. & Iacoboni, M. 2017.
      Increasing generosity by disrupting prefrontal cortex. *Social Neuroscience*
      12(2): 174–181.
32   Christov-Moore, L., Sugiyama, T., Grigaityte, K. & Iacoboni, M. 2017.
      Increasing generosity by disrupting prefrontal cortex. *Social Neuroscience*
      12(2): 174–181.
33   Hamlin, J. K., Wynn, K. & Bloom, P. 2007. Social evaluation by preverbal
      infants. *Nature* 450(7169): 557.
34   Hare, B. 2017. Survival of the friendliest: Homo sapiens evolved via
      selection for prosociality. *Annual Review of Psychology* 68: 155–186.
35   Singer, T. & Fehr, E. 2005. The neuroeconomics of mind reading and
      empathy. *American Economic Review* 95(2): 340–345.
36   Rand, D. G., Greene, J. D. & Nowak, M. A. 2012. Spontaneous giving
      and calculated greed. *Nature* 489(7416): 427.
37   Christov-Moore, L., Sugiyama, T., Grigaityte, K. & Iacoboni, M. 2017.
      Increasing generosity by disrupting prefrontal cortex. *Social Neuroscience*
      12(2): 174–181.

Chapter Eight

1   www.theguardian.com/world/2007/nov/10/schools.schoolsworldwide
2   Langman, P. 2012. Two Finnish school shooters. www. schoolshooters.
      info.
3   www.theguardian.com/world/2007/nov/10/schools.schoolsworldwide
4   www.theguardian.com/world/2007/nov/10/schools.schoolsworldwide
5   http://news.bbc.co.uk/1/hi/world/europe/7082795.stm
6   Langman, P. 2012. Two Finnish school shooters. www. schoolshooters.
      info.
7   Strenziok, M., Krueger, F., Deshpande, G., Lenroot, R. K., van der Meer,
      E. & Grafman, J. 2010. Fronto-parietal regulation of media violence
      exposure in adolescents: a multi-method study. *Social Cognitive and Affective
      Neuroscience* 6(5): 537–547.
8   Koolhaas, J. M., Coppens, C. M., de Boer, S. F., Buwalda, B., Meerlo, P.
      & Timmermans, P. J. 2013. The resident-intruder paradigm: a standardized
      test for aggression, violence and social stress. *Journal of Visualized
      Experiments* (77): e4367.
9   Langman, P. (2013). Thirty-five rampage school shooters: Trends,
      patterns, and typology. In School shootings (pp. 131–156). Springer, New
      York, NY.
10   Langman, P. (2013). Thirty-five rampage school shooters: Trends,
      patterns, and typology. In School shootings (pp. 131–156). Springer, New
      York, NY.
11   Langman, P. 2018. Different types of role model influence and fame
      seeking among mass killers and copycat offenders. *American Behavioral
      Scientist* 62(2): 210–228.
12   Langman, P. 2018. Different types of role model influence and fame
      seeking among mass killers and copycat offenders. *American Behavioral
      Scientist* 62(2): 210–228.
13   Björkqvist, K. 2015. White rage: bullying as an antecedent of school
      shootings. *Journal of Child Adolescent Behavior* 3(175): 2–6.

14   Iacoboni, M. 2009. *Mirroring People: The new science of how we connect with others.* Farrar, Straus and Giroux, New York.
15   Comstock, G. 2005. Media violence and aggression, properly considered. *Perspectives on imitation: from neuroscience to social science* 2: 371–380.
16   Guadagno, R. E., Lankford, A., Muscanell, N. L., Okdie, B. M. & McCallum, D. M. 2010. Social influence in the online recruitment of terrorists and terrorist sympathizers: implications for social psychology research. *Revue Internationale de Psychologie Sociale* 23(1): 25–56.
17   Decety, J., Pape, R. & Workman, C. I. 2018. A multi-level social neuroscience perspective on radicalization and terrorism. *Social Neuroscience* 13(5): 511–529.
18   Guadagno, R. E., Lankford, A., Muscanell, N. L., Okdie, B. M. & McCallum, D. M. 2010. Social influence in the online recruitment of terrorists and terrorist sympathizers: implications for social psychology research. *Revue Internationale de Psychologie Sociale* 23(1): 25–56.
19   Iacoboni, M. 2009. *Mirroring People: The new science of how we connect with others.* Farrar, Straus and Giroux, New York. 147.
20   Nagle, A. 2017. *Kill All Normies: Online culture wars from 4chan and Tumblr to Trump and the alt-right.* John Hunt Publishing, UK.
21   www.economist.com/open-future/2018/08/03/how-the-grotesque-online-culture-wars-fuel-populism
22   www.revealnews.org/article/they-spewed-hate-then-they-punctuated-it-with-the-presidents-name
23   Rushin, S., & Edwards, G. S. 2018. The effect of President Trump's election on hate crimes. www.ssrn.com 3102652.
24   From @realDonaldTrump Twitter feed, 14 July 2019, 12: 27pm
25   https://time.com/3923128/donald-trump-announcement-speech
26   Wilson, R. A. 2019. HATE: Why we should resist it with free speech, not censorship by Nadine Strossen. *Human Rights Quarterly* 41(1): 213–217.
27   Losin, E. A. R., Iacoboni, M., Martin, A., Cross, K. A. & Dapretto, M. 2012. Race modulates neural activity during imitation. *Neuroimage* 59(4): 3594–3603.
28   Losin, E. A. R., Iacoboni, M., Martin, A., Cross, K. A. & Dapretto, M. 2012. Race modulates neural activity during imitation. *Neuroimage* 59(4): 3594–3603.
29   www.revealnews.org/blog/hate-report-the-presidents-inspiring-schoolyard-bullies
30   Forster, M., Grigsby, T. J., Unger, J. B. & Sussman, S. 2015. Associations between gun violence exposure, gang associations and youth aggression: implications for prevention and intervention programs. *Journal of Criminology*: 1–8.
31   Lenzi, M., Sharkey, J., Vieno, A., Mayworm, A., Dougherty, D. & Nylund-Gibson, K. 2015. Adolescent gang involvement: the role of individual, family, peer and school factors in a multi-level perspective. *Aggressive Behavior* 41(4): 386–397.
32   Lenzi, M., Sharkey, J., Vieno, A., Mayworm, A., Dougherty, D. & Nylund-Gibson, K. 2015. Adolescent gang involvement: the role of individual, family, peer and school factors in a multi-level perspective. *Aggressive Behavior* 41(4): 386–397.
33   Lenzi, M., Sharkey, J., Vieno, A., Mayworm, A., Dougherty, D. & Nylund-Gibson, K. 2015. Adolescent gang involvement: the role of individual, family, peer and school factors in a multi-level perspective. *Aggressive Behavior* 41(4): 386–397.

34   Rush, E. & La Nauze, A. 2006. Corporate paedophilia: sexualisation of children in Australia. www.tai.org.au/documents/downloads/DP90. pdf.

35   Jackson, S. & Vares, T. 2015. Too many bad role models for us girls: girls, female pop celebrities and sexualization. *Sexualities* 18(4): 480–498.

36   www.elle.com/uk/life-and-culture/culture/news/a39643/miley-cyrus-psychological-damage-of-playing-hannah-montana

37   Dijksterhuis, A. 2005. Why we are social animals: the high road to imitation as social glue. *Perspectives on Imitation: From neuroscience to social science* 2: 207–220.

38   Dijksterhuis, A. 2005. Why we are social animals: the high road to imitation as social glue. *Perspectives on Imitation: From neuroscience to social science* 2: 207–220.

39   Kilford, E. J., Garrett, E. & Blakemore, S. J. 2016. The development of social cognition in adolescence: an integrated perspective. *Neuroscience & Biobehavioral Reviews* 70: 106–120.

40   Rosen, M. L., Sheridan, M. A., Sambrook, K. A., Dennison, M. J., Jenness, J. L., Askren, M. K., Meltzoff, A. N. & McLaughlin, K. A. 2018. Salience network response to changes in emotional expressions of others is heightened during early adolescence: relevance for social functioning. *Developmental Science* 21(3): p. 12571.

41   Rosen, M. L., Sheridan, M. A., Sambrook, K. A., Dennison, M. J., Jenness, J. L., Askren, M. K., Meltzoff, A. N. & McLaughlin, K. A. 2018. Salience network response to changes in emotional expressions of others is heightened during early adolescence: relevance for social functioning. *Developmental Science* 21(3): p.e12571.

42   www.nypost.com/2017/09/23/how-a-decade-of-the-kardashians-radically-changed-america

43   Ingham, H. 1995. The portrayal of women on television. Lawrence Erlbaum Associates, Mahwah, New Jersey.

44   Michael, N. 2013. Is feminism keeping up with the Kardashians? Female celebrities' portrayal of beauty and its influence on young females today. Doctoral dissertation, University of Pretoria.

45   www.cbsnews.com/news/parents-need-to-drastically-cut-kids-screen-time-evices-american-heart-association

46   Juarez, L., Soto, E. & Pritchard, M. E. 2012. Drive for muscularity and drive for thinness: the impact of pro-anorexia websites. *Eating Disorders* 20(2): 99–112.

47   Cheng, H. & Mallinckrodt, B. 2009. Parental bonds, anxious attachment, media internalization and body image dissatisfaction: exploring a mediation model. *Journal of Counseling Psychology* 56: 365–375.

48   Lokken, K. L., Worthy, S. & Trautmann, J. 2004. Examining the links among magazine preference, levels of awareness and internalization of sociocultural appearance standards, and presence of eating-disordered symptoms in college women. *Family and Consumer Sciences Research Journal* 32: 361–381.

49   Giles, D. C. & Close, J. 2008. Exposure to 'lad magazines' and drive for muscularity in dating and non-dating young men. *Personality and Individual Differences* 44: 1610–1616.

50   www.bbc.co.uk/news/magazine-23046602

51   www.bbc.co.uk/news/magazine-23046602

52   www.bbc.co.uk/news/magazine-23046602

Chapter Nine

1   www.sbs.com.au/topics/life/culture/article/2018/10/23/jameela-jamil-i-was-beaten-senseless-kids-being-pakistani-family
2   www.sbs.com.au/topics/voices/culture/article/2018/10/23/jameela-jamil-i-was-beaten-senseless-kids-being-pakistani-family
3   www.ozy.com/provocateurs/jameela-jamil-is-not-afraid-to-go-there/95338
4   www.medium.com/@petersonestee/the-good-place-actress-jameela-jamil-is-not-here-for-the-kardashians-antics-169864c86aa3
5   www.telegraph.co.uk/triathlon/2016/10/18/meet-john-mcavoy-the-former-criminal-who-is-aiming--to-become-th
6   www.youtube.com/watch?v=4gqk4WPnrpM
7   Johnson, S. K., Buckingham, M. H., Morris, S. L., Suzuki, S., Weiner, M. B., Hershberg, R. M., Fremont, E. R., Batanova, M., Aymong, C. C., Hunter, C. J. & Bowers, E. P. 2016. Adolescents' character role models: exploring who young people look up to as examples of how to be a good person. *Research in Human Development* 13(2): 126–141.
8   Bricheno, P. & Thornton, M. 2007. Role-model, hero or champion? Children's views concerning role-models. *Educational Research* 49(4): 383–396.
9   www.bbc.co.uk/sport/football/46897512
10   http://blog.nationalgeographic.org/2013/12/06/nelson-mandela-and-the-power-of-forgiveness
11   www.time.com/2865972/angelina-jolie-humanitarian
12   www.unhcr.org/541ad18c9.html
13   Hilmert, C. J., Kulik, J. A. & Christenfeld, N. J. 2006. Positive and negative opinion modeling: the influence of another's similarity and dissimilarity. *Journal of personality and social psychology* 90(3): 440.
14   www.harvardpolitics.com/united-states/youth-demand-climate-action-in-global-school-strike
15   www.independent.co.uk/environment/greta-thunberg-trump-latest-threat-climate-change-un-summit-speech-a9121111.html
16   www.bbc.co.uk/newsbeat/article/40580286/stormzy-chosen-as-person-of-the-year-by-university-of-oxfords-afro-caribbean-society
17   www.theguardian.com/music/2019/oct/10/stormzy-makes-cover-of-time-magazine-as-next-generation-leader-great-thunberg-annual-list
18   Owen, D. & Davidson, J. 2009. Hubris syndrome: an acquired personality disorder? A study of US Presidents and UK Prime Ministers over the last 100 years. *Brain* 132(5): 1396.
19   Owen, D. & Davidson, J. 2009. Hubris syndrome: an acquired personality disorder? A study of US Presidents and UK Prime Ministers over the last 100 years. *Brain* 132(5): 1396.
20   Mandela, N. 2011. *Conversations with Myself.* Anchor, Canada.
21   Frankl, V. E. 1985. *Man's search for meaning.* Simon and Schuster, New York
22   Murden, F. 2018. *Defining You: How to profile yourself and unlock your full potential.* Nicholas Brealey, London.
23   Błażek, M., Kaźmierczak, M. & Besta, T, 2015. Sense of purpose in life and escape from self as the predictors of quality of life in clinical samples. *Journal of Religion and Health* 54(2): 517–523.

24 Westerhof, G. J., Bohlmeijer, E. T., Van Beljouw, I. M. & Pot, A. M. 2010. Improvement in personal meaning mediates the effects of a life review intervention on depressive symptoms in a randomized controlled trial. *The Gerontologist* 50(4): 541–549.

25 Smith, B. W., Tooley, E. M., Montague, E. Q., Robinson, A. E., Cosper, C. J. & Mullins, P. G. 2009. The role of resilience and purpose in life in habituation to heat and cold pain. *The Journal of Pain* 10(5): 493–500.

26 Koizumi, M., Ito, H., Kaneko, Y. & Motohashi, Y. 2008. Effect of having a sense of purpose in life on the risk of death from cardiovascular diseases. *Journal of Epidemiology*: 0808270028–0808270028.

27 Boyle, P. A., Buchman, A. S., Wilson, R. S., Yu, L., Schneider, J. A. & Bennett, D. A. 2012. Effect of purpose in life on the relation between Alzheimer disease pathologic changes on cognitive function in advanced age. *Archives of General Psychiatry* 69(5): 499–504.

28 Bamia, C., Trichopoulou, A. & Trichopoulos, D. 2008. Age at retirement and mortality in a general population sample: the Greek EPIC study. *American Journal of Epidemiology* 167(5): 561–569.

29 Murden, F. 2018. *Defining You: How to profile yourself and unlock your full potential*. Nicholas Brealey, London.

30 @jameelajamil official Twitter handle

Chapter Ten

1 www.bbc.co.uk/news/world-asia-49968836
2 www.bbc.co.uk/news/world-asia-50009944
3 www.bbc.co.uk/news/world-asia-50009944
4 www.nytimes.com/2006/01/10/science/cells-that-read-minds.html
5 Vos, T., Barber, R. M., Bell, B., Bertozzi-Villa, A., Biryukov, S., Bolliger, I., Charlson, F., Davis, A., Degenhardt, L., Dicker, D. & Duan, L. 2015. Global, regional and national incidence, prevalence and years lived with disability for 301 acute and chronic diseases and injuries in 188 countries, 1990–2013: a systematic analysis for the Global Burden of Disease Study 2013. *The Lancet* 386(9995): 743–800.
6 www.psychiatrictimes.com/mental-health/mental-illness-will-cost-world-16-usd-trillion-2030
7 www.mentalhealth.org.uk/blog/what-new-statistics-show-about-childrens-mental-health
8 www.headstogether.org.uk/about
9 www.telegraph.co.uk/news/2017/04/16/prince-harry-sought-counselling-death-mother-led-two-years-total
10 Iacoboni, M. 2009. *Mirroring People: The new science of how we connect with others*. Farrar, Straus and Giroux, New York. 267.
11 Mesoudi, A. & Thornton, A. 2018. What is cumulative cultural evolution? *Proceedings of the Royal Society B: Biological Sciences* 285(1880): 20180712.
12 Eaude, T. 2009. Happiness, emotional well-being and mental health – what has children's spirituality to offer?. *International Journal of Children's Spirituality* 14(3): 185–196.
13 www.nytimes.com/2013/05/14/opinion/my-medical-choice.html
14 www.sciencedaily.com/releases/2016/12/16121421 3749.htm
15 Evans, D. G. R., Barwell, J., Eccles, D. M., Collins, A., Izatt, L., Jacobs, C., Donaldson, A., Brady, A. F., Cuthbert, A., Harrison, R. & Thomas, S.

2014. The Angelina Jolie effect: how high celebrity profile can have a major impact on provision of cancer related services. *Breast Cancer Research* 16(5): 442.

16 Roberts, H., Liabo, K., Lucas, P., DuBois, D. & Sheldon, T. A. 2004. Mentoring to reduce antisocial behaviour in childhood. *BMJ* 328(7438): 512–514.

17 http://archive.nytimes.com/www.nytimes.com/learning/teachers/featured_articles/19990505wednesday.html

18 http://users.nber.org/~rdehejia/!@$devo/Lecture%2009%20Gender/gender%20and%20politics/HKS763-PDF-ENG2.pdf

19 http://censusindia.gov.in/2011-prov-results/paper2/data_files/india/Rural_Urban_2011.pdf

20 Kaul, S. & Sahni, S. 2009. Study on the participation of women in Panchayati Raj Institution. *Studies on Home and Community Science* 3(1): 29–38.

21 http://archive.nytimes.com/www.nytimes.com/learning/teachers/featured_articles/19990505wednesday.html

22 Beaman, L., Duflo, E., Pande, R. & Topalova, P. 2012. Female leadership raises aspirations and educational attainment for girls: a policy experiment in India. *Science* 335(6068): 582–586.

23 http://archive.nytimes.com/www.nytimes.com/learning/teachers/featured_articles/19990505wednesday.html

24 www.arlingtoncemetery.net/ekcoulter.htm

25 Freedman, M. 1999. *The kindness of strangers: adult mentors, urban youth, and the new voluntarism*. Cambridge University Press, UK.

26 www.arlingtoncemetery.net/ekcoulter.htm

27 www.evidencebasedprograms.org/document/big-brothers-big-sisters-evidence-summary

28 www.bbbs.org/2017/07/meet-2017-big-brother-year-terence-cincinnati

29 www.bbbs.org/2017/07/meet-2017-big-brother-year-terence-cincinnati

30 Grossman, J. B. & Tierney, J. P. 1998. Does mentoring work? An impact study of the Big Brothers Big Sisters program. *Evaluation Review* 22(3): 403–426.

31 DuBois, D. L., Holloway, B. E., Valentine, J. C. & Cooper, H. 2002. Effectiveness of mentoring programs for youth: a meta-analytic review. *American Journal of Community Psychology* 30(2): 157–197.

32 Bird, J. D., Kuhns, L. & Garofalo, R. 2012. The impact of role-models on health outcomes for lesbian, gay, bisexual, and transgender youth. *Journal of Adolescent Health* 50(4): 353–357.

33 Bird, J. D., Kuhns, L. & Garofalo, R. 2012. The impact of role-models on health outcomes for lesbian, gay, bisexual, and transgender youth. *Journal of Adolescent Health* 50(4): 353–357.

34 Craig, S. L. & McInroy, L. 2014. You can form a part of yourself online: the influence of new media on identity development and coming out for LGBTQ youth. *Journal of Gay & Lesbian Mental Health* 18(1): 95–109.

35 www.bbc.co.uk/news/uk-48742850

36 Lines, G. 2001. Villains, fools or heroes? Sports stars as role-models for young people. *Leisure Studies* 20(4): 285–303.

37 Saunders, J., Hume, C., Timperio, A. & Salmon, J. 2012. Cross-sectional and longitudinal associations between parenting style and adolescent girls'

physical activity. *International Journal of Behavioral Nutrition and Physical Activity* 9(1): 141.

38   Young, J. A., Symons, C. M., Pain, M. D., Harvey, J. T., Eime, R. M., Craike, M. J. & Payne, W. R. 2015. Role-models of Australian female adolescents: a longitudinal study to inform programmes designed to increase physical activity and sport participation. *European Physical Education Review* 21(4): 451–466.

39   Vescio, J. A. & Crosswhite, J. J. 2002. Sharing good practices: teenage girls, sport and physical Activities. *ICHPER-SD Journal* 38(3): 47–52.

40   Stronach, M., Maxwell, H. & Taylor, T. 2016. 'Sistas' and aunties: sport, physical activity, and indigenous Australian women. *Annals of Leisure Research* 19(1): 7–26.

41   Meier, M. 2013. Sporting role models as potential catalysts to facilitate empowerment and tackle gender issues. Doctoral dissertation, Technische Universität München.

42   Biskup, C. & Pfister, G. 1999. I would like to be like her/him: are athletes role models for boys and girls? *European Physical Education Review* 5(3): 199–218.

43   www.ft.com/content/70e92e3c-e38b-11e8-a6e5-792428919cee

44   Cheng, A., Kopotic, K. & Zamarro, G. 2017. Can Parents' Growth Mindset and Role-modelling Address STEM Gender Gaps? *EDRE Working Paper* 2017–07.

45   Incidentally the softer skills such as creative thinking, problem-solving and negotiating are heavily reliant on having a well-developed mirror system.

46   www.weforum.org/agenda/2018/02/does-gender-equality-result-in-fewer-female-stem-grads

47   Stoet, G. & Geary, D. C. 2018. The gender-equality paradox in science, technology, engineering, and mathematics education. *Psychological Science* 29(4): 581–593.

48   http://news.microsoft.com/europe/features/girls-in-stem-the-importance-of-role-models

49   Personal interview with Amy Cuddy and Fiona Murden, November 2019.

Chapter Eleven

1   www.theguardian.com/uk-news/2019/mar/08/how-a-survivor-of-knife-crime-became-a-role-model-for-children

2   www.theguardian.com/uk-news/2019/mar/08/how-a-survivor-of-knife-crime-became-a-role-model-for-children

3   www.bbbs.org/2017/09/big-motivated-mistakes

4   Meier, M. 2013. Sporting role models as potential catalysts to facilitate empowerment and tackle gender issues. Doctoral dissertation, Technische Universität München.

5   Nelson, S. K., Layous, K., Cole, S. W. & Lyubomirsky, S. 2016. Do unto others or treat yourself? The effects of prosocial and self-focused behavior on psychological flourishing. *Emotion* 16(6): 850.

6   Nelson, S. K., Della Porta, M. D., Jacobs Bao, K., Lee, H. C., Choi, I. & Lyubomirsky, S. 2015. It's up to you: experimentally manipulated autonomy support for prosocial behavior improves well-being in two cultures over six weeks. *The Journal of Positive Psychology* 10(5): 463–476.

7   Crocker, J., Canevello, A. & Brown, A. A. 2017. Social motivation: costs and benefits of selfishness and otherishness. *Annual Review of Psychology* 68: 299–325.

8   Crocker, J., Canevello, A. & Brown, A. A. 2017. Social motivation: costs and benefits of selfishness and otherishness. *Annual Review of Psychology* 68: 299–325.

9   Whitbourne, S., Sneed, J. R. & Skultety, K. M. 2002. Identity processes in adulthood: theoretical and methodological challenges. *Identity: An International Journal of Theory And Research* 2(1): 29–45.

10   www.psychologytoday.com/us/blog/fulfillment-any-age/201003/mentoring-and-being-mentored-win-win-situation

11   Greenfield, E. A. & Marks, N. F. 2004. Formal volunteering as a protective factor for older adults' psychological well-being. *The Journals of Gerontology Series B: Psychological Sciences and Social Sciences* 59(5): S258–S264.

12   www.dur.ac.uk/hr/mentoring/mentoringguidelines/mentoringbenefits

13   Bayley, H., Chambers, R. & Donovan, C. 2018. *The Good Mentoring Toolkit for Healthcare.* CRC Press, Florida, US.

14   MacCallum, J. & Beltman, S. 2002. Role-models for young people: What makes an effective role-model program. The National Youth Affairs Research Scheme.

15   Meier, M. 2013. Sporting role models as potential catalysts to facilitate empowerment and tackle gender issues. Doctoral dissertation, Technische Universität München.

16   Murden, F. 2018. *Defining You: How to profile yourself and unlock your full potential.* Nicholas Brealey, London.

17   Fineman, S. 1993. *Organizations as Emotional Arenas.* Sage Publications, California.

18   Murden, F. 2018. *Defining You: How to profile yourself and unlock your full potential.* Nicholas Brealey, London.

19   www.bbbs.org/2017/09/big-motivated-mistakes

20   www.episcenter.psu.edu/sites/default/files/ebp/Implementation%20Manual%20BBBS%20Sec7%20Aug2013%20TL-RLS.pdf

21   Benard, B. & Marshall, K. 2001. Big Brothers/Big Sisters mentoring: the power of developmental relationship. National Resilience Resource Center, University of Minnesota.

22   www.hbr.org/2014/10/a-refresh-on-storytelling-101

23   www.nationalarchives.gov.uk/education/heroesvillains/transcript/g6cs3s4t.htm

24   Martela, F. & Ryan, R. M. 2016. Prosocial behavior increases well-being and vitality even without contact with the beneficiary: causal and behavioral evidence. *Motivation and Emotion* 40(3): 351–357.

Chapter Twelve

1   In order to do this I would recommend looking at a books such as Defining You (which I wrote to help people explore these areas), taking courses or finding a personal coach, or even role model, to help you.

2   https://www.cnbc.com/2017/06/23/4-ways-comic-books-shaped-elon-musks-vision-of-the-future.html

3   https://www.cnbc.com/2017/06/23/4-ways-comic-books-shaped-elon-
     musks-vision-of-the-future.html
4   https://www.cnbc.com/2017/06/23/4-ways-comic-books-shaped-elon-
     musks-vision-of-the-future.html

Conclusion

1   Christian, D. 2012. Collective learning. *Berkshire Encyclopaedia of
     Sustainability.* Berkshire. 10: 49–56. Great Barrington, MA, US.
2   https://2019.spaceappschallenge.org/locations/larisa
3   Konrath, S. H., O'Brien, E. H. & Hsing, C. 2011. Changes in dispositional
     empathy in American college students over time: a meta-analysis.
     Personality and Social Psychology Review 15(2): 180–198.
4   www.nami.org/learn-more/mental-health-by-the-numbers

Acknowledgements

Thank you to Jo de Vries for her untiring support in pushing yet another idea through to reality. Emma for being there at the start. Anna for being a responsive and helpful editorial director and Emily a gentle copy editor. Professor Anthony Forster for the many stimulating conversations that always spark exciting trains of thought. All of the academics who have guided me on the mirror neuron's functionality, most of all Professor Marco Iacoboni who has been generous, humble and brilliant.

Thanks to Brenda, a role model of positivity, Izzi for reading things while they still made no sense, Mum for being there for all of us. My girls – I love you so much and Chris, you literally do complete me.

Thank you to all those who I have mirrored throughout my life, most of all the family who shaped my early years – Peter, my Mum, my Dad, Gail and Malcolm.

Index